DAYS OF FIRE

DAYS
OF
by Samuel Katz
FIRE

1968
DOUBLEDAY & COMPANY, INC., GARDEN CITY, NEW YORK

Published as DAY OF FIRE by
Karni Publishers Ltd., Israel
1966

To the Memory of My Parents
Alexander Zyskind and Luba Breslov Katz

My thanks to Miss Elly Gross and Mrs. Ora Zohar of Tel Aviv for their helpful comments while the manuscript was in preparation, and to the staff of the Jabotinsky Institute for their ever-ready response to my requests for source material. I owe a special debt of gratitude to Mrs. Thelma Mintz of Herzlia for courageously undertaking to decipher and type my original manuscript.

FOREWORD

Between the writing of this book and its publication in English, a change of revolutionary dimensions has taken place in Palestine. In the Six Day War of June 1967 the Israel armed forces, performing what appears to be one of the great military feats in history, again defeated three Arab aggressors, put an end to the partition of western Palestine, brought Israel's effective frontiers down to the Jordan in the east, raised them on to the Golan Heights in the northeast, and in the south extended them to the Straits of Tiran and the Suez Canal.

Viewed only six months after the event, the drama of 1967 seems so much a continuation of the great transformation of 1948 that the historian in fifty years' time may well see the intervening nineteen years of Israel's confinement behind the partition frontiers as an aberration, a temporary distortion of the historic process of the mutual restoration of the Jewish people and country. He will be able the more sharply to discern the paradox that the victories and the consequent reunification of Palestine west of the Jordan, were achieved by a people initially unwilling to go to war and psychologically unprepared for its consequences. He will certainly be able to gauge the depth of the sharp change that has followed the great events of 1967 in the way of thinking of the people of Israel, in its attitude to the world, and to its own problems.

A tangible rapprochement has taken place between the generations. The fathers, who in 1948 brought the state to birth, never quite freed themselves of the remembered anguish of a Diaspora engulfed in tears and blood and ashes, carried the memory of the painful progress of the upbuilding of the Jewish national home under the British, and bore the scars of battle of the fighting underground and of the War of Independence. To their sons, the state of Israel in which they were born or brought up, with its grotesque frontiers and problems was the ready-made natural framework of their lives. Suddenly they were forced to taste something of the very threat of extermination which is so scarring a memory of their fathers. In May 1967, to the sound of the shrill Arab threats to destroy them and their state, to the accompaniment of Egyptian troops massing into position on Israel's southern borders, fathers and sons reached instinctive understanding of each other.

The great crisis of May and June lit up in the new generation an insight, a special awareness that Israel is not struggling for prestige or for markets or for domination, or to hurt other people, but for her very right to live, and that her extreme strategic vulnerability makes every battle crucial. This awareness no doubt added the extra dynamic of mind and will to her soldiers—from the planners in the General Staff to the last private soldier in the field—that brought such swift and sweeping victory in the Six Day War. It was surely also one of the sources of the seemingly infinite spirit of bravery, of self-sacrifice, of comradeship in battle which shone through countless incidents in the six days' fighting: again a striking projection of the spirit which moved the generation of the revolt against Britain and the War of Independence.

The events of 1967 seem therefore to have halted in Israel what appears to be a universal trend in the current phase of Western culture. There has become manifest here an uninhibited mutual recognition and mutual respect between the generations. There is no melancholy gray-head-shaking at the rebellious inexplicabilities of the youth. There is no jargonic sneering and jeering at the parents. There is an undeclared, often unexplored, yet quite patent sense of historic continuity between the acts and outlook of the generation of 1948 and that of 1967.

The "presence" of 1948 in the events of 1967 is, however, of a greater and a deeper importance. The real, historic, decisive lesson that must be learned derives not from the Six Day War but from the compromise of 1948 as it was reflected in the preceding three weeks of threatened doom and incredible tension.

Suddenly the inherent precariousness of the physical foundations of the state became evident. The armistice-line boundaries established after the War of Independence not only left Israel without any natural defenses but at the mercy of neighbors strongly protected by nature. Even a mediocre antagonist, striking the first blow, could cut the Jewish state in half. To those few who, in 1937, following Jabotinsky, had warned against this danger in the first partition scheme and who, in the Irgun in 1947 had again invoked it against the acceptance of the UN partition scheme—it was of no comfort at all that the danger had at last incubated. For here in the spring of 1967, after years of preparation, were our enemies on all three landward sides, armed to the teeth in overwhelming superiority of numbers and matériel, massing their forces and screaming their intention to wipe us literally off the face of the earth.

In preliminary implementation of their threats the Egyptians demanded the withdrawal of the United Nations peacekeeping force from the armistice lines between Israel and Egypt and from the Tiran Straits. When the UN Secretary General summarily fulfilled their demand, they announced the closing of the Tiran Straits to Israeli shipping, thus blockading our southern port and cutting our sea communications with the east and the south.

Precisely at this point, the Western powers, who in 1957 had guaranteed the status quo, including the freedom of the Tiran Straits (and indeed of the Suez Canal), and had in this way secured Israel's agonized agreement to withdraw from Sinai and from the Gaza "strip," made it plain that they would not lift a finger to implement their guarantee. Indeed, they found it impossible to convene a meeting of the Security Council of the United Nations.

Here once again an inherent political weakness of Israel was revealed—perhaps even more emphatically than in 1948. The Arabs have thirteen votes in the United Nations. They control the major sources of Western Europe's oil. They control the shortest sea route from the East—through the Suez Canal—and the oil pipelines to the Mediterranean coast. They count a total population—and therefore a potential market—of one hundred million. Sprawled across the breadth of North Africa, they are in many ways the gateway to influence in that Continent. Such attributes create a far wider area for satisfying material and political interests in a pragmatic, divided world than the values, however disproportionately large, that Israel can offer. These qualities have won for the Arab states the support of many countries, notably of the Soviet Union and her satellites, and the constant courting of Western powers.

The consequence was that in spite of the tide of sympathy that in May and June flowed strongly among the ordinary people of many countries in East and West alike (not to mention an unprecedented outburst of emotion among the Jews throughout the world) if Israel's security had been to any serious degree dependent on the fulfillment of foreign promises or international guarantees or the practical application of declared friendship, she would have been crushed as an independent state and her population ravaged and murdered.

It was this prospect unfolding in the three weeks while Israel waited and the Arab leaders made bloodcurdling promises on the radio to their people hour after hour, on television, and in the newspapers which spelled out the conditions for Israel's self-preservation. It is this experience from which sprang the central motif of all thinking in Israel after the Six Day War: Never Again.

It is surely a fantastic notion, and a measure of the unreality and cant in international debate, that Israel, having for the third time since 1947 saved herself by her exertions and by the ingenuity and courage of her youth should once again as though in a series of friendly football games, be asked to hand over to her would-be destroyers the territorial prerequisites for a new attempt on her life.

Logic and morality apart, this demand is of course also contrary to both the principles and the practice of international relations. In our own time, the Treaty of Paris after the First World War, the Charter of the United Nations itself, and the behavior of the victorious nations toward the defeated aggressors of World War II— all bear the same precept and example. Twenty-two years after the end of that war, no significant territorial change imposed by the victors has been amended—notwithstanding the apparent evaporation of aggressive attitudes in Germany or Japan.

The reintegration of the rest of western Palestine into Israel, and the consequent absorption of a large community of Arabs who for two decades have been indoctrinated with extreme hatred for the Jews, will be no easy task. But this is the first time that Jew and Arab confront each other without physical barriers or a "third party" dividing them. Already the Arab population of the towns and villages of Judea and Samaria have begun to discover to what extent they were misled about the characteristics and intentions of the people of Israel. The way to understanding may now be open. The inhabitants of the areas captured by the Israel Army have now had an opportunity, moreover, of seeing how the 300,000 Arabs who lived in Israel before the Six Day War have gradually come to terms with Israel rule, that they are prospering materially and culturally, that they enjoy civic rights and freedom—which most Arabs in their own states do not have.

They have seen in reunited Jerusalem, which alone has so far been formally incorporated into Israel, the benefits of co-operation with a Jewish authority prepared to bury the past and open a chapter of co-operation and co-existence between Jews and Arabs.

Those who casually assume the impossibility of conciliation between a Jewish majority and an Arab minority do not realize that the Arab's fears on this score stem in some part from his knowledge of the way minorities have been—and are—ill-treated in the Arab states. Given a firm commitment by the Israel government to extend its authority and to apply its laws to the whole country and its peoples, the Arab population will soon be able to discover that it is no tragedy at all to live as a minority when you are treated as equal citizens and when your own people enjoy sovereignty in thirteen states of their own.

It will need a great effort both by Israel and by international agencies to liquidate the problem of the "refugees" of 1948. They will have to be resettled, and it is very likely that a substantial part of them will prefer to emigrate. The bulk of the people concerned are within the frontiers controlled by Israel, and freed from the dictates of the Arab politicians who in 1948 brought about—then perpetuated and exploited—their plight. Here too it is possible for the first time to come to grips with the problem. It is in Israel's interest, as well as a demand of common humanity, to formulate a comprehensive solution speedily and not to postpone it against the day when the Arab states accept Israel's offer to make peace—a consummation as remote today as ever it was.

A more complicated problem for the Jews in Israel is how to ensure that Israel shall remain a Jewish state. The fear that the far lower birth rate of the Jews will enable the Arabs (numbering about one third of the total population of united Palestine) to overtake them, has made some of them doubt whether it is feasible or desirable to retain Judea and Samaria. The positive answer (apart from a reduction in Arab birth rate as a result of a rising standard of living) is of course twofold. First a drastic social change to encourage substantial increase in the Jewish birth rate. This will no doubt begin to emerge in the next few years. But more than ever before the eyes of Israel are turned outward. Again, as throughout the past fifty years—we must have immigrants. The Jews of the West have never responded in large numbers to the challenge of Israel. Now it may be that her very future as the Jewish state will depend on the strength of the feeling of Jews of the West that they are also part of the rebirth of the Jewish homeland.

We dreamed this dream in 1948. Will it come true now? This is the most pointed question posed in the aftermath of the War of 1967.

Samuel Katz

CONTENTS

LIST OF ILLUSTRATIONS

THE IRGUN BEGINS   (following page 54)

Vladimir Jabotinsky

David Raziel

The author with Peter Bergson (H. Kook) and H. Lubinsky; Warsaw, October 1937.

Avraham Stern

Menahem Begin

The author on an IZL mission in France; 1946.

An Irgun poster for distribution in Central Europe.

Kidnaped British officers after their release on remission of death sentences on Michael Ashbel and Joseph Simhon; June 1946.

Jacob Tavin ("Eli") a member of the IZL High Command who was responsible for blowing up the British Embassy in Rome.

Shmuel Ariel, the IZL "ambassador" to France.

Some of the men who went to the gallows during the British mandate.

Two maps illustrating British policy toward the Jews:

Formation of the Arab League; and

The refusal to take action against Auschwitz and the railways leading there from Budapest, compared with the operation to help the Polish rising in Warsaw.

THE STRUGGLE FOR A STATE   (following page 246)

The attack on Goldsmith House, the British Officers Club; Jerusalem, March 1947.

The Irgun "barrel bomb" designed to lob over the high fences around British army and police buildings.

Irgun attacks a British police tender in the heart of Tel Aviv; 1947.

Looking down Ben Yehuda Street, Jerusalem.

Part One

THE BEGINNING

1

The Beginning

I came to Jerusalem for the first time on a winter morning in January 1936. The weather was raw and melancholy. The sky was overcast, with a steady drizzle, the pavements were muddy. I soon discovered how well this day fit the mood of the times.

A cloud of fear seemed to hang over the city. Its Jewish inhabitants, and many of its Arabs, were restless and apprehensive. For weeks all the Arab newspapers had been publishing articles vilifying the Jews with more than customary passion. Arab politicians were publicly advocating a campaign of violence, the coming clash being the dominant theme in the Arab cafes and market places throughout Palestine. Commercial and professional relations between the communities were coming to a standstill, and Arab businessmen were warned to disassociate themselves speedily from dealings with Jews. At the Vienna Cafe, Jerusalem's journalists, lawyers, officials, socialites, and spies for various interests foregathered at the day's end to exchange news and gossip, and Arab newspapermen, like some whispering Greek chorus, muttered gloomy prognostications to their Jewish colleagues.

I had come from Johannesburg to open in Jerusalem the office of Michael Haskel, the appointed South African honorary consul, whom I was to serve as secretary. The work I was able to do during those first weeks was not difficult or taxing, and most of my time and thought was taken up in understanding the political elements—British, Arab, and Jewish—in the palpably charged atmosphere. I found myself acclimatizing rapidly to the uneasy way of life in Jerusalem, to the endless political discussion, to the constant whisper of rumors and to the general ambiance of unreality which was engendered by the conflict of interests—British Mandatory rule, Arab emergent nationalism, and Jewish dreams of a national home.

My first three months in Palestine indeed proved to be the last nervous period of peace there. There followed successive phases of bloodshed, war, and political upheaval that were to last for nearly thirteen years.

On the morning of Sunday, April 19, 1936, I traveled from Jerusalem to Tel Aviv by the interurban taxi service to meet Haskel. When we reached Mikveh Yisrael, the agricultural school on the outskirts of Tel Aviv, we were stopped by a Jewish policeman who told us that Jewish cars had been stoned by Arabs on the road and that several passengers were injured. We waited an hour for a British police escort car, which then led a queue of cars into Tel Aviv.

The town itself was in a tumult. The stoning incident was a minor one in comparison to what was happening in neighboring Jaffa, where a menacing Arab crowd had gathered outside the district commissioner's office, alleging the killing of Arabs in Tel Aviv. The crowd stood there even after officials had denied the story, and groups of young men roved the town, falling on individual Jews. Seventeen were stabbed to death that day.

Haskel was enraged by the news of the Arab violence. What was happening followed the pattern of earlier events during the eighteen years of British rule. There was a tradition of elaborate British inaction except in preventing Jewish retaliation to Arab attack.[1] Haskel was impatient to return to Jerusalem, where he was to meet the Chief Secretary of the Mandatory government, Hathorn Hall. We telephoned British Police District Headquarters in Jaffa who provided an escort only as far as Jaffa, where the streets were all but deserted, its shops shuttered. Major Foley, the police commandant, assured us that all was quiet, so we drove back to Tel Aviv.

There, Haskel telephoned one of the leaders of Haganah B—the nonconformist splinter of the semi-clandestine Haganah (the "official" self-defense organization of the Palestine Jewish community) —and explained his desire to reach Jerusalem. Soon a car, driven by Aryeh Ben Eliezer, a member of the organization, sped us away.

When Haskel called on the Chief Secretary the next day, he roundly denounced the British Government, declaring that he would make it his business "to publish throughout the world" the fact that Britain was not only betraying her obligation to facilitate the establishment of the Jewish national home, but was inciting the Arabs to murder, while preventing the Jews from hitting back.

Hathorn Hall, the Chief Secretary, maintained that the government had the situation in hand, and declared that the trouble would be over in a couple of days. At this Haskel exploded again.

"Your people do not even know what is going on!" he protested. "Your police chief in Jaffa yesterday refused me an escort to Jerusalem, saying everything was already under control. Yet the Arabs were still attacking Jewish cars on the road."

Hall smiled. "But you reached Jerusalem safely."

"Of course I did," said Haskel. "I was given an armed escort by the Haganah."

The report I wrote on Haskel's angry conversation with Hathorn Hall could hardly have caused even a raised eyebrow in the External Affairs Department in Pretoria. The South African Government knew that Michael Haskel had long been a forthright critic of the British regime in Palestine for its failure to implement Britain's promise "to facilitate the establishment of a Jewish National Home in Palestine . . ."

Haskel was also highly critical of the Zionist leadership headed by Chaim Weizmann, because he considered they had accepted the British betrayal too passively. He himself was a follower of Vladimir Jabotinsky, the leader of the opposition in the Zionist Movement. A man of considerable wealth, he gave Jabotinsky's party, the Revisionists, large financial support, although this did not affect his contributions to the regular Zionist funds, nor his many public benefactions and private philanthropies, which regarded no barriers of race or creed.[2] His appointment in 1933 by the South African Government as its honorary representative in Palestine was a gesture of friendship by the Union to the Zionist Movement and also to the Jews of the country at a time when anti-Semitism was becoming world-wide in the wake of the Nazi control of Germany.

Haskel's views on the British regime in Palestine, moreover, had the approval of the Afrikaner Nationalist leaders, who nursed their own historic antagonisms against the British and were not averse to setting up a potential irritant in Jerusalem.

The association between Haskel and myself was founded in our shared admiration for Vladimir Jabotinsky, one of the heroes of Jewish history. I had been captivated by Jabotinsky on his first visit to South Africa in 1930, when I was a fifteen-year-old student at the university. I was invited to hear him lecture at a private gathering of the Betar Youth Organization. Jabotinsky, one of the great orators of the age, was capable of holding vast audiences spellbound for hours. I was enthralled by the irrefutable logic of his words, and the restraint with which he conveyed their searing content.

The essence of his message was that we youngsters living in the comfort and comparative security of the South African sunshine had a responsibility to the masses of Jews who had remained in Eastern Europe, where they were exposed to perpetual attacks, economic and social—hated, despised and persecuted. There they faced the threat of gradual economic extinction. For those who would not accept this fate passively, there were two solutions: either to become Communists or to rebuild their lives in Palestine, in a state of their own.

But, said Jabotinsky, the hope of such a Jewish state as envisaged in Britain's World War I promise was receding as successive British governments constricted and confined it; and the Zionist leaders were too weak and spineless to combat these restrictions.

In Jabotinsky there was, for the first time since the death of Theodor Herzl, a leader who said that the Jews must cease being political victims and must instead create and change the political circumstances in which they found themselves. He called for complete dedication to the idea of a Jewish state, working for it and, if necessary, fighting for it.

Jabotinsky believed in Britain's ultimate integrity. He argued that in the end British statesmen would realize that honor and self-interest demanded the fulfillment of British promises. But he maintained that the Zionist leadership must be firm. By the irony of history it was Jabotinsky's disciples, implementing his principles, who took up arms against Britain when it was clear that she no longer intended to keep faith with the Jews.

Without hesitation I became a dedicated soldier in the cause which Jabotinsky espoused, speaking, writing, organizing, at first in the Betar Youth Organization, later in the Zionist-Revisionist Party. My studies were neglected, and my university career came to an ignominious end.

I met Haskel soon afterward; his explosive youthfulness bridged the gap in age between us—he was in his middle fifties—and we became good friends. It was not long before I became his political secretary.

It thus fell to me to manage the consular office in Palestine and, indeed, to fulfill all of Haskel's official functions. I issued visas and passports and sent reports to the South African Government on the unfolding political situation. It was now dominated by the so-called "Arab Revolt" which broke out that April.

The year 1936 seems an almost visible turning point on the road to World War II. After Britain and France had angered Mussolini by their hostility to his attack on Abyssinia and deepened his self-confidence by their failure to prevent his conquest, he took Italy into the German camp. Hitler gambled on the decadence of Britain and France for the success of his plan for world domination, a resolution fortified in the spring of that year, when he marched without opposition into the demilitarized Rhineland. The Spanish Civil War exploded in the summer, lighting all of Europe with a bloody, corrosive glow. "Non-intervention" prevailed. It was against this background that the "Arab Revolt" in Palestine began.

The "Revolt" was a bizarre alliance between the Arab leaders and the British administration—against which the Arabs were presumed to be rebelling!

The British Government's purpose was not, of course, to hand over control of Palestine to the Arabs. They wished merely to limit Jewish progress so that the Jews might never be strong enough to claim the independence implicit in the Balfour Declaration. A Jewish majority in Palestine would be unmanageable. They must therefore remain a minority, and Palestine would remain under British control as long as Jews and Arabs could be kept at each other's throats.

To realize this objective, the Arab national movement had to be fostered and the myth of Arab claims to a country they had briefly ruled a thousand years earlier had to be maintained. The validity of this claim is too seldom examined in the light of historical facts. Through centuries of Turkish rule it had never occurred to the Arabs to throw off that yoke, nor to exert themselves to prevent vast areas of the country from becoming wasteland. Even in the first glow of Arab resurgence in 1918 after the collapse of the Turkish Empire, the Arab leaders had no qualms in endorsing the idea of a Jewish state in Palestine. King Feisal of Iraq even signed a treaty of friendship with Dr. Weizmann.

During the British military occupation of Palestine after the First World War, the administration of the country was in the hands of a group of generals who could not tolerate the thought of Jews with European ideas and political ambitions creating a Jewish national home ruled from London, and their antagonism was soon reflected in British policy and behavior.

Jewish reaction was weak and vacillating, and by the early 1930s British policy had crystallized. London hoped to impose authority by maintaining a state of tension in the country.

But when, in 1933, there was a sudden influx into Palestine of Jews fleeing from Hitler's Germany, the world became aware of European Jewry's peril. The tragedy of the German Jews was destined to become the dynamo of Jewish development in Palestine. Palestine began to witness a surge of Jewish progress which, unchecked, would within a few years find the Jews in a commanding position there, with British control mortally threatened. Whitehall reasoned that something dramatic and apparently irresistible would have to be set in motion to justify a conclusive containment of the Jews.

Thus was the "Arab Revolt" born. Its devious detail was left to develop with circumstances, its ebb and flow and direction controlled so as not to endanger one crucial objective—the perpetuation of British rule.

The mechanics of the revolt were simple. The Arab nationalist leaders were headed by the Mufti of Jerusalem, who had been deliberately encouraged by the British, such assurances giving point and direction to the incitement of the Arab masses against the Jews. The slogan of the Arab movement was "Ad-dowlah ma'anah [The government is with us]," whispered throughout the Arab coffeehouses and market places. But when this "unofficial" encouragement by the British failed to arouse enough nationwide hostility to the Jews, the divide and rule strategy was clearly called for so that the "Arab Revolt" could be manipulated to terrorize the Arab population itself. Thus, in the towns a general strike was engineered and shops were closed by pickets. The majority of these "Palestine rebels" had been imported from Iraq and Syria and billeted in the Arab villages. Soon, "Ad-dowlah ma'anah" came to have a dual significance. Arab merchants discovered that the forced closing-down of their businesses was regarded as perfectly legal by the Mandatory government. Appeals by Arab villagers for protection or for arms to defend themselves against their "guests" were met with stony silence by the authorities. Indeed, so well organized was the terrorization of the Arabs themselves that in the three years of the "Revolt" the "rebels" killed more Arabs than Jews!

The British went through all the motions of a great effort "to restore law and order." Troops poured into the country, with a succession of new and famous generals in command. Troops and police were always in evidence after an attack, but had strict orders to do no more than defend themselves.

A popular point of attack for the Arab bands was near Bab el Wad, in the narrow valley in the Judean Hills about fifteen miles from Jerusalem, on the only road to the coast. The Arab sharpshooters would sit behind the rocks on the crest of the hill and shoot at cars, which traveled in close convoy, "protected" fore and aft by a British military escort. The burst of Arab rifle or machinegun fire invariably took its toll, and the British soldiers would shoot back desultorily—and drive on—while the attackers returned tranquilly to coffee in their village.

An anonymous British soldier gave a complete description of the pattern of the Arab Revolt in 1936. In an article in the London *New Statesman and Nation*,[3] he wrote:

"At night when we are guarding the line against the Arabs who come to blow it up, we often see them at work but are forbidden to fire at them. We may only fire into the air, and they, upon hearing the report, make their escape. But do you think we can give chase? Why, we must go on our hands and knees and find every spent cartridge-case, which must be handed in or woe betide us."

There were, of course, variations in the way the British carried out their plans. Punitive operations were mounted from time to time, when the "revolt" conflicted with some immediate British interest, local or international.

The government insisted that the duty of "maintaining law and order" was its alone. As the British authorities intended in any case to keep the actual work of Arab destruction within bounds, they came, in course of time, to close their eyes to some elementary Jewish defense activities. Certain agricultural settlements were permitted a fixed quantity of arms with which to repel Arab attacks, and in the towns a small number of supernumerary policemen—*ghafirs*—were enrolled to carry out patrol duties. But the violence of the revolt did not diminish. Jews were killed from ambush in the towns and on the highways, Jewish buildings dynamited, communi-

cations cut, fields burned, trees uprooted; and finally came mass
Arab attacks on Jewish settlements.

The major theme of official Jewish policy came into harmony with
the British Grand Design. After a very brief period of hesitation
the Agency decided on a policy called *havlaga* (self-restraint).
This did not mean passivity. The Haganah[4] was active, maintaining a twenty-four-hour protective guard on institutions in the towns,
and a constant lookout in the agricultural settlements, and ready at
any moment to repel attackers. But *havlaga* forbade carrying the
war back to the attackers. They drove the enemy off (if he attacked in mass) but they did not pursue him; they did not liquidate
his bases, nor counterattack. The orders to the Haganah were similar
to those given to the British soldiers. The only difference was that
the Jews were not expected to hand in empty cartridge cases!

Havlaga was an understandable phenomenon, the natural result
of a coalition of various interests controlling Jewish affairs. First,
there were the *aliyah shniya* (the second wave of Zionist immigration), the generation of pioneers who came to Palestine from Eastern
Europe in the decade before the First World War. Today in Israel
aliyah shniya refers to a self-designated "elite" who believe not
only that they laid the foundations of the state of Israel but that
they represent the quintessence of idealism and morality, not to
mention political wisdom. They were in the beginning an intellectually
vigorous group who placed their stamp on early Zionist culture and
they and their disciples were in 1936 the leaders of the community.
They were revolutionaries, who had usually come from religious
Jewish homes in the small towns of czarist Russia. They had avidly
consumed all the forbidden literature of the age, and had been in
revolt against Czarism and against the insecurity and the humiliating
status of the Jews. They had turned against the empty incantations
of organized religion; they had rejected the unproductive life of the
middle class, scorning commerce and shopkeeping, even some of
the professions. They were in revolt because they were socialists;
they were in revolt also because they had been fired by the Zionist
ideal, despite the fact that Zionism was still anathema to many of
their generation and indeed to most of their own parents.

These ardent revolutionaries came to Palestine to restore the
wilderness, to return to the land, to set up a socialist society. "Restoring the wilderness" became the watchword of these pioneers and
its significance, in toil and sweat, in disease and death, is now too

easily forgotten. Forced into ideological debate with other sections of the population, the more dedicated immigrants became further convinced of the validity of their *Weltanschauung* and of the revolution they were initiating. True, some went to the despised towns or even back to Europe, but those who remained became more conscious of the magnitude of the role they were playing in Jewish history.

Those early years, compounded of an intense emotional upheaval, of great physical exertion and material hardships, left a deep imprint, a certain fanaticism about the new values created in Jewish life, inculcating a certain superciliousness toward newcomers and toward all who did not follow their way of life. Eventually there arose a deep hostility to all who dared oppose the ideas—for which they had given and suffered so much.

The truth is that the achievements of these dedicated people were great. In the wilderness in which they toiled every new hut set up, every new tree planted, every new blade of grass, every square yard of land reclaimed from the swamp, was a tangible victory. The emotions of the farmer as he watches his crops grow and ripen were multiplied in the hearts of these revolutionaries. They saw their pioneering efforts as the foundation on which Jewish political existence could be built. But with their gaze turned inward, they were not capable of making a realistic assessment of the forces ranged against Zionism. Confronted by a clear-sighted, purposeful antagonist determined to set bounds to Jewish regeneration, they did not even identify the antagonist, let alone pause to recognize his motives.

Moreover these settlers were under the spell of the illusion of British sympathy with Zionism, and persuaded themselves that this interest in Zionism was a moral one. They believed that their social revolution had endeared itself to the British people, and that the virtues they personified (if only they could be sufficiently publicized) would cement British friendship.

Consequently the Jewish Agency agreed to the policy of *havlaga,* believing that as long as Zionist action did not go beyond the defense of what existed, the British would have no desire to destroy that shaky status quo. British statesmen were able to keep the Zionist leaders complacent.

The Zionists' faith in their own wisdom was buttressed by British policy during the revolt not to call a complete halt to Jewish immigration. A trickle of Jews from persecuted Europe was permitted to flow into the country. But the final, conclusive blow came early in

1939, when the British Government announced that 75,000 more Jews were to be allowed into Palestine—15,000 every year till 1944; after which time the gates would be closed.

Had history been merciful, events would have produced for the Jewish people a political leader equipped to hold in balance the application of *aliyah shniya* philosophy. Chaim Weizmann was not such a man.

Weizmann, like the *aliyah shniya* pioneers, was an understandable phenomenon of the times. Raised in a village in czarist Russia, he had as a young man opposed Herzl. He, too, had been a "practical" Zionist, one of those who believed that tangible achievement in rebuilding Palestine would bring political reconstruction. He mocked the idea that political rights were an essential prerequisite for creation of a viable state.

Weizmann, however, had been quick to grasp the opportunity presented by the First World War. He had negotiated with the British for recognition of Jewish aspirations in Palestine, and he played a major part in the discussions which led to the Balfour Declaration of 1917—which both sides recognized as being the charter for the founding of the Jewish state in Palestine.

By that time, Weizmann had traveled far from his East European origins. He found personal freedom in England, opportunities to pursue his career as a scientist, success as a research chemist, and official recognition of a memorable contribution to the British war effort. He identified himself with the British way of life and with British interests, and this identification became a guiding principle in his public career. Unfortunately it led to an emotional remoteness from the masses of his own people.

As a young immigrant scientist, Weizmann had adopted British citizenship, and during the years when he was acknowledged as representative and spokesman of the Jews, he carried a British passport in his pocket. There was no formal need for this; but he could not deny himself any part of the "Britishness" which he prized so highly. Indeed it was only after his election as President of the Jewish state in 1949 that he ceased to be a British subject. During the long period when Zionist thought and emotion were focused on the suffering millions of Jews in Poland, to whom Zionism was a matter of life and death, Weizmann, internationally recognized as their leader, never visited that country. It was not that he was blind to the tragic facts. Indeed his basic comprehension was acute, and he did not shut his eyes to the British betrayal of the Balfour Declaration. In his autobiography,[5] published in the evening of his days, he reveals how often he gave private expression to his bitterness, how free he was of illusions. He recalls conversations with British statesmen indicating their indifference to Jewish suffering, their irresponsible attitude toward their Palestinian obligations—the deceit inherent in their relations with him. He accuses the high commissioner of Palestine, General Wauchope, of sending fabricated reports on the 1936 outbreaks to the League of Nations and he even goes so far as to describe the British policy of that period as "an appalling fraud on the hopes of a martyred people."[6]

Yet at the time he resigned himself to the belief that British policy must prevail, that when the last word of criticism had been spoken, when all persuasion had failed, British policy must be accepted by the "martyred people."

This, with only rare deviations, remained his creed to the end. Combined with the *aliyah shniya* philosophy it made the British Government's task considerably easier. Thus the "Arab Revolt" became a most formidable event.

2

The Irgun Is "Official"

The policy of *havlaga* of non-retaliation to Arab violence which the Jewish Agency adopted, was not at first clearly articulated. The Hebrew newspapers, by repetitive propaganda, tried to persuade the public that the tortuous reasoning of the Jewish Agency was political wisdom. The task of the propagandists was difficult. Day after day they were compelled by events to protest against Arab terrorism and against British Government policy. Editorials in the official Jewish Agency Press could not disguise their perplexity at the British Government's equivocal behavior. The articles were sprinkled with question marks—"How long will the Government tolerate . . . ?" "Why does the Government . . . ?" and "How does the Government explain . . . ?"

Many months were to pass before there were significant reprisals against the Arab terrorists by dissident Jews. For the dilemma of the dissidents in this initial stage was indeed grave. To allow the revolt to proceed with its toll of blood and destruction must consolidate the Arab population and lead to political catastrophe. Yet the decision to act independently of the Jewish Agency was a difficult one, for the Agency controlled the main sources of strength and finance, and held the goodwill of most of the press. To abandon these supports demanded a courage which the leaders of "Haganah B" did not possess.

Haganah B was the result of a split in the Haganah six years earlier. Its members were composed of Revisionists (the largest single group), General Zionists, Mizrachists (members of the religious party), and a sprinkling of politically unattached young men and women. Its military leaders were all Haganah veterans with long records of service in defense, subject to a civilian committee of political personalities, of whom the most prominent were Rabbi Meir Berlin and Israel Rokach (mayor of Tel Aviv), although it was generally assumed that on major policy they would accept the rulings of Vladimir Jabotinsky.

Throughout the years of comparative quiet, Haganah B had been generally indistinguishable from its parent in its methods and practical training. Yet its occasional use of a new title—Irgun Zvai Leumi (National Military Organization)—indicated the emergence of a new inspiration and purpose. It had no national funds on which to draw; it financed itself from voluntary contributions and from inevitably meager subsidies by the sponsoring political parties.

When the Arab attacks began in earnest, many leaders of Haganah B expected both organizations to sanction retaliation. But Haganah failed and remained hidebound by the Jewish Agency's policy of self-restraint. As a result, differences of opinion developed within the leadership of the Haganah B. Some members believed that retaliation, however necessary, was impossible without official Haganah consent. Others were persuaded that self-restraint was the correct policy. The advocates of direct action were almost all in the lower echelons, having assumed—as they later told me—that whatever decisions the leaders took were approved by Jabotinsky. These men were impatient with the passivity imposed on them, for Haganah B pursued the line of Haganah A for nearly a year after the first Arab outbreak.

After only forty-eight hours in Jerusalem, I found myself at the very heart and center of Haganah B, for the office in which I was loaned a room by Haskel's friend Peretz Cornfeld (one of the civilian leaders of the organization) was used in the evenings as a headquarters.

Not long after my arrival, I opened the consular office for the South African Government. I decided not to enroll in the Haganah B. I was determined to do nothing to embarrass Haskel with his own government and tried to be friendly yet aloof toward the clandestine movement, a resolution I kept for a year, although I was in close contact with Cornfeld and others in Haganah B.

As the months went by and the policy of self-restraint became habitual to both organizations, the leaders of Haganah A began talk of reuniting with Haganah B. Negotiations eventually opened tentatively in the autumn of 1936 and came to a head in the spring of

1937. One day, at Cornfeld's request, I sent a code cable (through Haskel) to Jabotinsky then visiting South Africa, in which the Haganah B leaders recommended that he accept the terms of Haganah A.

To the dismay of Avraham Tahomey, territorial commander of Haganah B, who, only a few months earlier, had signed an agreement accepting Jabotinsky's ultimate authority, Jabotinsky rejected the recommendation. He had not intervened against the policy of self-restraint and indeed (as transpired later) his feelings on the subject of retaliation were mixed, but Jabotinsky could not agree to be tied irrevocably by the policies of Haganah A.

Tahomey and his colleagues decided to disregard Jabotinsky and join with the Haganah. But in the ranks tension was high, for while the senior commanders were determined to return to the Haganah, their juniors wanted to remain independent. A tug of war for power began in the organization, and in the end only about one quarter of the three thousand members of Haganah B followed Tahomey. A minority fell away, and the organization continued under the new name of Irgun Zvai Leumi.

One evening in May 1937, as I was about to leave my office, Vladimir Jabotinsky's son, Eri, who was head of the Palestine Betar (Zionist Youth Group), suddenly arrived from the north with Dr. Shimshon Yunitchman and two colleagues for consultations with the officers of the Irgun. They wished to remain incognito, and Eri had decided that the best way for them to keep out of sight was to spend the night in my office.

When I reached the office early next morning, they were on the point of leaving, but in the corridor talking to my secretary, David Koenig (himself a member of the Irgun), was a squarely built man a few years my senior. He held out his hand and said "My name is David. I think we ought to meet for a talk." This was my first meeting with David Raziel, now the Jerusalem commander, a member of the new national command of the Irgun Zvai Leumi. Within a few weeks of my first meeting with Raziel, I reported to Haskel in a letter:

"Of all the younger generation here, Raziel is the first who has impressed me as a leader. He is on quite a different plane from all the others I have met. He is the new type of Jew: a soldier. He is tough, he knows what he wants. He is full of 'professional' knowledge and he is disseminating it."

Raziel was an unusual and talented man. If he had not been needed as a soldier, he would have achieved great success as a writer and teacher. The scion of a rabbinical family, intensely orthodox, he might have become a great rabbi or a great historian. In his studies at the Hebrew University he excelled in philosophy and mathematics. As a young man he had decided that Jewish redemption could be achieved only by the sword. He therefore studied military history, military science, military biography, weaponry, logistics, and guerrilla tactics.

He did not study military lore out of idle curiosity. He was consciously preparing himself to teach others. He wrote (together with his colleague, Avraham Stern) textbooks on the revolver and on methods of training. He conducted courses in the use of small arms and in the manufacture of homemade explosives. He was a scholar who could discuss the strategy and tactics of the Napoleonic wars, and write a commentary on Clausewitz. He fretted and chafed at the tardiness of the historic process. Although accepting Jabotinsky's leadership, he did not believe that party political action alone could achieve Jewish statehood. He was convinced that this could be attained only after an armed struggle with the British and he would have preferred to build the Irgun to meet the inevitable clash, rather than concentrate on retaliation against the Arabs.

Although I did not share Raziel's view about the inevitability of the clash with the British he and I did agree that the policy of self-restraint would lead to disaster and that the Arab terror must be met by vigorous countermeasures.

This was a formidable task. The material resources of the Irgun were pitifully weak, the number of full-time officers totally inadequate, the acquisition of arms and explosives was possible only on the most limited scale. Also the British were well informed about the consolidation of the Irgun and its purpose. They had already set their Intelligence Service to work against the Revisionist Party, which they believed was the nursery of the Irgun; and there was evidence of some Jewish co-operation in this espionage. These were the enormous odds against the Irgun, the only organization with the will (but not the resources) to challenge the British.

My relations with Raziel developed easily. I secured a monthly contribution for the Irgun from Haskel and I provided Raziel with an office. His other *pied à terre* was at the home of Mrs. Spitzer, headmistress of a large private school for girls in the Geulah quarter, whose daughter Shoshana was to become Raziel's wife. He often took his midday meal there, and the school was used in the evenings as an Irgun training center. British detectives were on the lookout for him. One day they came to the apartment and showed Mrs. Spitzer a snapshot of Raziel asking her if she knew him. Mrs. Spitzer looked hard at the photograph and in an unusually loud voice regretted that she could not identify it. Mrs. Spitzer was a big woman with a vigorous, determined personality. She kept the British at the door long enough for David (who had been eating his lunch) to make his escape over a rear balcony.

After this the room in my office served for several months as Raziel's sole headquarters. The arrangement was far from foolproof. There was no exit from the little back room except through my room, and no way out of the office except through the front door. Raziel took great care going to and from the building, and he had grown a mustache; but these were frail defenses. I was glad that throughout this period Haskel did not come to Palestine, but when on his visit early in 1938 I told him of the imprudent use to which I had put the office, he was at first shocked, then delighted.

Having gone so far in my "double life," I suggested to Raziel that I might as well also join the ranks of the Irgun. He did not approve and proposed a compromise. A number of older men, most of them Revisionists, were unable for various reasons to join the Irgun as regular members, and had formed a so-called "civilian group," which he suggested I join. Its leading spirit was Eliel Freiman, the manager of the Banco di Roma and also the Generali Building, who had placed a room in the building at the disposal of the group. There in the summer nights a dozen of us gathered to learn how to use small arms. I was the youngest of the group. The others, professionals or businessmen, were in their thirties or forties. The oldest member was Dr. Yitshak Landau, a cheerful physician from Danzig who enlivened the dry atmosphere of the lectures with witty personal comment. His son was to preside twenty-four years later as a member of the Supreme Court of the state of Israel at the trial of Adolf Eichmann.

I had meantime undertaken yet another assignment—writing a weekly article for a South African newspaper that was launched during a triumphant tour of the country in mid-1937 by Jabotinsky.

The paper was called *The Eleventh Hour*—a phrase that symbolized the theme dominating Jabotinsky's mind and heart—the imminence of catastrophe in Europe and the lengthening of the shadows in Palestine. Jabotinsky himself gave much time and thought to this new paper. Never had a Jewish community, far from the centers of Jewish travail and with only secondhand knowledge of the realities of the Palestine situation, received such an intensive and controversial education.

My contribution was an anonymous weekly commentary on events called "On the Spot in Palestine." Later I wrote additional articles, as the spirit moved me, under my old pseudonym, "Ben Elkanah," or a new one, "Justin Priestly."

Jabotinsky stayed in South Africa, delivering speeches and lectures that held audiences spellbound throughout the country, until the end of June. In May I received a letter from him:

> I hope you will forgive me if I make a confession: that I have been trying to suggest to Mr. Haskel that it would be a great thing for all of us if you came for a year to Jo'burg. It seems that we have proved able to lay here a foundation for a strong N.Z.O.[1] movement, and I am sure that this provides you with a field and a range of action you could achieve wonders with. Especially the "11th Hour" needs you. I have been reading your reports and articles and must very earnestly congratulate you on the perfect clarity, the forcible simplicity, the *"Sachlichkeit"* with which you present the most complicated situations. I think you are much more than a journalist; but you also are a born journalist and a very good one.
>
> Think it over and, when you write to Mr. H. about it, drop me a line.

I agreed to discuss the matter with Jabotinsky in Egypt, where he planned to stop on his way back to Europe in order to meet members of the various Palestinian organizations of which he was leader. The British had refused him permission to enter Palestine.

When I met Jabotinsky in Egypt, I was able to persuade him that I would probably be more useful in Palestine than in South Africa. In return he persuaded me to act as his secretary for the five days of his stay in Egypt. As it happened they were eventful days.

The publication that week of the report of the British Royal Commission in Palestine, headed by Lord Peel, made clear both the realities of British policy and the convoluted nature of Zionist psychology. The document itself cast a long shadow into the future.

The Royal Commission had been appointed to "investigate" the Arab Revolt. And since a truce might be interpreted as a sign of Arab weakness (with consequent damage to the prestige of the Mufti and his colleagues) the British called in the neighboring Arab vassal kings to "appeal" to the Palestine Arabs to call off the "strike." Thus the Arab states were for the first time accorded the right of inexpensive interference in the affairs of Palestine. The strike was dutifully called off, and the Mufti and his Higher Committee retained their intransigent status. The British authorities permitted the fighting bands, led by Fawzi el Kaukji, to return unmolested to Iraq and Syria, there to rest and reorganize for the next round in the battle.

The six gentlemen of the Royal Commission then spent some months listening to Arab and Jewish views and after a further period for sifting their findings, produced the report. It contained a brilliantly conceived scheme which would assure continued British control of the country.

They proposed that the Mandate (and thus even the theoretical supervision of the League of Nations over the British Administration) should come to an end. The country must be split into three parts: an Arab state in the major part to be joined to Transjordan; a Jewish state along the coastal strip; and reserved areas in which Britain would continue to rule directly. Haifa "temporarily" and Jerusalem permanently should be governed by Britain, with a British "corridor" from Jerusalem to Jaffa, all communications in the three areas being under British control. The Jewish state would have to finance both the British and the Arabs: all customs dues to be collected by the British, and a subsidy given by the Jews to the Arab state. The tiny area assigned to the Jews (about 2800 square miles) was the most densely populated part of the country—so that its capacity for taking in newcomers was infinitesimal. Strategically it would be wholly at the mercy of the Arabs who dominated the hill country. The "state" would thus be almost completely dependent on British protection.

The impact of the Peel Commission Report was dramatic, not so much in changing the political climate in Palestine, but in demonstrating the intellectual subservience of the Zionist leaders to Britain. The Zionist leaders changed their basic policy overnight. Weizmann had over the years suggested a variety of formulas, all of which conformed with revealed British policy. In the years before 1937 he had preached "parity"—a nebulous ideal in which Jews and Arabs would forever enjoy equal political status, while Britain retained her role as supreme arbiter. But "parity" was swept aside the moment His Majesty's Government adopted the partition scheme. Then Weizmann discovered that a Jewish state such as the Peel report suggested, was an ideal solution.

The conversion of David Ben-Gurion, a man second only to Weizmann in status and influence in the Zionist leadership, was even more spectacular. The differences in temperament and style between him and Weizmann have often obscured the fact that in essentials there was little to choose between them. Ben-Gurion clung to borrowed ideas even more tenaciously than Weizmann. Up to the eve of the Royal Commission's hearings he too was quietly preaching "parity." In his address to the Commission the single clear thought was his emphatic rejection of the idea of a Jewish state[2] which he described as politically unnecessary, morally undesirable, and potentially against Jewish interests.

Still, no sooner had the gentiles proposed a Jewish state, one in which all the qualities Ben-Gurion had scorned must surely be manifest, then, like Weizmann, Ben-Gurion discovered that in this suggestion lay the answers to all his problems.

Jabotinsky studied the Royal Commission's report in Egypt. He was quietly jubilant about it. Only he among those who had addressed the commission had explained, in a precise analysis of Jewish needs and of British undertakings, why there could be no other realization of Zionism or to the partnership with Britain than a Jewish state. He alone had—for the first time—argued before a British forum the thesis that if Britain would not or could not fulfill her Mandate her right to rule Palestine was forfeit.[3] Now, he saw a ray of light through the maze of the commission's conclusions. To a crowded public meeting in the Alhambra Theatre, in Alexandria, he explained what it was:

"We shall have to fight this scheme, though it is so fantastic that nothing will come of it," he said. "But it has one great positive feature: it contains an official stamp of British approval for the idea of a Jewish state."

Later on that summer, the combined influence of Weizmann and

Ben-Gurion won the day for the idea of the partition of Palestine at the Zionist Congress. In the British House of Commons, partition was denounced not only as a betrayal of Britain's undertakings but as impractical. The friends of the Zionist Movement in the House of Commons, bewildered though they were by official Zionist acceptance, fought resolutely against the scheme. Briefed by Jabotinsky, Winston Churchill, in one of his many acts of revolt against his party, proposed a delaying amendment to the Government's proposal in Parliament.[4] The acceptance of this amendment dealt partition a crippling blow.

Still the Zionist leaders persisted in pretending to the world that opposition to partition stemmed only from enemies of Zionism.

There was one element of truth in this theory. The Arab leaders rejected the partition plan outright. Nine months had passed since the declaration of the "truce," and the Arabs were ready to take the offensive again. As smoothly as they had departed, Fawzi el Kaukji and his bands returned to Palestine and the campaign of violence against the Jews was resumed. No new strike was organized, but Arab activity was marked by better organization, by a greater diversity of tactics, and by an even more systematic liquidation of Arab nonconformists.

3

Strife Within the Irgun

In the face of renewed Arab activity, the Irgun retaliated with sporadic small attacks in various parts of the country. The British administration acted at once, and fell upon the Revisionists, who were openly critical of the policy of *havlaga*. The party newspaper, though often ingeniously circumspect in its language, refused to conceal its obvious militancy. The British closed down the paper and prohibited public meetings except by permit. Dawn raids were made on the homes of scores of Revisionists, who were arrested and promptly sentenced by the District Commissioners to imprisonment without trial.

Prisoners were forced to sleep on vermin-infested mattresses laid out on stone floors, with only enough food for subsistence. In any approach to the prison governor they were expected to crouch outside his door until he was ready to receive them, although this ruling was soon ignored when the prisoners refused to comply.

The British chose their victims indiscriminately, making arrests at will. First were the associates of Dr. Aba Achimeir, who six years earlier had proclaimed that resistance to the British administration was a Zionist imperative, and that going to jail for such resistance was in itself a contribution to the ultimate breakdown of the anti-Zionist regime. Achimeir and his Brit Habiryonim, the most militant wing of the Revisionist Party, had at the time carried out a number of demonstrative acts against the regime. Though they had long been inactive as a group, their names and addresses were available to the British. The British also made use of lists of men active in the Revisionist Party.

I was able to judge the British method of arrest at close quarters. One Friday midday, on the point of leaving the office for the weekend, I had an unexpected visitor, a young Jewish policeman named "Bubby" Bergman, a Betari from Latvia whom I had met before. He was attached to the police station near the Generali Building, where Inspector Gordon, a Jew, was in charge. By his public habits Gordon seemed obsessed by the desire to be an Englishman and was certainly determined to identify himself absolutely with British objectives. On that Friday he had told his second-in-command, Inspector Langer, that he had an order to arrest forty Revisionists by Sunday morning. He himself was about to leave Jerusalem for the weekend and the execution of the order devolved on Langer. Langer, unlike Gordon, was a veteran resident of Jerusalem and so knew who all the important Revisionists were. He was ordered to make up a list of names, despite his protests against this indiscriminate method of arrest.

Langer had no difficulty in compiling such a list. I was appalled when Bergman showed it to me. It contained the names of thirty-eight men whose arrest would have paralyzed the Revisionist activities in Jerusalem. Bergman carried a message from Langer: he had no alternative but to carry out arrests but was prepared to allow the Revisionists themselves to substitute less important names for those on his list.

I approached Hayyim Shalom Halevi, one of Raziel's first colleagues in the Irgun and a member of the party committee. No substitute list was made, but when the police arrived in the pre-dawn hours on Sunday morning to make the arrests, all but one of the chosen victims had flown, although they drifted back within a few days.

The Jewish Agency reacted almost as furiously as the British did to the Irgun activities. Irgun reprisals were generally approved by the man in the street, and they increased the restiveness in the ranks of the Haganah itself. But the Agency regarded reprisals as treachery, even though few believed in their policy of self-restraint which even the British treated with contempt. Indeed Dr. Weizmann in his memoirs, published twelve years later, wrote: "Violence paid political dividends to the Arabs while Jewish havlaga was expected to be its own reward. It did not even win official recognition."[1] Looking back, the Agency's persistence in this suicidal policy seems fantastic.

At that time, fantasy seemed to be the only reality. Those were the days when Hitler was preparing to enslave Europe, and in Britain the warning voice of Churchill cried vainly in the wilderness for a national defense policy. Weakness, shortsightedness, and appeasement ruled in a Europe deafened and cowed by Nazi aggression and lies. If the political leaders of the great and powerful Western European states were complacent and self-satisfied, how could better qualities be found in the Jewish leaders, who were dominated by an inferiority complex, and battered and bewildered by successive British betrayals?

The Jewish Agency seemed delighted with the news of prisons filled with Jewish prisoners. *Davar,* the organ of the *Histadrut,* laced its pathetic protests at the British inaction against the Arab rioters with calls to the British to carry on with the good work.

After the Irgun reprisals, there was a subsidence of Arab terror. The London *Times* commented laconically that Jewish reprisals had had some effect. The censor did not allow this interesting judgment to be printed in Palestine.

The Irgun was now swept into its first crisis. It arose from the incompatibility of Robert Bitker for his post as commander-in-chief. It is difficult even now to conceive precisely what qualifications were required in the leader of a still-amorphous organization, hounded by the British, hated by the Jewish authorities, materially impoverished, and still uncertain of the direction of its activities. Robert Bitker was a soldier and not a politician, new to the country, and ignorant of Hebrew.

His relations with his staff were strained. Bitker was impatient for action, and was particularly irked by the Irgun's financial problems.

Without the knowledge of his staff, Bitker authorized an attempt to confiscate the funds carried by a bank messenger in a busy Tel Aviv street. The attempt was made by a group of young men who were not members of the Irgun but had been associated with Brit Habiryonim. Three of the men were caught and sent to prison.[2]

The agitation of the Irgun staff, and of the Revisionist leaders, was heightened by the mystery of the fate of a young Irgun member named Frankel. In an act of retaliation, Frankel had killed a Jaffa Arab in Tel Aviv. The police who had found clues to his identity arrested his ailing mother as a hostage. The Irgun staff decided to spirit Frankel out of the country. They asked Dr. Altman to provide the money for his flight, but Frankel was later found drowned in the Yarkon River. The mystery of his death has never been solved.

There were signs of an unofficial camarilla and the evolution of two conflicting policies within the organization. However well-meant, Bitker's methods were not working, and the Irgun staff and the Revisionist Party leaders decided to call for his removal. They resolved to send me as their direct emissary to Jabotinsky, then on one of his frequent visits to Poland. I was asked to leave by the first plane for Poland on this unpleasant mission.

I arrived in Warsaw in the afternoon and took a room at the Polonia Hotel. I found Jabotinsky in a shabby hotel on the Vistula River, about to leave for Lodz, where he was to give a lecture.

I told him the object of my surprise visit as we sat in a compartment on the train. His face grew tense, and when I had finished my unhappy tale he said in very angry tones: "By what right did you bring this to me at all? Have you no idea of what is right or wrong in a military organization? When will you people learn that any complaint you have to make, any complaint at all, you must submit to your superior officer? All that you have told me you should have asked Bitker to convey to me. I can assure you that he would have passed it on. Maybe he is not the right man for the job, but he is a man of honor." He was silent for a moment. Then he said, "I shall treat your case as though I had it through the correct channels. Let us go over it again."

He subjected me to a searching cross-examination for the rest of the trip.

At Lodz we were met by Jacob Spektor, a member of the NZO Presidency,[3] who took us to his home, and later to the theater where Jabotinsky was to speak. Jabotinsky was in the midst of his campaign to alert the Jews of Eastern Europe to their surrounding danger and to persuade them to evacuate. In his speeches he described the spreading blight of anti-Jewish discrimination, and pointed out that even the non-violent variety which he called "the anti-Semitism of things," could not be halted. The virulent dissemination of Nazism—"the anti-Semitism of men"—had only hastened a process which in Eastern Europe had been marching forward with increasing speed. He saw that in countries such as Poland, with its three and a half million Jews, anti-Semitism was integral to the economic and social development of the population, and gentile statesmen, even when well-meaning, could not defeat it. The exclusion of Jews from the economic life of "East-Central Europe" was an objective process not related even to specific hatred of the Jew, but when hatred and violence were added to this process, it meant death.

To Jabotinsky, the determined devotee of nineteenth-century liberalism, the collapse of that liberalism was a bitter personal experience. Yet there was no escape; and he stubbornly faced the issue. The Jews must leave "East-Central" Europe.

He went further. The Jews must smash the British locks on the gates of Palestine. He knew that most of the statesmen of Eastern Europe were appalled at their own inability to hold back the tide of anti-Semitism, and he set out to enlist the co-operation of these leaders in creating a volume of international pressure which Great Britain would, in the end, be unable to withstand.[4]

Jabotinsky had some success with the statesmen. It was the Jews who would not listen! Never in his stormy career had Jabotinsky encountered such vilification as he did while lecturing in Eastern Europe. The Jewish leaders, the Zionist politicians, rose up in wrath and horror to denounce him. They accused him of playing into the hands of the anti-Semites, of giving them a warrant to get rid of the Jews and of sabotaging the struggle for equal rights.

Many of the Zionist leaders did not believe in this "struggle for equal rights." Weizmann himself seemed resigned to the hopelessness of the Jewish condition in Eastern Europe. We in South Africa had indeed already heard Weizmann argue this point of view in 1932. The plight of the Jews in Eastern Europe, he said then, was not necessarily the consequence of anti-Semitism. He had testified before the Royal Commission that the "million superfluous Jews" in Poland were the result of the rising Polish middle class taking the place of the Jews in the economic life of the country. His answer to this problem as to all other problems, was determined by his resigned acceptance of the main lines of British policy in Palestine. In contrast to Jabotinsky's call: "Get out, save yourselves before you are destroyed, let us together break open the gates of Palestine," Weizmann said of these Jews (to the Royal Commission in secret session):

"They are dust, economic and moral dust in a cruel world. Only a branch will survive. This we must accept."[5]

Some of the Jewish leaders in Poland, however, blindly believed in their own truth. They could not face the fact that the struggle for equal rights was not only hopeless but did not exist. Only two of them found the courage in later years to make public acknowledgment of their tragic error: Yitzhak Gruenbaum, then the foremost leader and spokesman of the Polish Jews, and Sholem Asch, the great Polish-born Yiddish novelist. Asch responded to the urgent pleas of the Zionist leaders to come to Poland from America and use his powerful influence in the community to counteract Jabotinsky's "dangerous" doctrine. A rebellious humanist philosopher, himself the center of many controversies and the victim of much vilification, Asch was not a political thinker and accepted uncritically the pacific defeatism preached by Weizmann. Many years later, in Israel, we became good friends and he told me:

"For twenty-five years I believed that Weizmann was the realist and Jabotinsky, for all his gifts, an impractical dreamer. Now I realize it was exactly the other way round."

I returned with Jabotinsky to Warsaw and, strolling in a public park in the middle of a workday morning, I learned something of the cold hopelessness of the Jews of Poland. Jews, mainly young men, sat on the benches, singly or in groups, reading newspapers, talking or simply idling. They had no work and no prospects. My companion told me that among them there were university graduates who found it impossible to start on their careers—there was no room for them. The government service was closed to them. They were largely barred from academic posts. Of the three million and more Jews in Poland, almost all living in the towns, sociologists and relief organizations had established that one third were "living below the bread-line," dependent on the charity either of the thin wealthy layer in its own community or of the Jews of the Western countries. Another third which, in the preceding decades, had achieved positions of some stability in the professions or in commerce, were being forced out of them. Such a condition of hopeless mass poverty was not unprecedented in Europe. Vast emigration movements, as from Ireland and Italy, had provided a solution. For the Jews of Poland, and of Eastern Europe, the gates of the countries of the world were all but barred.

My last meeting with Jabotinsky took place late in the evening. When I entered his room I saw that he already had a visitor: a pale, tense-faced young man of about my own age, Menahem Begin, the head of the Polish Betar, whom I had met a few days earlier very briefly, in the street. A forceful orator with determined opinions, Begin was beginning to play a dynamic part in the world movement, especially as the proponent of Irgun action.

I hesitated at the door, but Jabotinsky beckoned me in. Years later Begin told me that he said to him, "It's all right. I have no secrets from him."

Jabotinsky told me he had acceded to the request I had brought him and nominated Moshe Rosenberg as Bitker's successor. He now questioned me at length about the work of the Irgun, its method of recruitment and organization, its relations with the Revisionist Party. Suddenly he interrupted: "Don't tell me any more. There are things I don't want to be told. You never know. I might one day be caught and tortured for information."

On this note we parted. My last recollection is of him standing at the head of the stairs as I went down, giving me a last wave of the hand and a wistful smile. I was never to see him again.

4

Reprisals and an Execution

The Arab "revolt" had got out of hand. The British District Commissioner in Galilee was assassinated by the Arabs, and British reaction was swift. They pounced on the members of the Arab Higher Committee and deported them to the Seychelles Islands. The Mufti escaped, although it was known that he was in the Old City of Jerusalem, where British forces were said to be watching all exits. Nevertheless the Mufti managed to reach Bludan, in Lebanon, where he resumed the political leadership of the "revolt." A number of important Arabs were urging peace with the Jews, and these had first to be silenced or intimidated. A large-scale murder campaign began against the Mufti's opponents.

One winter's morning, I found a note under my office door from Jack Simon, the United Press correspondent in Jerusalem, asking me to meet him in Beit Hakerem. Simon was one of my earliest friends in Jerusalem—an erudite Sephardic Jew and a brilliant newspaperman. He was steeped in Arab culture, liked the Arabs, among whom he had many contacts, and believed that if Britain ceased to interfere, Jews and Arabs might still live in amity in a Jewish state.

When I arrived at Beit Hakerem I found Simon waiting in his car. We drove off and he explained the reason for the secret rendezvous. The previous night an Arab friend on the staff of one of the Jerusalem Arab dailies, and now attached to the Mufti's headquarters, had come to Simon's house. He reminded Simon that he had always been a convinced though secret opponent of the Mufti. His hostility was now exacerbated by the murder of some of his friends. Being persona grata at the Mufti's headquarters, he had become privy to a scheme to liquidate the Mufti. Simon's friend planned to take an active part in the plot, but he needed a getaway and two hundred pounds. As proof of his sincerity he insisted that the money be paid him only after the deed was done.

The sum he wanted was quite considerable, roughly equivalent in purchasing power to 10,000 Israeli pounds today. Nevertheless, I foresaw no great difficulty in finding it. I was not troubled about the moral aspect. The problem was more pragmatic to my mind. Political assassination, even of a deserving victim, is not necessarily productive of good results. The proposal might well have far-reaching political repercussions.

Back at my office I wrote a cable, in a private cipher I had long since grafted onto Bentley's Commercial Code, and sent it off to Haskel's branch office in London, asking for a ruling by Jabotinsky. When it came, after a delay of several weeks, I was informed: "Jabotinsky says no. Would you like to see the Arabs bumping off Weizmann or Shertok?"

This argument did not impress me. If the Arabs could have assassinated Jewish leaders they would have done so. Jabotinsky was no doubt swayed by his strong opposition to personal terror. I have similar feelings on the subject, but the Mufti was a glaring exception. Looking back now on the Mufti's later aid to Hitler in planning the extermination of the Jews of Europe, I am all the more sorry I did not accept the proposal at once instead of asking Jabotinsky.

The "revolt" which had quieted after the Irgun's summer reprisals, was resumed with a new intensity in the autumn of 1937. The Irgun, its uncertainties resolved by Jabotinsky's firm decision on retaliation against Arab attack, launched its campaign of large-scale reprisals on November 14. This campaign was to continue intermittently until the outbreak of World War II nearly two years later. It opened with the explosion of a homemade bomb constructed by Raziel himself, in the Arab market place in the Old City of Jerusalem, killing and wounding scores of Arabs.

The Jewish Agency openly dissociated itself from this campaign. The Irgun, under its new leadership, tightened its organization and conspiratorial discipline. It was a rare courage it demanded from its members—to carry on day after day surrounded by hatred, vilification, and denunciation from their own people. There are many unsung heroes in the story of the Irgun. Jacob Rass, an eighteen-year-old boy, was one of them. Detailed to carry out an attack in the Arab market place of Jerusalem, he disguised himself as an Arab villager and wheeled a vegetable barrow into the market, a homemade bomb concealed among the vegetables. Something in his manner apparently aroused the suspicion of an Arab woman, who began screaming, *"Yahud, Yahud."* A crowd closed in on Rass, who was shot while trying to escape. Badly wounded by several bullets, he was taken to the hospital by British police, and there operated on. His guards waited for the doctor's permission to question him. Knowing this, weak from the loss of blood and fearful lest in his weakness he might give away the names of comrades, he quietly undid his bandages and slowly bled to death.

It is not easy to reconstruct the pattern of my own life at that time. During the day I attended strictly to the affairs of the office. Outside of office hours, in addition to my writing for the *Jewish Herald,* I was accepting more and more tasks both for the Revisionist Party and the Irgun. I knew the British police had me on their files as a Revisionist sympathizer. I had come to believe that Haskel's maintenance of the office was no longer justified. I urged him to come to Jerusalem. When he did and I pressed this view upon him, he rejected it. But he did agree that he should, at long last, come to Palestine to settle. He promised to try to do so in six months. With that I had to rest content.

My night journeys to Tel Aviv became more frequent once Raziel moved to underground headquarters there. I made it a rule always to be in my office punctually in the morning, and to be seen often at the Cafe Vienna in the early evening. This meant traveling to Tel Aviv after dark, when the curfew brought public transport—and indeed the movement of all but the few who had curfew passes—to a complete standstill.

I had exploited my semi-consular status to obtain a pass as soon as this curfew was imposed, but I had no car. I did not wish to use the car Haskel had bought, but my problem was solved by my journalist friend Jack Simon, who, although he never once asked me questions, made himself available whenever I needed his help.

It was he who took me across the border on most of my journeys to Lebanon and Syria. My official capacity in the consular office enabled me to secure visas without difficulty and gave me some protection from interrogation at the frontier, so that I could establish a regular and uncomplicated channel of Irgun and Revisionist communication with Europe.

At this time, as danger threatened the Jews of Europe, some of the young people succeeded in eluding both the Nazis and the British and make their way to Palestine to join the youth groups there.

The *pelugot giyus*[1] of the Betar were the embodiment of all the high ideals which Jabotinsky had formulated for the new generation of Jews he visualized—the breed which, "out of the pit of dust and decay," would arise "proud and generous and strong." Their central principle was utter dedication. For two years, without the compulsions of state or society, in the face of hostility and derision, they voluntarily gave themselves to national service and to the undertaking of difficult and dangerous assignments. The most concentrated effort was the revival of the neglected Jewish development in Galilee, largely ignored by the official Zionist institutions which applied themselves to the Jezreel Valley (the Emek) and the Sharon.

The Betar *pelugot,* at Metullah, at Mishmar Hayarden, at Rosh Pinna, injected a new dynamic into the area, toiling to revive the production of tobacco, previously abandoned by the Histadrut, and becoming the only producers of olive oil in the country. Elsewhere the *pelugot* hired themselves out to the farmers. In other parts of the country, like Zichron Yaakov and Kefar Sava, where the Histadrut had failed in its efforts to establish Jewish labor, the *pelugot* tackled the problems involved. Yet their two years' service earned them no special rights and no personal advantages. They worked in collectives under the most primitive conditions.

In the Old City of Jerusalem members of the group acted as "security," the Pelugat Hakotel (the Wailing Wall platoon) being the self-appointed guard of the Jewish community there. It provided protection for Jewish pilgrims at the Wailing Wall and maintained a permanent watch over the heavily outnumbered Jewish quarter, in constant danger of Arab attack.

Whenever I could I traveled up to Galilee to visit the *pelugot* there. I fell in love with Galilee, its rugged heights, its rolling plains, its sense of historical continuity. Most often I visited Rosh Pinna, which, established in the 1880s, was bathed in an Old World mellowness. The cobbled main street, under an overhanging canopy of tall eucalyptus trees, gave a sense of unchanging tranquillity, remote from the bustling dynamic of Palestine.

A young poet, Shlomo Skulsky, was to write in a poem called *Rosh Pinna,* today a popular song:

> *The height will not be conquered*
> *If no grave is on the slope.*

The Arab attacks, especially these against the agricultural settlements, had developed a dangerous rhythm, although the "legal" force of Jewish auxiliary police, together with their "illegal" comrades in the Haganah, were usually able to repel such attacks. For months on end men and women worked by day and watched by night, fortitude and bravery under attack a daily phenomenon.

In the towns the pattern was different. There were no mass attacks and no response at all from the Haganah to the continuous series of shootings from ambush and hit-and-run destruction.

The British Army now played a larger part in the Administration's policy. A number of pitched battles were fought with Fawzi Kaukji's bands, which suffered heavy losses, necessary price for the British image of revolt.

The "revolt" was kept within bounds but not crushed. The Arab fighters never numbered more than a thousand in the whole country at any one time and Jewish static defense was sufficient to prevent their doing irretrievable damage. The heavily publicized battles waged by the British made the uprising seem genuine, but at a heavy cost in Jewish property and Jewish, Arab, and British lives.

A dynamic British officer named Orde Wingate was given a routine posting to Palestine in 1936. Fired by the historic dream of Zionism and inspired by a mystic identification with the Jewish people and their destiny, he risked his life and his military career in a daring effort to break the strait-jacket of the static Jewish defense. Wingate preached the idea of taking the war to the attackers, and by sheer force of personality convinced a Haganah group in the *Emek* (who at first resisted his proposals as "illegal") to accept his leadership. He led them in a number of raids on Arab villages suspected of serving as bases for the Arab bands.

Wingate's career in Palestine was abruptly cut short, and he was recalled to England. His brief personal experience had revealed to him the truth about his government's policy. On the eve of his enforced departure he made an impassioned effort to make the Haganah leaders understand that the Jews, if they wished to achieve a Jewish state, would have to fight Britain for it. To the end of his adventurous life—tragically cut short in World War II—this conviction, and his love and concern for the Jewish people, found repeated and fervent expression in all he did and said.

Wingate was friendly with the Zionist leaders and offered them advice while criticizing them with the outspokenness of a faithful friend. Incapable of following their tortuous reasonings, he once said to Ben-Gurion: "You are a traitor to your people."

The Zionist leaders absorbed none of Wingate's political wisdom, nor learned anything from the treatment he received from the British Government. They did indeed continuously publish warnings to the British that forbearance was reaching the breaking point, yet the Jewish Agency openly incited the British to institute even sterner measures against the Revisionist Party, whom they identified as sponsors of Irgun retaliations.

The tension did reach the breaking point at the pleasant village of Rosh Pinna which was attacked almost nightly, and its fields set on fire. Between the village and the fields there was a British army camp. At each attack a British force would arrive on the scene. Sometimes they arrived in time to join in driving off the attackers. They were always in time to prevent any pursuit.

One of the sixty Betarim in the *pelugah* at Rosh Pinna in that spring of 1938 was a youth of twenty-one, Shlomo Tabachnik, who had adopted the Hebrew name of Ben-Yosef. His "grave on the slope" marked a turning point in our relations with Great Britain. Ben-Yosef had, only the year before, made his "illegal" way from Poland across the Syrian border into Palestine. A quiet, unobtrusive, straightforward young man, he was filled with bitterness and frustration in the face of continuous Arab aggression against his village.

As an act of protest, one afternoon in April, he and two younger members of the *pelugah,* Avraham Shein and Shalom Zuravin, went out to the main road and fired at an Arab bus. No one was hit, but he and his friends returned to the village to be arrested. For this attack he was hanged by the British two months later, despite world-wide appeals for clemency.

On the eve of the execution, Robert Briscoe, the Jewish mayor of Dublin and an NZO leader, suggested to Jabotinsky the possibility of legal precedents stemming from the days of the Irish Rebellion. With the help of Lord Nathan, then still a Labor Member of Parliament, they began to search for a legal loophole, and asked for a stay of execution to give them time. Ben-Yosef's lawyer, Philip Joseph, made a similar plea. All were denied.

Chief Rabbi Herzog in Jerusalem asked for the execution to be delayed for a day as it was *Rosh Hodesh*,[2] when no rabbi could give the boy religious consolation. It was denied.

Ben-Yosef alone remained calm and poised. When a group of journalists visited him on the eve of the hanging at Acre Prison, it was he who comforted them.

"Do not console me," he said, "I need no consolation.

"I am proud to be the first Jew to go to the gallows in Palestine," he said. "In dying I shall do my people a greater service than in my life.

"Let the world see that Jews are not afraid to face death," he said.

In his cell the journalists saw that he had written on the wall: TO DIE OR TO CONQUER THE HEIGHT.

On the morning of the execution, he washed, brushed his teeth, and drank a cup of tea. As he walked the few yards to the death cell he sang the Betar hymn, and on the gallows he called out, "Long live the Jewish state. Long live Jabotinsky."

The Jewish community in Palestine was horrified. There was a spontaneous strike of workers and shopkeepers, but the Jewish Agency leaders warned against disturbing "the peace," and new denunciations appeared against the Revisionists. Ben-Yosef's courageous act was derided as a foolish sacrifice of a life, and no more.

Ben-Yosef's execution brought about a complete change in my feelings. I had been convinced that he would be reprieved. When the news of his death came, I was filled with a rage I had never known. I knew then that the belief I had cherished that a more militant Zionism could effect a change of heart in the British was a delusion. The British would have to leave Palestine if we were ever to achieve a Jewish state.

As though the hanging of Ben-Yosef had been a signal, the Arab terrorists released a wave of attacks of undiscriminating ferocity. Five Jews were massacred in their sleep. Seven were killed in an attack at a settlement. Nine were killed in a bus. There were shootings, stabbings, bombings, burnings everywhere.

The Irgun retaliated. Scores of Arabs were killed and many more wounded in a series of attacks. Bombs exploded in the Jerusalem market place and in Haifa. The Jewish Agency press denounced these acts, while the British reacted by filling the prisons with Revisionists.

Dr. Aryeh Altman, the leader of the Revisionist Party in Palestine, left the country to join Jabotinsky on his third mission to South Africa. The burden of running the organization fell on his two colleagues, David Bukspan and Binyamin Lubotsky.

While Bukspan labored under a heavy administrative burden, Lubotsky played a more colorful role. A brilliant public speaker, and a lucid forceful writer, he had been, in 1937, one of the first of the Revisionists to be jailed by the British. The appalling prison conditions seriously weakened his health, but this did not affect the tempestuous pace of his labors, which included regular service as the Revisionist Party representative on the Irgun Command.

My relationship with him and with Bukspan was now very close. On a steaming Thursday morning in July I received a message that Lubotsky was ill and that he wished me to go to Tel Aviv without delay to see him. I used Haskel's car and driver and arrived at Lubotsky's apartment in the early afternoon. He was not there. His wife was agitated. She told me that the police were on his heels, and he had gone into hiding. She gave me the address of the friend with whom he had taken refuge, but Lubotsky was not there, having gone to a new hiding place. With some difficulty I found out where he had gone last and reached him in an apartment on the outskirts of town. Pale and harassed, he was greatly relieved to see me.

"I can't stay here any longer," he said. "I know the police will soon be here too. Can you get me out of this?"

"Come with me to Jerusalem," I suggested. "I'll find you a place there."

We arrived in Jerusalem before evening, having decided that I would get him a room in my own pension.

Lubotsky told me that because of his ill health, he could no longer serve any useful purpose to the organization. He proposed leaving the country and working for the movement abroad. He planned to call on the Latvian consul in Jerusalem, Mordechai Caspi, to arrange for a visit to Riga, his birthplace and an active Revisionist center. I urged him to postpone his visit to Caspi until the following week, and he agreed albeit reluctantly.

But Lubotsky was arrested, and my own comparative immunity

was undermined. He did not observe our compact and on the day after our arrival had left the pension for Caspi's office, where he had been given a passport. The blow fell the next night. There was a knock at the outer door of the apartment, and when I opened it, two Englishmen brushed past me.

I knew one of them, a man named Ayre, the younger of the two, having met him a week or two earlier in the Cafe Vienna. A pleasant young man, he was a newcomer to the country, and looked ill at ease. Still, he greeted me cheerfully and said at once to his companion: *"He's* all right." The other, a bespectacled man in his thirties with a calculating, piercing eye, pointed to a room. "Who lives there?" he asked. I told him: "Miss Aharoni, a student."

"And where do you live?"

"Here," I said.

He walked past me into my room, over to my desk, and opened the drawer.

"I'm sorry," I said. "I can't agree to your searching my room."

"Why not?" he returned.

I went silently to my desk, took out my passport and showed him the endorsement which said that the holder was the Secretary to the Commissioner for the Union of South Africa. Ayre took him aside and whispered to him. He grunted and he and Ayre went back into the hall.

Again he asked me, pointing at Lubotsky's door:

"Who lives there?"

"A Mr. Cohen from Tel Aviv."

They knocked at his door, went in, and closed the door behind them.

I stood at the door of my room, but could hear nothing. They stayed there for nearly fifteen minutes. Then they emerged, Lubotsky leading the way, and went straight out of the apartment.

I sat in my room, utterly despondent, and angry with Lubotsky for having brought this on himself by his impatience.

The senior detective returned within twenty minutes.

"I want to talk to you," he said. "He's broken down. He's admitted that he's Lubotsky. Now you can probably tell me where Berman is."

I tried to deny Lubotsky's identity, but the detective brushed my words aside. "We'll leave that," he said. "Now what about Berman? We know Berman is in this building. They're still looking for him upstairs."

"Berman? I know a Berman, but what has he to do with this?"

"Which Berman?" he said.

"The son of the rabbi," I replied. Yitshak Berman was a young Revisionist, who, as a student, had been associated with the Achimeir group and once, in 1932, had spent a night in jail for taking part in a demonstration at the university. He had only a few months earlier returned to Palestine after completing his law studies in London.

"That's the one," said the detective. "And he's in this house."

I realized that the CID was more active than I had suspected, though not more efficient. Obviously Berman had been pointed out by somebody to a police agent when he was in my company. The agent had confused me for him and then a watch had been kept on me, presumably in the vicinity of the pension. "Berman" had thus been seen going into the eight-story building which housed the pension and had not come out. The detective's logic was irrefutable, except that I was not Berman.

"I'll tell you something," the detective said. "We know how the Irgun Zvai Leumi is run. The leader is Berman. He gives the orders. Lubotsky does the propaganda. He writes the inciting articles and makes the inciting speeches. The man who carries out the orders"—he whipped off his glasses and looked at me hard—"is a man named Raziel. Do you know Raziel?"

"Raziel?" I said. "An Italian? I don't know the name."

"Why an Italian? A Jew. He's the one who's been putting those bombs in the Arab market."

"D'you know," I said, "after what you told me about Berman and Lubotsky I've a feeling your sources of information are a bit doubtful. Raziel? I wouldn't be surprised if there's no such person."

"Our information is good enough. Only how far can we get if we get no co-operation from you people?"

"The way you people behave, why should the Jews co-operate with you?"

"You wouldn't talk like that if you saw the mess the bomb made among the Arabs in the Old City. I did."

"What have you done about the mess the Arabs have been making among the Jews? In any case," I added, "putting people away without a trial is not going to get you anywhere. You're not saying that Lubotsky threw any bombs?"

"But he's an inciter. I read his articles."

"Oh," I said. "You read Hebrew?"

"No. They're translated for me."

"So you ought to be arresting everybody who writes articles, if that's what you call incitement."

"I don't know about that," he said. "I don't read all the articles."

"You should," I said. "You might learn why the Jews don't co-operate with you. I send all this material as part of my job to the South African Government. I could let you have a copy."

"Do," he said.

"Where should I send it to?"

He whipped off his glasses for the last time.

"Don't make any effort to find out my name or where I am," he said.

I was speechless. He suddenly beamed as though he had won a victory, and walked out of the apartment.

I was left in a state of great anxiety. I was certain that the detective's "man-to-man" talk had been influenced by my "consular status," but my "image" as a comparatively passive sympathizer with the Revisionist point of view had been smudged.

I could not discover precisely what my file at the CID now contained, although Jack Simon tried unsuccessfully to find out. My secretary, Koenig, discovered that I was being tailed and one afternoon a week later Simon told me:

"Since two o'clock today two new numbers have been added to the list of telephones tapped. One is Morkos (an Arab official at the Italian consulate). The other is yours."

Determined now to bring my dual existence to an end, I wrote to Haskel and asked him to come to Palestine. He invited me to meet him in South Africa, to which I agreed.

I made preparations for an absence of three months. I was sure that I could now persuade Haskel to agree to resign from his post. I would then return to Palestine, close up the office and devote my energies to the Irgun.

5

On the Brink of War

When I arrived in Johannesburg, in October 1938, Haskel was even more responsive to my pressure than I had expected. He was in the middle of a financial crisis, and there was little hope of his being able to live in Jerusalem even part of the time. He agreed to resign his consular post and close the Jerusalem office.

Soon after my arrival, Haskel left for London. He returned with a proposal from Jabotinsky. I was to come to London to launch and edit a weekly newspaper for the New Zionist Organization. After some hesitation I agreed. A number of circumstances delayed me, and I did not arrive in London until March 1940. By then Hitler's war had been in progress for six months. The world we knew had fallen apart.

Meantime the year 1939 had brought the culminating phase of the Arab "revolt," and the revelation of the British purpose in Palestine—for which indeed the revolt had been fostered. The Irgun reacted in Palestine by a number of minor attacks on British installations. Jabotinsky publicly gave them his blessing. He now also resolved his own doubts about indiscriminate retaliation against Arab attackers. For the first time publicly, he announced in effect his support for the Irgun point of view. He wrote:

> The worst of all horrors known to history is *galuth,* dispersion. The blackest of all the characteristics of galuth is the tradition of the cheapness of Jewish blood: *hadam hamutar,* the permitted blood the spilling of which is not prohibited and for which you do not pay. To this an end has been made in Palestine. Amen.[1]

At this time, too, the New Zionist Organization intensified its efforts to save at least some of the Jews in Europe. Up to the outbreak of the World War and indeed until the Balkans were com-

pletely overrun by Hitler in 1941 the immigration network maintained jointly by the NZO, and the Irgun continued to bring Jews
from the European hell to Palestine. By 1939 many thousands had
already been rescued. For an organization with meager financial
resources it was a task that required devotion, courage, daring, and
ingenuity. Persuasion, bribery, and smuggling became the daily task
of the organization's agents. Offices were opened throughout Eastern Europe to register prospective immigrants. Transit camps were
established near frontiers. Negotiations were conducted with con-
suls from South American countries for the granting of visas to
facilitate the acquisition of transit visas in Europe. These were
granted on condition that their recipients would not use them to
travel to South America.

The agents of the network scoured the Mediterranean and Aegean
ports for boats to be chartered. In Palestine the Irgun planned and
executed the reception of the immigrants on the coast, organized
their dispersal as they stepped ashore.

All these activities were carried out despite the unfailing vigilance
of the British on the Palestine borders and their interventions elsewhere. Often ships voyaged for weeks before being able to breach
the British guard.

This enormous rescue operation was vilified by the old Zionist
Organization, whose leaders opposed the very concept of evacuation, trying to dissuade Jews from seeking passages on ships and
warning wealthy Jews against contributing funds to our organization.
The Revisionists, they cried, were taking money under false pre-
tenses, they were endangering the lives of Jews by packing them
like sardines into small, leaky, unseaworthy ships, they were bringing pregnant women and prostitutes into Palestine.[2]

Such propaganda had considerable effect, as Captain Jeremiah
Helpern, then working in Europe at the center of Aliyah B operations, discovered. He approached a French member of the Roth-
schild family for a contribution to the fund and was refused. The
baron told Helpern that the ships on which the immigrants were
being taken were overcrowded and lacking in adequate lavatory
facilities. He could not aid or encourage such an unsalubrious undertaking. But Helpern's impassioned denials finally caused him to re-
lent with a donation. A year later, in the late spring of 1940, the
baron was one of the fortunate few who, on the fall of France,
succeeded in obtaining passage on a small, crowded vessel which

took him to safety in the United States. It is not known whether he first inspected the ship's lavatories, but he did at least survive to ponder the ironies of fate.

So did the Zionist leaders. Six years later, when the mass of trapped Jews of Europe had been murdered, they launched large-scale "illegal" immigration into Palestine. They were attacked unmercifully by British propaganda in an almost word-for-word copy of their own propaganda against us in 1939.

In May 1939, Malcolm MacDonald, the British Colonial Secretary, published his White Paper on British policy in Palestine. It proposed that the Jewish restoration in Palestine was to be brought to an end. In the next five years the final 75,000 Jews were to be allowed into Palestine. After ten years an independent state would be set up—on two conditions: that peace had been fully restored and that Jews and Arabs could work together.

The Jewish reaction was revealed in an outburst of pain and rage, echoed by the British opponents of the government's Palestine policy on both sides of the House of Commons. The Labor opposition announced that, should it come to power, it would not be bound by this policy and the Mandates Commission of the League of Nations withheld its consent to it. For any nation respecting its international obligations, the White Paper was thus illegal.

After the release of the White Paper there was a brief softening of Jewish denunciations of our Aliyah B. At this time the Haganah itself organized a number of transports. According to Colonel Wedgwood in the House of Commons, of fifteen thousand immigrants brought in "illegally" during the five months ending in June 1939, 4500 were brought by the Haganah, 7000 by the Revisionists, 3500 "privately." The Jewish Agency attacks on our Aliyah B were resumed when MacDonald canceled the regular six-monthly "legal" immigration quota, now exceeded by the number of "illegals."

In Palestine the universal bitterness about the MacDonald White Paper was reflected in the new firm tone employed in Jewish Agency pronouncements. Ben-Gurion in particular spoke in militant terms of the struggle against the British. When one or two attacks against British buildings were actually carried out by the Haganah, we dared to hope that we had reached a point where a united fighting front was possible. But this was an illusion. The vilification of Irgun "terror" continued unabated.

The Irgun suffered a serious blow when the British arrested Raziel, his deputy Avraham Stern, and almost all their colleagues in the Irgun High Command. Yet the vitality of the organization proved adequate even after this depletion and retaliation against both British and Arabs continued. Abroad, the machinery of "illegal" immigration was expanded, as was the propaganda department. In Poland a lively weekly newspaper was launched under Irgun aegis and was distributed throughout Eastern Europe. In Geneva in August, after the Zionist Congress had spent a day listening to violent denunciations of the Irgun, the delegates discovered the whole city plastered with Irgun posters. It seemed the beginning of a new era in Zionist history, the era of resistance. A few weeks later it was washed away by Hitler's invasion of Poland.

With the outbreak of Hitler's war, the presidency of the New Zionist Organization announced its identification with the struggle against Germany and decided to strive for the achievement of a separate Jewish army to establish Jewish identity in the war. To this end a delegation headed by Jabotinsky planned to leave London for the United States. Meantime the Aliyah fund campaign in South Africa was intensified by the arrival of Robert Briscoe—once a fighter for Irish independence, later mayor of Dublin and now for several years an adherent of Jabotinsky—and the return of Nahum Levin, who six months earlier had completed a brilliant period of service in South Africa as a national organizer.

Haskel was disturbed by Jabotinsky's intended departure from London. He had no high opinion of the people at the London headquarters of the movement. With Jabotinsky leaving for an indefinite period, he felt the group would be seriously weakened. Moreover, S. Y. Jacobi, Jabotinsky's closest lieutenant, who enjoyed wide confidence, had died suddenly. Late in January 1940, Haskel cabled Jabotinsky, pressing upon him the necessity for creating a reliable working body in London.

Jabotinsky's cabled reply went further than Haskel had expected. Haskel himself and Briscoe were co-opted to the presidency. In London an administrative committee was to run the movement as long as Jabotinsky and his delegation were away. Levin and I were appointed to this administrative committee. He was to head the Organization Department; I was in charge of press and propaganda.

In a second private cable Jabotinsky characteristically warned me of the financial hardships at the London headquarters with its "exiguous budget." I had recently married Doris Kaplan, and he was no doubt worried at my wife's having to face the difficulties of a London housewife after the comforts of South Africa. She, however, was as eager as I had become to play a part at the significant center of things. Three weeks later we sailed from Capetown.

6

Death of a Great Leader

The nature of the Nazi enemy left the Jewish people no choice in the Second World War. We had to be on the side of whoever was fighting Hitler. We were consequently taken for granted.

This was the central source of our political weakness and of our sustained political defeats during the war. It was not difficult for Britain to stifle our national identity. Over and beyond the natural desire for the sympathy of neutral nations, however, Britain needed help and looked for it to the United States. America was still neutral, a substantial proportion of the population isolationist, and many Americans (for a variety of reasons) anti-British. President Roosevelt was outspokenly anti-Nazi, but could not at first move toward serious aid for Britain in advance of public opinion.

In the four months he spent in the United States, Jabotinsky sought to bring American pressure to bear upon the British Government to accept the offer of a Jewish army. Widespread support for the idea would make it difficult for the British to refuse the addition of a large body of volunteers. Such a refusal would not square with Britain's vigorous efforts to obtain American aid.

There were no signs of change in the attitude of the British Government on Palestine. Ignoring the fact that, as trustees of the League of Nations, they had been refused legal warrant for the White Paper of 1939, they made it plain even after war broke out that its tenets would be applied in letter and spirit. In mid-February 1940 they published the land regulations envisaged by the White Paper, which prohibited the purchase by Jews of land in all but five per cent of the area of western Palestine—in the area, that is, already largely in Jewish hands.

Nor did the outbreak of war lessen the intensity of the British Government's efforts to prevent Jews fleeing from Europe to Palestine. The Foreign Office brought pressure on the Turkish and Greek governments to forbid their shipowners to help Jews break the British blockade. Throughout that winter and early spring boatloads of Jews ready to set off down the Danube in "illegal" boats found themselves abandoned by the Greek or Turkish ship captains. Hundreds of Jews, at one time two thousand, their transit visas for Romania or Bulgaria expired, were squeezed on to barges on the Danube while the organizers of "illegal" immigration cast about feverishly for other seagoing boats, now at a premium. British threats of imprisonment for any ship's captain caught in Palestine waters (several were in fact in Acre Prison) acted as effective deterrents against sympathizers. Week after week went by in these frozen miniature hells, before finally, by some miracle of ingenuity and the humanity or overwhelming cupidity of the captain of some old vessel, the "Danube refugees" were successful in reaching Palestine.[1]

These manifestations by the British Government of utter indifference to the fate of Jewish refugees must have encouraged Hitler in the first steps of "processing" the Jews of Poland that first winter of the war. Jews were being herded into ghettos. There were forced marches, executions, arbitrary collective murders.

These facts were known in the West from American and Jewish news agencies, but, except for some reports in the *Manchester Guardian,* the British press and public figures maintained an almost unanimous silence.

Even now the official Zionists continued their campaign of sabotage against our organization of "illegal" immigration. Their activity was not now public and indeed came to our notice only through an error of one of the Jewish Agency functionaries. Henry Montor, the vice-chairman of the United Jewish Appeal in the United States, wrote a letter to Rabbi Baruch Rabinowitz of Hagerstown, Maryland, to explain why the Revisionist campaign for funds for "unregistered" immigration should not be supported, presumably unaware that Rabbi Rabinowitz was a man of independent mind and very knowledgeable.

"Selectivity," Montor wrote, "is an inescapable factor in dealing with the problem of immigration to Palestine"; and the Revisionists did not "select" their passengers. The letter then went on to attack the conditions on the ships, the character of the immigrants, and the motives of the organizers.

The date of this letter is February 1, 1940.[2]

We do not know how many such letters were written while the men maligned were freezing on the Danube with their charges or languishing in Acre Prison. It is important, however, to measure the disastrous impact of this campaign on the work of rescue.

In London, Levin and I made our own decision. No money had been set aside for the newspaper, but within three weeks of my arrival in March 1940 we had worked out a plan for a weekly. Abraham Abrahams, the head of the Political Department and Levin agreed to act with me as an editorial board. On April 19, 1940, we published the first issue of the *Jewish Standard*. For the first time in its history Jabotinsky's headquarters in London had its own publication.

I was fortunate in the editorial collaboration I enjoyed. Abe Abrahams, one of the brilliant men of the Zionist movement, contributed the main political article for many weeks. Samuel Landman, the oldest of our colleagues, brought us a first-rate diplomatic correspondent: A. M. Gerothwohl, a professor of history at the University of Wales. He retained the anonymity in which he contributed also to the *Scotsman* and the *Daily Telegraph,* and his article arrived like clockwork every Tuesday afternoon.

Jabotinsky wrote me at intervals, giving advice and encouragement, but his reply to my request for articles for the *Standard* was disturbing.

"The *Standard*," he wrote on May 31, "is good and getting ever better. I am sorry and feel ashamed for being so useless but just now my writing hand is withered; it has often happened before, and when this mood is upon me there's nothing doing."

There was no sign of the financial aid which Jabotinsky and the delegation had promised us from New York. Progress was made in the political campaign, Jabotinsky's public speeches evoking considerable enthusiasm, even when he forcefully predicted America's entry into the war. "The Yanks are coming!" he exclaimed. More important, he found support from the British ambassador in Washington, Lord Lothian, who sensed the value of Jabotinsky's independent co-operation in mobilizing support for the Allied cause, and apparently reported favorably to his government.

During that time, Chaim Weizmann pursued his own campaign in London, pressing the British to create a Jewish division in the British Army. Though this was not the same thing as a separate Jewish army, it was a step in the right direction, and we were willing to co-operate with him. Sympathetic British Members of Parliament also pressed the desirability of united Jewish action.

Why Weizmann, at this critical moment, should have made such co-operation impossible is difficult to understand. He said he accepted the idea and assured his British friends that he would work to that end. He promised our emissaries, Robert Briscoe and the veteran Russian Zionist Dr. M. Schwartzmann, as well as his own supporter, Joseph Sagall, who worked hard to bring about co-operation, that he would cable a proposal to Jabotinsky. Although he agreed on a text, he did not send the cable, and was thereafter "unavailable," even on the telephone.

The war swept into its next active phase. Hitler quickly overran Norway and Denmark. In Britain the Chamberlain government was voted out and Winston Churchill became Prime Minister. In May, the Germans launched their onslaught on the Low Countries and France. Three weeks later the British forces were driven from the Continent. By the end of June, Hitler was master of Western Europe; and the British prepared for a Nazi invasion.

In those weeks, when the British were shocked by shattering defeats, the call for a Jewish army sounded thin and unreal. In America, the possibility of Britain losing the war did not seem remote. In a letter to me, while the Dunkirk evacuation was in progress, Jabotinsky said, "If the war will go on there will be a Jewish Army," but in the same letter he bemoaned "this crumbling universe."

On August 2, Eliahu Ben Horin, a member of the delegation that accompanied Jabotinsky to America, addressed a long and most despondent letter to Abrahams and Levin. He confessed that the delegation had failed the London team completely. The most important reason for their failure was, he said, Jabotinsky's "state of mind and state of nerves . . ."

"You know better than I do," [he wrote] "his state of mind, his hesitation, etc. before he finally left London. Now multiply it by 100 and you may get the right idea. He suddenly became more and more aware of the fact that he is almost 60 and he became terribly impatient in everything we did. A feeling that he has no time to lose and that his life may be over before he achieves what he wants became with him almost an obsession."

In those first months of the war Jabotinsky seemed consumed with anxiety. "It eats deep into my heart," he wrote me, "to know how useless I am in giving no support to people of such loyalty as you all in London or those in Palestine, or elsewhere . . ."

There were private griefs too. His son Eri was still in Acre Prison for his part in helping Jews escape from the European hell. His wife, stricken by heart trouble, lay ill in London. The ravages on his health after a decade of incessant strain and pain and tortured prophetic anxiety were made manifest now. On August 4, two days after Eliahu Ben Horin wrote his gloomy letter to London, Jabotinsky died.

Within a few years of his death, life itself wrote an epitaph in swift and terrible vindication of his tragic vision, in triumphant justification of his faith. As time and events have moved on and away from his lifetime, as his image in ever sharper perspective has emerged from the mists of falsification and misrepresentation, our sense of his immortality has become the heritage of our people. Jabotinsky, a generation after his death, towers with Theodor Herzl in solitary eminence over the stormy Jewish landscape of our century.

Jabotinsky's will was a simple document. It gave directions for the disposal of his few possessions. He added a brief request.

"I want," he wrote, "to be buried or cremated (it is all the same to me) just wherever I happen to die; and my remains (should I be buried outside of Palestine) may not be transferred to Palestine unless by order of that country's eventual Jewish Government."

The date of this will was November 3, 1935, but it was not published until some years after his death. It was an entirely private act of faith, performed in a climate of circumstances far removed from his dream of statehood, of independence or national self-determination. Jewish suffering, humiliation and poverty in Europe, and in Palestine the developing anti-Zionist policy of the British, did not bode well for Jewish independence. As for Zionist policy, it had reached its lowest ebb of resignation. From that source indeed came the most vigorous detractions of Jabotinsky's vision. Zionist leaders, including Ben-Gurion as well as Weizmann, were preaching the strange creed of "parity" which, at best, promised the perpetuation of British rule.

It is consequently understandable that even after the dream of the state had come true, Ben-Gurion, for the fifteen years he was Prime Minister, should have refused to honor Jabotinsky's testamentary request.

The strangest chapter in Jabotinsky's biography is the one which his opponents tried to rewrite after his death. The official versions of the history of the Zionist movement and of the making of the state of Israel try to "eliminate" Jabotinsky's role by often ignoring him. This expedient was apparently essential to the image which Weizmann and Ben-Gurion wished to maintain. When Weizmann was elected the first President of the state of Israel, in 1949, his inaugural speech mentioned various men who had "brought us to this point." Jabotinsky was not among them.

Sooner or later the record had to be set straight. Too many people were conscious of Jabotinsky's role, even if only because they had opposed him. Moreover, Ben-Gurion's very refusal to bring about the return of his remains to Israel awakened the interest and curiosity of the new generation which had not known him.

When in 1963 Ben-Gurion was replaced as Prime Minister, his successor, Levi Eshkol, announced the recognition by the "eventual Jewish Government" of Jabotinsky's wish as expressed in his will. On the twenty-fourth anniversary of his death, in 1964, Jabotinsky's remains, and those of his wife (who died in 1950), were brought to Israel and buried on Mount Herzl in Jerusalem.

Men, women, and children came from every corner of the country to walk past his coffin as it lay on an illumined platform near the sea in Tel Aviv. Except when the remains of Theodor Herzl were interred in 1949, the country had never before experienced such a demonstration of homage. The people and the government of the Jewish state at last were able to pay a part of their debt of honor to this man. The state itself was symbolized in the funeral procession by its third President, Schneour Zalman Shazar, who that day no doubt remembered how, on hearing the news of Jabotinsky's death in 1940, he forgot the political gulf between them and wrote in impetuous grief:

"The full-toned violin that once seemed destined to play the leading role in the orchestra of Jewish revival has suddenly broken."[3]

7

A Split in the Party

In August 1940, bereaved and grief-stricken, we were confronted with the immediate consequences of Jabotinsky's death. There was no constitutional or logical successor to Jabotinsky. He had failed to groom able lieutenants to follow him.

The headquarters of the organization were in London, and with the departure of the delegation for America the administrative committee in the London headquarters had in fact been set up by the presidency to be the governing body of the movement. It had also given authority to the U.S. delegation to decide on major policy as long as Jabotinsky was with them. Without him they were simply a delegation from London, no longer empowered to make major decisions. Yet without any warning, they announced themselves as the sole and exclusive leadership of the organization, calling for the dissolution of the administrative committee and, by implication, the closing of the *Jewish Standard.* Only in May 1941, after nearly nine months of acrimonious correspondence, did the New York delegation agree to a conference in South Africa, to which each group of the organization would send a representative.

Meanwhile, we continued with our work despite the German blitz on London. The *Jewish Standard,* although sentenced to death from New York, met its budget by sheer miracle and weathered the German bombing as well. At first the German's main target was the East End, where our own printers had their works.

In the beginning, the workers took shelter every time the air-raid sirens wailed, but later they ignored these and went on working, just as most London people did. In our block of flats we went to the shelter only twice in all those months. Except when on fireguard duty or when we fought a fire in a nearby building, we slept in our beds.

In those months, we campaigned against the British Government's "enemy aliens" policy. In prewar years a substantial number of refugees from Germany and Austria had been admitted into the country. Now, under the threat of German invasion and fearing the incursion of spies or disguised soldiers among them, the government took drastic precautions. The refugees were given the forbidding title of "enemy aliens" and many were interned and sent off to the Isle of Man. The *Jewish Standard,* in concert with the *Jewish Chronicle,* maintained a constant attack on this policy of the British Government. Later came some relaxation of these panicky measures, many "enemy aliens" were released and permitted to serve in unarmed Pioneer battalions, although many others spent dreary years in internment.

At the same time we developed an affection and an admiration for the British. In the first nights of the blitz there were no antiaircraft defenses in London, but the courage and good humor of the British never deserted them, not even when they were threatened by a German invasion.

They are not a politically conscious or well-informed people and certainly not very demonstrative, yet that summer and autumn their love and understanding of freedom broke through spontaneously. The ordeal and the challenge, the sense of comradeship in danger, created an atmosphere at once tense and exhilarating. Churchill's inspired exhortations in the dark weeks after Dunkirk are history. Yet the "finest hour" of which he spoke could not have come about without the spark of greatness in the people themselves. Living with the British in those months was like being transported into some ancient heroic age.

Our work proceeded along three main lines: we argued for a Jewish army, a planned postwar evacuation of the Jews of Europe, and the establishment of a supreme Jewish National Council. Such a council could be set up only by the existing organizations, for a democratically elected congress was not practicable. This meant an arrangement between us and the Jewish Agency.

The incessant campaign for a Jewish army through Abrahams' parliamentary lobbying as well as by the *Jewish Standard* seemed to evoke some response at last, and the idea began to be discussed in the British press.

That autumn, Weizmann was promised fulfillment of his demand for a Jewish unit within the British Army. Winston Churchill, Anthony Eden, the Foreign Secretary, and Lord Lloyd, the Colonial Secretary, all gave him assurances. By the turn of the year an officer was appointed to command the unit. Weizmann agreed to keep the negotiations secret. In the spring of 1941 Lord Lloyd died suddenly. His place was taken by Lord Moyne, who had opposed the scheme from the start. Several months later the project was formally dropped.

No reason was ever given to Dr. Weizmann, whose angry public reaction had no effect.

On May 31, 1941, I boarded a P & O liner at Greenock, bound for Capetown. My brief was clear. I was to explain to our South African colleagues the development of events inside the organization, and try to achieve an emergency conference in Johannesburg. When Ben Horin, representing the American delegation, arrived there we would invite the Palestine NZO, the Betar, and the Irgun, to send their representatives.

I spent five months in South Africa. I failed completely to set up a conference of the various branches of our movement, for the Palestinians would not come to South Africa, and Ben Horin refused to go to Palestine.

My disillusionment and unhappiness were overwhelming. I began to think about resigning. In October, my colleagues in London abandoned the National Council policy. Abrahams cabled me from London that "we" were prepared to return to the Zionist Organization, a move much favored by many defeatist Revisionists.

There was other sad news. While still in Capetown, I learned that David Raziel had been killed in action during the pro-German revolt in Iraq. When the rebellion in Iraq broke out, the British appealed to Raziel—recently released from Acre Prison—to go to Iraq to organize guerrilla activities behind the Arab lines. Raziel agreed to go. In Iraq, even before he could begin carrying out his mission, his car was bombed from the air and he was killed instantly.

At the time of his death, Raziel commanded an attenuated and divided Irgun. The organization was split into two vigorously conflicting factions.

Vladimir Jabotinsky   David Raziel

e author with Peter Bergson (H. Kook) and H. Lubinsky; Warsaw, October 1937.

Avraham Stern   Menahem Begin

The author on an IZL mission in France, 1946.

ארגון צבאי לאומי

IRGUN ZWAÏ LËUMI BE-EREZ JISRAËL

ORGANISATION MILITAIRE NATIONALE JUIVE D'EREZ JISRAËL

JEWISH NATIONAL MILITARY ORGANISATION OF EREZ JISRAËL

An Irgun poster for distribution in Central Europe.

Kidnaped British officers after their release on remission of death sentences on Michael Ashbel and Joseph Simhon; June 1946.

Left, Jacob Tavin ("Eli") a member of the IZL High Command who was responsible for blowing up the British Embassy in Rome. Right, Shmuel Ariel, the IZL "Ambassador" to France.

Eliahu Hakim, March 1945

Mordechai Alkochi, April 1947

Some of those who went to the gallows during the British Mandate:

Yehiel Dresner, April 1947

Dov Gruner, April 1947

Eliezer Kashani, April 1947

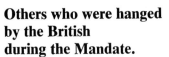

Others who were hanged by the British during the Mandate.

Moshe Barazani, April 1947

Meir Feinstein, April 1947

Avshalom Haviv, July 1947

Yaacov Weiss, July 1947

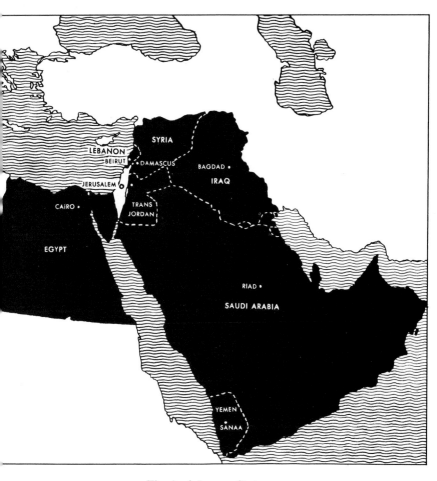

The Arab League States

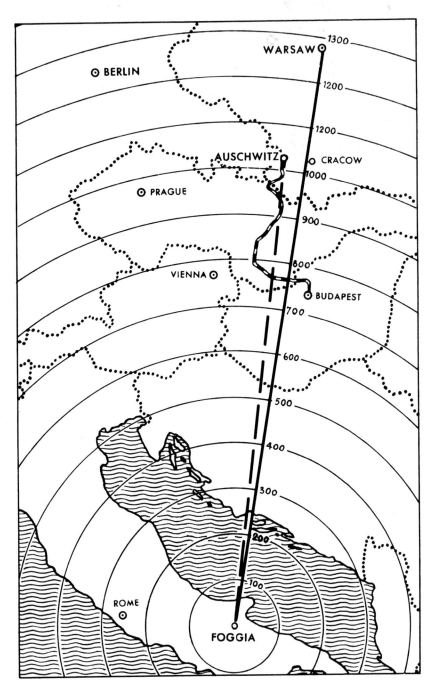

Map indicating distances from British air bases at Foggia to Auschwitz and Warsaw
British flew missions over Warsaw to support Polish Underground but ignored
pleas to bomb railways leading to Auschwitz.

The dissident group, later to become famous as the Lehi (Loham-mei Herut Yisrael—Fighters for the Freedom of Israel) or, as the British preferred to call them, the "Stern Gang"—was led by Avra-ham Stern, for years Raziel's closest colleague and second-in-command.

Stern was a colorful figure. A brilliant student, equally at home in Greek as in Hebrew classics, he wrote lucid prose and sometimes stirring poetry.[1] He believed in the destiny of a restored Jewish people and in the obligation to self-sacrifice of every young Jew. He believed in the logic and justice of his own strategy for achieving Jewish independence.

Stern had decided that our national objective would be achieved only by an armed struggle against the British, scorning diplomatic action. On an Irgun mission to Poland at the end of 1938 he tested Jabotinsky's reactions to his view. Jabotinsky rejected it. He thereupon began to preach secretly not only Irgun independence of the Revisionist Party but the abandonment of Jabotinsky, whom he now regarded as no better than Weizmann. Although ostensibly accepting the relationship between the Irgun and the party which had been hammered out between Raziel and Jabotinsky, in Paris in January 1939, Stern continued to build up clandestine cells of his militant group in Poland.

In Palestine, while languishing in Acre Prison, Stern appeared to have concurred in the decision of the Irgun High Command, taken at the outbreak of the German war, to declare a truce with Britain in the face of the greater common enemy. Later Lehi versions of this period deny that Stern ever agreed to this policy. In any case, by 1940 Stern parted company with Raziel, and launched a fierce propaganda campaign against the pause in the struggle with Britain. Raziel resigned and was with difficulty persuaded by telegraphic appeals from Jabotinsky in New York to resume the command. He went on to meet his fate on the road to Baghdad.

Stern's own thesis was simple. The future of the Jews would be decided by the struggle for independence in Palestine. The obstacle to independence was not Germany but Britain, and any truce with Britain meant a cessation of the fight for independence. It meant allowing Britain to pursue her policy to remain in control in Palestine. Therefore Britain remained the enemy.

In the summer of 1941 Stern decided to translate his ideas into practical politics: he would make a deal with Hitler. He proposed that Hitler send a large fleet of ships with tens of thousands of Jews into the Mediterranean, in order to break through the British blockade and upset their naval dispositions. Stern sent a representative, Naftali Lubentschik, to Vichy-controlled Syria to seek contacts with Italian and German agents, but Lubentschik was arrested. In the autumn Stern discussed the plan with Nathan Friedman-Yellin (later the central figure in the triumvirate leadership of Lehi) and proposed that he make his way to the Balkans and establish the necessary contacts there. Friedman-Yellin got as far as Syria, where he too was arrested and sent back to imprisonment in Palestine.[2]

Stern's thinking was dominated by a single-minded patriotism and by his insistence that Jewish policy should be sovereign; that the Jewish people should decide their own fate, uninhibited by sentiment or by traditional associations. As he saw it, helping Britain could not bring Jewish independence; a deal with Hitler might.

Stern's plan was of course a fantastic oversimplification of the tragic dilemma which we all faced. It was born of desperation. It failed to see the overriding, all-embracing menace of Nazism to the survival of our people, ignoring the elementary realities of the situation. An agreement with Hitler was impracticable; to make the scheme feasible Hitler would have had to remove from his forces in North Africa the shipping on which they were dependent for their supplies, which in turn meant that he would have had to give up North Africa altogether. The hunger for Jewish sovereignty clouded Stern's judgment. He was also hampered by inadequate organization and lack of unanimity among his lieutenants. In addition, the British authorities, encouraged by the hostility of the official Jewish organizations to Stern, made vigorous efforts to crush the group. Stern, related by marriage to a Haganah leader, was offered sanctuary in a kibbutz, provided he suspend his activities. Though hounded from pillar to post, he refused and continued to pursue his course. In February 1942 he was trapped by British police in an apartment in the center of Tel Aviv and shot "while trying to escape."

8

Europe's Jews Left to Their Doom

In London once again, I saw that the situation of our organization was grim. The administrative committee had all but ceased to exist. Levin, wearied by Abe Abrahams' deviousness, had resigned. Abrahams, who had throughout my absence been in control of the paper, received me with considerable coolness. There seemed no alternative: I resigned as well.

My wife and I and the Levins were unemployed, with no source of income. We were owed substantial sums by the organization for accumulated unpaid salaries—one of the reasons why the *Jewish Standard* had survived. It was a long time before we were paid, and for several months our state was most precarious. We moved to a friend's evacuated house and set up housekeeping in joint frugality and co-operation. In the summer of 1942 Levin secured a post as manager of a plastics factory at Dunstable. Soon afterward my wife, originally a mathematician, became technical secretary to the general manager of Osram's Lamp Works, while I found a job in the library of the *Daily Express*.

The year 1942 began in defeat and disaster for Britain and the newly belligerent United States, the Germans slowly cutting the supply lines across the Atlantic. In the Far East the Japanese swept all before them. In the Soviet Union the Germans, despite heavy setbacks, achieved their deepest penetration. In North Africa, they had pushed the British back to well within the borders of Egypt.

But by the end of the year all this had changed. The Americans won great naval victories in the Pacific; the Germans at Stalingrad suffered the worst military disaster in their history, and began their long retreat. In North Africa both Germans and Italians were decisively defeated at El Alamein. American and British troops landing in Algeria brought with them the bright promise of the enemy's final expulsion from Africa. The Japanese overreached themselves and spread their forces beyond their capacity to defend their lines.

Throughout that summer, the threat of German invasion of Palestine hung over the country. During those months, when policy was guided by immediate military considerations, the British made their only serious effort to co-operate with the Jews in planning the country's defense. But once the danger was over, the British Army's sense of a common interest with the Jews of Palestine faded.

The official Zionist leaders now adopted a bold attitude. Weizmann reverted to his demands of twenty years earlier, speaking of a Jewish commonwealth, and prophesying the establishment of an Arab federation into which such a commonwealth could be integrated. He pursued the idea, suggested to him by the British adventurer St. John Philby, of an alliance with Ibn Saud, the Arab desert ruler, to proclaim Saudi supremacy in the Arab world and to assure Zionist consummation within its orbit. Weizmann also preached the need for a transfer after the war of at least two million Jews to Palestine from Europe.

Zionist aims were reformulated in the Biltmore Program of 1942, which called for Palestine as a Jewish commonwealth at the end of the war, with the control of immigration in the hands of the Jewish Agency.

Weizmann and Ben-Gurion were later to give differing interpretations to the Biltmore resolution. To Ben-Gurion it meant that the transfer of two million people was to be "immediate" upon the conclusion of the war, while Weizmann envisaged a more gradual transfer, about 100,000 a year.

There was nothing new in the Biltmore scheme, which was a belated acceptance of Jabotinsky's teaching adopted by Weizmann and readapted by Ben-Gurion. Characteristically, even Weizmann's part in the process has been obscured by the historians. The Biltmore Program has been offered as a shining example of Ben-Gurion's originality of thought.

What *was* new in this program was Ben-Gurion's temporary realization that if Britain persisted in her policy and the United States proved unable or unwilling to press a change upon her, the Jews would have to take charge of their fate.

They must be prepared, Ben-Gurion told the Jewish Agency Executive in May 1941, "for the other way, the way of conquest. The youth must be trained to do what is possible when the time comes."[1]

In 1942, the Nazi leaders decided formally (at a meeting in the Wannsee suburb of Berlin) on the systematic extermination of all the Jews in the territory they occupied, and in April the mass deportations began.

Once the truth of the wholesale killings was known, the Allied governments decided to take concerted action. On December 16, 1942, Anthony Eden, the British Foreign Minister, made a statement in the House of Commons. He spoke in the name of all the Allies, whose attention, he declared, had been drawn to numerous reports from Europe.

> . . . that the German Government, not content with denying to persons of the Jewish race in all territories over which their barbarous rule has been extended the most elementary human rights, are now carrying into effect Hitler's oft-repeated intention to exterminate the Jewish people in Europe.
>
> From all occupied territories Jews are being transported in conditions of appalling horror and brutality to Eastern Europe. None of those taken away is ever heard of again. The able-bodied are slowly worked to death in labor camps. The infirm are left to die of exposure and starvation or are deliberately massacred in mass executions.
>
> The number of victims of these bloody cruelties is reckoned in many hundreds of thousands of entirely innocent men, women and children.

Mr. Eden announced what the Allied governments proposed to do in consequence.

> The above-mentioned Governments and the French National Committee, condemn in the strongest possible terms this bestial policy of cold-blooded extermination. They declare that such events can only strengthen the resolve of freedom-loving peoples to overthrow the barbarous Hitlerite tyranny.

An impulsive Member of Parliament, Mr. Sampson Cluse, at once proposed that the Members "rise in their places and pay silent testimony to this horror and to their determination to defeat Hitler." The government made no objection to this daring proposal. The Members rose and stood for two minutes.

The British Government's concern did not extend to the trapped Jews. The 760 Jewish men, women, and children who had been spirited out of Romania by the Irgun-Revisionist rescue organization had set sail for Palestine. Jewish Agency appeals to allow them entry were rejected by the British Government. Because of engine trouble the ship put in at Istanbul, while the Jewish Agency continued to press for permission for them to enter Palestine. It was refused by Lord Moyne, acting for the British Government. After two months the Turkish authorities ordered the ship to return to Romania and had her forcibly towed into the Black Sea. There, while still in Turkish waters, she blew up and sank. There was one survivor. Jewish grief and anger at the tragedy of the *Struma* echoed all over the world. The Palestine government felt compelled to explain why Palestine was barred to these otherwise certain candidates for murder or starvation. First, there might be German spies among them; second, Palestine was short of supplies. Weizmann reacted bitterly. "One stands aghast," he said, "at the attitude which the Palestine Government is taking up repeatedly and systematically towards those unfortunate Jewish refugees who flee from the clutches of the German or Rumanian Nazis, try at the risk of their lives to find refuge in Palestine and are very often, within sight of its shores, cruelly, inhumanly driven back into the sea and the jaws of death."

In April 1943, British and American representatives met at Bermuda avowedly to seek means of helping refugees. They established two guiding principles. First, the British principle that the White Paper policy in Palestine must not be disturbed; second, the American principle that the immigration restrictions of the United States (which had of course no legal obligations to Jews or anybody else) must not be relaxed.

Only a few days before the conference, Mr. Churchill was definitively reiterating the White Paper policy, in a letter to Lord Moyne. "I have always regarded [the White Paper] as a gross breach of faith committed by the Chamberlain Government . . . Our position is that we have carried on for the time being in the exigencies of war the policy of our predecessors and have made no new pronouncement on the subject. My position remains strictly that set forth in the speech I made in the House of Commons in the debate on the White Paper. I am sure the majority of the present War Cabinet would never agree to any positive endorsement of the White Paper." He then concluded his letter: "It runs until it is superseded."[2]

No attempt was made to conceal the futility of the Bermuda Conference. The American Assistant Secretary of State, Adolph A. Berle, Jr., said:

"I should be less than frank if I did not give you the blunt and cruel conclusion which is the only honest answer. Nothing can be done to save these helpless unfortunates except the invasion of Europe, the defeat of German arms and the breaking, once and for all, of the German power. There is no other way."[3]

In Britain, a fortnight later, answering a full-dress debate in Parliament, Anthony Eden made a polished gesture of tolerance toward the Members who had criticized government inaction.

"It is right and proper," he said, "that people should feel strongly about the subject [of refugees]. There would be something wrong with the British character if we ceased to feel strongly about this thing. I know that some members of the House think that the Government is perhaps rather insensitive in this matter. I can assure them that this is not so. We shall do all that is in our power to deal with it, short of any interference with our war-effort."

Such statements were acts of deception.

The British and the American governments were aware that large numbers of Jews in Europe could still be saved, for many plans for saving Jews were thrust upon them. These were deliberately rejected. Most British leaders in their subsequent memoirs have characteristically forgotten to mention this phase of Anglo-American co-operation. From American sources a little of its horrifying detail has emerged.

A member of the United States Cabinet, Henry Morgenthau, Jr., Secretary of the Treasury, writes bluntly in his *Diaries* that after the facts of Nazi extermination of the Jews had become known to the American Government, "officials dodged their grim responsibility, procrastinated when concrete rescue schemes were placed before them, and even suppressed information about the atrocities in order to prevent an outraged public opinion from forcing their hand."

In March 1943, he relates (a month, that is, before the Bermuda Conference), "the World Jewish Congress cabled to Washington that there was a real chance of rescuing 70,000 Jews in France and Rumania, provided funds could be got into Switzerland. The money was collected and ready to go. It would not be available to the officials in Nazi-occupied Europe who would co-operate with the plan, but it had to be deposited in their names."[4]

The Treasury gave its consent, but the plan was blocked in the State Department. On this we are given an authoritative apologia by Cordell Hull, the Secretary of State himself. He writes in his memoirs:

"President Roosevelt and I had many conferences on the subject of Hitler's attempt to exterminate the Jews. We eagerly studied all ideas and information that might be in the least helpful in relieving their inconceivable situation.

"The inescapable fact was, however, that Jews could not leave German-occupied Europe unless they escaped across borders into neutral Spain, Switzerland or Sweden or unless the German authorities permitted them to leave. And the Germans permitted Jews to leave only when they were amply paid to do so. We were reluctant to deposit sums of money to the credit of the Nazis, even though the deposits were to be made in Switzerland, were to be liquidated only after the end of the war and apparently could not be used by the Nazi leaders. Moreover the State Department did not have the large amounts of money and the personnel needed to carry out a plan of reaching and bribing the German officials in charge of the extermination program."[5]

These objections (according to Morgenthau's account) were presumably overcome. Six months after the original approach, the State Department cabled to Harrison, the American Minister at Bern, "the Treasury's clearance of the financial phases of the evacuation program."

"But by now," he continues, "the British Ministry of Economic Warfare wanted to take the matter up in Washington. Harrison requested specific instructions as to whether he should proceed without the British. The license was still held up. Meanwhile the news from Europe was increasingly depressing. Cables from Bern disclosed, for example, that 4000 children between the ages of two and fourteen, had been taken from their parents in France and deported in sealed trains, locked in windowless boxcars, sixty to a car, without adult escort, without food, water or hygienic provisions. We gritted our teeth and kept putting on all the pressure we could."

"But the worst was still to come." The British Foreign Office asked the Ministry of Economic Warfare to write a letter to the

American Embassy in London, and the American Embassy in London cabled its contents to the State Department. The letter said:

"The Foreign Office is concerned with the difficulty of disposing of any considerable number of Jews should they be released from enemy territory. For this reason they are reluctant even to approve of the preliminary financial arrangements, though these are now acceptable to the Ministry of Economic Warfare."

No more was heard of the seventy thousand.

Mr. Morgenthau, a Jew, was clearly not kept fully informed; perhaps he was deliberately deceived. He obviously did not know that before these painful negotiations were begun, a decision on the highest level had been made—in principle, that Jews in Europe who could be saved must be left to die. A hint of this comes to us through the private notes kept by Harry L. Hopkins, President Roosevelt's confidential adviser, of a meeting in Washington which he attended with Roosevelt, Hull, and Sumner Welles (Assistant Secretary of State) on the American side, with, on the British side, Anthony Eden, Lord Halifax (the British ambassador) and William Strang of the Foreign Office.

"Hull raised the question of the 60 or 70 thousand Jews that are in Bulgaria and are threatened with extermination unless we could get them out, and very urgently pressed Eden for an answer to the problem. Eden replied that the whole problem of the Jews in Europe is very difficult and that we should move very cautiously about offering to take all Jews out of a country like Bulgaria. If we do that, then the Jews of the world will be wanting us to make similar offers in Poland and Germany. Hitler might well take us up on any such offer and there simply are not enough ships and means of transportation in the world to handle them.[6]

"Eden said that the British were ready to take about 60 thousand more Jews to Palestine but the problem of transportation, even from Bulgaria to Palestine, is extremely difficult. Furthermore, any such mass movement as that would be very dangerous to security because the Germans would be sure to attempt to put a number of their agents in the group. They have been pretty successful with this technique both in getting into North and South America."[7]

There is no reference to the reply of the Americans. We now know the results.

The implications of the extermination of the Jews of Europe were simple and far-reaching. At the rate at which it was proceeding, it was reasonable to assume that there would be few or no Jews left in Europe to press once more against the gates of Palestine once war was ended; the prospect of freezing the Jewish minority in Palestine as it stood looked brighter than ever. The Zionists would be far less capable of resisting. A few minor concessions would no doubt ensure their amenability. There remained the Arabs. With the Jews decimated, the Arab could be assured of the certain fulfillment of the central promise of the White Paper: the eternal Arab majority in Palestine. With this promise, and the further promise to eliminate the French from the Levant, Eden could hope to achieve British dominance in the area under the banner of Arab independence. On February 19, 1943, two months after his statement in the House of Commons on the Nazi atrocities, Eden announced Britain's interest in the establishment of Arab political unity. Nineteen months later, the Charter of the Arab League was published in Alexandria. It contained the expected proclamation of war on Zionism. It also contained unequivocal acceptance of the terms of the British White Paper of 1939.[8]

9

Stirring a Tempest

I worked on the *Daily Express* until the summer of 1945. In 1944 I joined the editorial staff as a sub-editor. My spell on the paper was a valuable, many-sided experience. I learned a good deal about the techniques of a high-powered newspaper. What was more important, I broadened considerably my knowledge of the everyday Englishman. The *Daily Express* comprised a fair cross-section of the people of London. Living among them at their daily work, sharing with them the highly charged emotional experiences of the war, becoming aware of their individual interests, troubles and reactions, one gradually sensed the subtle composite pattern of a people. I began to understand their qualities: kindness, vigilant wariness of authority, diffident patriotism.

I resigned myself to remaining in England till the war ended. There was no way, apparently, for me to return to Palestine, and I did not forget that the Jerusalem CID still had a file on me. My impatience increased, however, when the news came early in 1944 that the Irgun in Palestine had ended its truce with the British and begun a vigorous campaign of violence against the Mandatory administration.

In the late summer of 1944, there seemed to be an opportunity to return. Rome had fallen, the Allied armies had invaded France, Paris was liberated; the final defeat of Germany was now a matter of time. In October I was offered a position on the *Palestine Post*. There ensued inexplicable delays in the granting of an exit permit, until finally the passport office informed me that such a permit would be granted only when the Palestine authorities issued a visa for me, to be applied for by my prospective employer. On November 14, I cabled Gershon Agronsky, the editor of the *Post,* to approach the

Palestine government. A week later he cabled his withdrawal of his offer because of the "prevailing conditions" in the country.

There, a political hurricane had indeed struck. On November 6, two members of Lehi, Eliahu Hakim and Eliahu Beth-Tsoury, had assassinated Lord Moyne, the British Minister Resident in Cairo. In his ministerial career Moyne had consolidated a long-standing hostility to Zionism by a harsh, unyielding attitude to any suggestions for the rescue of Jews fleeing from Europe. The violence of British reactions to Moyne's assassination seemed to terrify the Zionist leaders. They co-operated with the British, and Ben-Gurion seized the opportunity to launch a campaign against the Irgun.

Agronsky's withdrawal of his offer was understandable, considering my Revisionist antecedents. I swallowed my disappointment. I twice tried unsuccessfully that winter to obtain an appointment as a foreign correspondent which might bring me to Palestine. I continued my sub-editing routine on the *Express,* deciding to remain patient.

During the summer of 1944, the British Government set up the Jewish Brigade Group, the pallid and very belated fruit of the previous world-wide efforts for a Jewish military unit. It served to appease some Jewish resentments without upsetting the political pattern that Eden had designed. After an honorable performance in the Italian campaign the members of the brigade brought moral comfort to the liberated survivors of the concentration camps. They helped to ease their lot and later played a large part in organizing their movement across frontiers toward the centers for "illegal" immigration to Palestine. Two Jewish organizations had brought about the British decision to form the brigade, the Jewish Agency and the Committee for a Jewish Army.

The Committee for a Jewish Army was the brainchild of a remarkable young man, Hillel Kook, who had worked as Irgun representative at the New Zionist Organization headquarters in London in 1939–40. In the summer of 1940 he had gone to the United States, where he subsequently adopted the name of Peter Bergson.

After the death of Jabotinsky, Bergson and a group of former Revisionists and Irgunists in New York established the Committee for a Jewish Army, and went on to score the most striking political successes ever achieved by any Jewish organization in the United States.

The history of the official Zionist Organization in America was throughout World War II one of dismal and unmitigated failure. In early 1943, Emanuel Neumann, a veteran leader of the more activist wing, resigned from the American Emergency Committee for Zionist Affairs, giving as his reasons "recurrent factional and personal differences; vacillation in policy and action, failure to adopt a comprehensive program of activities."

There was, however, a deeper reason for this persistent decline. The leadership of the organization, particularly its central figure, Rabbi Stephen S. Wise, who followed the State Department policy, which was traditionally opposed to Zionism and throughout the war co-operated with the British. While presidential messages of stereotyped benevolence were published on the eve of Jewish festivals, or sent to Zionist gatherings where Democrat Stephen Wise presided, and concern was expressed for the Jewish lot, President Roosevelt had no sympathy for Zionism in its profound political and historic implications. After the United States had reached agreement with Ibn Saud for her exploitation of the gigantic oil resources of his desert kingdom, Roosevelt was concerned that nothing should be done which might seriously disturb Ibn Saud's anti-Zionist equanimity. Ibn Saud himself later told the members of the Anglo-American Committee on Palestine who visited him that when, at their famous meeting in Egypt in February 1945, he had upbraided Roosevelt for supporting Jewish immigration, Roosevelt had replied: ". . . I neither ordered nor approved of the immigration of Jews to Palestine, nor is it possible that I should approve it."[1]

At a press conference after the meeting, Roosevelt remarked that he had learned more about Palestine from Ibn Saud in five minutes than he had learned through all his years in government, an observation which said little for the official American Zionists who claimed to have his ear.

Rabbi Abba Hillel Silver, at that time the most dynamic of the Zionist leaders, was critical of the official Zionist approach. In 1944, Silver lobbied several congressional committees to pass a pro-Zionist resolution. The State Department did not approve and communicated its displeasure to Rabbi Wise. He promptly sent a telegram to the State Department, which stated that he and many associates did not wish action to be taken on any Palestine resolutions that were contrary to the recommendations of the State Department and President. The Under-Secretary of State, Stettinius, showed Silver the telegram.

"This," wrote Silver of Wise's telegram, "more than any other factor was responsible for shelving the Palestine resolutions. Dr. Wise's *shtadlanut* (policy of intercession) in Washington has been an egregious failure for many years, not only as far as Zionism is concerned. This weak-kneed *shtadlanut* policy has accomplished next to nothing for our people during these tragic years of slaughter and annihilation."[2]

Perhaps the moribund nature of the Zionist Organization of America actually helped bring success to Bergson and his group. A powerful body of support among congressmen, senators, and other public figures was built up and many gave liberally of their time and energy to press the Jewish cause upon the government and upon American public opinion. The Bergson group was also extremely effective with American Jewish intellectuals, who had previously shown little interest in Zionism. Ben Hecht, Louis Bromfield, Konrad Bercovici, Frances Gunther, Stella Adler, and many others became active exponents of the cause of Jewish nationalism.

The Bergson group succeeded in maintaining an almost permanent state of ferment among Jews in the United States, first for the idea of a Jewish army, second under the banner of the Emergency Committee to Save the Jewish People of Europe, and finally, after the Irgun revolt was launched in Palestine, as the Hebrew Committee of National Liberation.

It was largely as a result of their efforts that Roosevelt was persuaded in 1944 to set up the War Refugees Board, which, though limited in scope, did succeed in saving many lives.

The Bergson group had sent Jeremiah Helpern, a veteran Betar leader and a pioneer of Jewish seamanship, to London to establish a branch of the Committee for a Jewish Army and launch a campaign for a Jewish unit within the British Army. Helpern mobilized support among British public figures. His committee included clergymen, sixty-five Members of Parliament as well as Field Marshal Chetwode. The most important member of the Committee was Lord Strabolgi, who had been a staunch supporter of Zionism for more than twenty years. It was in answer to a motion by Strabolgi, in the House of Lords, that the Government first announced in July 1944 that they were considering the formation of a Jewish Brigade Group.

When this brigade was formally launched, the Jewish Agency claimed the credit, but Strabolgi, never a meek man, angrily denied their claim. Moshe Shertok attacked the Committee for a Jewish

Army on the grounds that it was associated with the Bergson group, it being evil *because it was anti-British!*

This was in November 1944.

The war in Europe ended in May 1945. In July a delegation arrived from the Palestine New Zionist Organization, consisting of my old friend, Dr. Aryeh Altman and Israel Rosoff, who, as a young man in Russia, had been a friend and colleague of Jabotinsky. Rosoff had news of the activities of the Irgun and Lehi in Palestine, though he was not in direct contact with either.

My conversations with Altman developed into heated arguments once I learned that his mission was in no way related to the underground struggle. Since the Irgun and the Lehi were pursuing the common aim of driving the British out of the country so as to make the Jewish state possible, I could not understand why the New Zionist Organization wished to function as a legal entity in apparent dissociation from the struggle.

Altman argued that the party's legality was useful. His contacts with the British authorities made it possible to put to them a different point of view from that of the Jewish Agency and in keeping with traditional Revisionism that a Jewish state was in the British interest. We agreed to differ.

Before the end of his stay, Altman made a proposal which opened the way to my return to Palestine.

He was now prepared to organize an emergency consultative conference in London to establish a temporary world leadership for the movement. He believed that the New Zionist Organization should return to the World Zionist Organization. He proposed that a referendum should be held to determine the wishes of its members, and urged me to accept both the editorship of the *Jewish Standard* and membership in the temporary World Executive until a regular world conference could be called. As soon as Abrahams had returned to the paper from a six-month suspension of his work, Altman promised, he would arrange for me to go to Palestine.

My point of view differed considerably from that of Altman's. I believed that in Palestine the New Zionist Organization should go underground, that its branches abroad should campaign for British evacuation of Palestine, gain support for Jewish resistance against them until evacuation was consummated, and raise money to finance the revolt. However, I knew that if I did not take over the *Jewish*

Standard, it might collapse, and by working on the paper, I would be free to pursue a policy closer to my outlook. At any rate, I would return to Palestine. I accepted his proposal.

We now heard reports regarding the pitiful remnants of our people. On the whole of the continent, including Soviet Russia, it was thought that there remained no more than three million of the nine million Jews who had lived there in 1939. Some 100,000 souls had survived in the death camps, living testimony to the failure of Zionism to rescue those who could have been saved.

The speedy removal of these survivors from the bloody soil of Europe became a pressing moral obligation. Surely the victors would not waste a moment in ensuring this act of humanity. Yet nothing happened. Three months after the end of the war, President Truman called upon the British Government to allow the 100,000 survivors of the death camps to enter Palestine. There was no response.

The survivors of the death camps waited 220 days, herded together in "displaced persons" camps, before the long-awaited "Statement of Policy" was made as to their future. In a statement by the British Foreign Secretary in the House of Commons on November 13, 1945, Mr. Bevin suggested that the "displaced persons" should aid in the rebuilding of Europe by remaining there. He announced the formation of a new commission to investigate the problem of the "displaced persons," six of its twelve members being Americans.

For the first time the Zionist leaders demonstrated that they were not deceived by a British device to gain time. On November 1, 1945, when the contents of the statement were already known, the Haganah had in collaboration with the Irgun and the Lehi proclaimed the launching of a resistance movement.

Mr. Bevin's statement of November 13 demonstrated that British policy had not changed since 1939. It was the most blatant display of perfidy our generation had experienced outside of the totalitarian states. The government was now Labor, led by the very men who had damned the MacDonald White Paper in 1939 and denounced it as a breach of faith to which they were not bound should they ever come to power. In April 1944, the Labor Party Conference had reiterated its opposition to the White Paper, and committed itself to a clear declaration of support for the Zionist aim, even to the extent of proposing to transfer the Arab population from Palestine, which was not a Zionist demand.

As late as May 1945, on the eve of a general-election campaign, Hugh Dalton had stated:

"The Executive has made its position abundantly clear. Having regard to the unspeakable horrors the Jewish people have suffered, it is morally wrong and politically indefensible to restrict entry to Palestine to Jews desiring to go there."

He then went on to insist that the Americans and the Russians co-operate in dealing with the Palestine problem. "It is indispensable," he said, "that steps be taken to get common support for a policy leading to the establishment of a free, happy and prosperous Jewish State in Palestine."

No Labor leader ever thought it necessary to explain the party's later reversal of policy. Bevin himself did indeed try to dispose of this question. He said unblushingly:

> There is not one resolution carried by the Labor Party that I know of that promised a Jewish State. If ever it was done it was done in the enthusiasm of a Labor Party Conference.

My work for the *Jewish Standard* and the New Zionist Organization proceeded in comparative tranquillity. Only once did it become stormy on a question of principle. In 1945, Professor Johan J. Smertenko, a colorful, somewhat boisterous advocate of Jewish opposition to British policy, came to London to set up an office of the American League for a Free Palestine, the popular organization created by Bergson's Hebrew Committee for National Liberation. I agreed to help him. This angered the local Revisionists, who were strongly opposed to the ideology of the Hebrew Committee, as were the official Zionists. The Hebrew Committee had developed an elaborate historical, sociological ideology, dividing Jews into two categories. First, the "Hebrews," who embraced the Hebrew nation and regarded themselves as repatriates from Palestine. Second, the "Jews," who were Jewish by religion or birth but did not wish to go to Palestine or otherwise to embrace Hebrew nationalism.

This division was supposed to be attractive to American Jewish intellectuals who gave their support to the Hebrew Committee, because it freed them from the fear that to support Jewish independence in Palestine would undermine their identity as Americans and require them to emigrate to Palestine.

I found this hard to believe. The American intellectual—Jewish and non-Jewish—emerged from the war with a sense of shock and even guilt at the incapacity of their world to prevent or mitigate the ravages of Nazi barbarism in Europe. The instinct to help the surviving Jewish remnant was rational. The logic of resistance to the British in Palestine was self-evident. Their support for the underground followed naturally.

I disliked the Hebrew Committee's philosophy from the beginning, deploring the unnecessary antagonisms it aroused. But I was filled with admiration for what the Bergson group had achieved in America and believed that we had a common objective. I thought it would be ridiculous not to co-operate with them.

Smertenko was one of Jabotinsky's earliest disciples in the United States, a man of great intellectual force, with a vigorous style and an explosive manner. We consulted frequently and held a joint press conference when, early in 1946, Ernest Bevin announced that he intended giving independence to Transjordan.

The truncation of Transjordan from the body of Palestine was an unabashed breach of international law. Transjordan was part of the Mandated territory. Britain's mandate did not give her any rights beyond its execution, or its return to the international authority, now the United Nations as successor to the League of Nations. Article 80 of the United Nations Charter provided against any unilateral change of status such as the British Government proposed. Moreover, Britain's announcement of independence for Transjordan was a public proclamation of contempt for the Anglo-American Committee then inquiring into the Palestine problem, and a blatant prejudgment of the committee's recommendations. That very month the Chairman of the Labor Party executive, Harold Laski, urging restraint and patience upon the Jews, had used the argument that the Anglo-American Committee's terms of reference were "wide enough to make possible the abandonment of that administrative separation between Palestine and Transjordan which was a grave initial error in British policy."[3]

There was an outraged reaction to Bevin's announcement, which continued until it was officially announced that a treaty had been signed with the independent state (the "Hashemite Kingdom") of Jordan. The nominal grant of "independence" to the 300,000 nomads of Transjordan enabled the Emir Abdullah to call himself King. British control of the country was now arbitrarily freed of the encumbrance of even formal international supervision. It would henceforth be governed only by a "treaty" wholly adequate to the British purpose.

To further our campaign against this new development I met several of the delegates to the first session of the United Nations Organization in London that spring.

The Mexican and the Polish delegates were, as I remember, especially well informed and sympathetic, but not a single government was prepared to make an issue of Transjordan.

At least one of these conversations helped broaden my own education. An interview was arranged for me with a leading member of the United States delegation, the veteran chairman of the Senate Foreign Relations Committee, Tom Connolly.

The meeting took place at his office in the conference building at 12:30 P.M. As he opened the door to me, I was startled to see the white mane, the ruddy cheeks, that fiction and cinema had taught me to expect of a southern senator. Senator Connolly shook my hand and clapped me on the shoulder.

"What can I do for you, Sam?" he asked.

I felt completely at ease. I gave him as full an outline as I could of the Jewish claim on the whole of Palestine, of the loss in 1920, through international intrigue, of the northern strip (now in Lebanon) which President Wilson had described as vital to Palestine viability, and of the gradual alienation by Britain of the territory across the Jordan.

Connolly listened intently. At times he doodled on a scribbler, at times he fidgeted with his spectacles. He did not interrupt me. I spoke for fifteen or twenty minutes, toward the end with some vehemence.

I finished. Connolly straightened up in his seat, looked at me for a moment, then abruptly at his watch.

"Ah—I'm afraid I have to go off to a luncheon appointment," he said. "That was very interesting, Sam, very interesting."

We both rose. He came around the desk, shook me warmly by the hand. He clapped me on the shoulder.

"Thanks for coming to see me, Sam," he said. "I'll do what I can for Egypt!"

The establishment of the kingdom of Transjordan seemed but another step in Britain's over-all plan for the Middle East. During the previous summer, in June 1945, the Churchill government had intervened in Syria and Lebanon to force France from her last toehold in that area.

It was an expulsion accomplished without finesse in breach of a wartime agreement with De Gaulle's French National Committee in which Britain agreed to leave Syria and Lebanon in the traditional French "sphere of influence."

France had announced her intention of granting independence to the two countries. At the end of World War II, she opened negotiations toward this end, although determined to secure what De Gaulle described as her "cultural, economic, and strategic interests."

The implications for Britain were clear. She had exerted herself to establish the League of Arab States as an instrument of her policy. During its incubation Britain's influence had been lessened by United States activities in Saudi Arabia. Nationalist pressure constantly threatened Britain's hold on Egypt. If now the two Levant states, instead of drifting into the British sphere, were to remain, however loosely, in the French orbit, it was possible that Britain might soon lose her influence in the Arab countries altogether.

General de Gaulle accused the British of having fomented Syrian and Lebanese opposition to the French proposals for them. Armed groups, helped by gendarmes and police (and carrying arms supplied over the years, despite French warnings, by the British) attacked French posts and personnel.

France took swift, drastic action. The resistance was quickly overwhelmed. Then the British delivered an ultimatum to the French Government: if French forces were not withdrawn, British forces would be sent into action against them. The French withdrew: they had only four to five thousand men in the Levant as against Britain's force of over half a million within striking distance.

The man who had directed the British "diplomatic" operation to supplant France in the Levant states was the ambassador, General Spears. No sooner had the Anglo-American Committee on Palestine opened its hearings in London in January 1946 than General Spears approached them with his advice. R. H. S. Crossman writes of him:

He was the only witness, so far as I can recall, of any nationality who did not trouble to conceal a clearly unsympathetic point of view about the Jews. We did not take him very seriously at the time, yet he alone proposed the drastic line of action against the Palestinian Jews which the Labour Government was to adopt six months later.[4]

The Anglo-American Committee did not realize that it was General Spears who personified British policy. They were soon harshly disillusioned. Despite Foreign Office pressure the committee's report contained two unanimous recommendations utterly unacceptable to the government. The first was for the abolition of the White Paper. The other was for the admission into Palestine of the 100,000 "displaced persons."

Bevin had promised the committee that if their recommendations were unanimous he would implement them. That, no doubt, was why he left it to the Prime Minister, Mr. Attlee, to announce the government's refusal to do so.

The fiasco of the Anglo-American Committee at least left no room for illusions about the mood of the British Government and its determination to carry out the policy of the White Paper to the end.

Abrahams returned to office in March 1946. Altman had kept his promise and secured me an immigration permit for Palestine. We left in late May. On board ship I studied the Palestine Emergency Regulations. The 1936 regulations had been tightened in 1945, expanded again in 1946. They were a draconian code of laws, an absolute concentration of power in the hands of the government, an indiscriminate conferment of authority on every soldier and every policeman in the street.

The hostility of the British Government to the remaining Jews in Europe was apparent in its regulations on "illegal" immigrants in Palestine. Any soldier, policeman or even immigration official was empowered to arrest without warrant anyone suspected of being an "illegal" immigrant, who could thereupon be jailed by administrative order, without trial.

In the event of a trial, the accused was obliged to prove his innocence.

Anyone harboring an "illegal" immigrant, even his own father or mother, was liable to an eight-year jail sentence. By comparison, the penalty for harboring a murderer was three years, unless he was a relative, in which case there was no penalty at all.

All rights of the individual had been abolished in Palestine. A man could be arrested at will, imprisoned without trial, sentenced for an indefinite period. He could be exiled and held in detention in exile for year after year without ever having been asked a single question, let alone called to appear in court.

The censorship was complete. All written material, including letters and telegrams, was subject to it. Nothing might be printed that the censor thought could be harmful to "law and order." Every newspaper was censored. Any excision by the censor had to be concealed from readers.

Travel within the country was severely restricted or controlled.

Any organization or society could be declared an illegal body without reason or explanation or right of appeal.

The High Commissioner could confiscate the property of anyone suspected of having broken any emergency regulation. Any army officer had authority to confiscate entire streets, suburbs or towns, if he had reason to believe that a shot had been fired from a house in the vicinity.

Any civilian could be tried on any charge before a military court. Although sentence had to be confirmed by the commander-in-chief the accused himself had no right of appeal, except perhaps to the House of Lords in Britain.

The crowning glory of the regulations were those dealing with the specific crimes for which there was to be a trial before a military court.

The death sentence could be imposed (1) on anyone shooting at someone, or at a place where people were to be found;

(2) on anyone throwing or placing a bomb or inflammable material with intent to injure people or damage property;

(3) on anyone carrying arms, ammunition, a bomb or explosive or inflammable material without a license from a military officer;

(4) on any member of a group or body of people one of whose *other* members had committed one of these capital crimes.

For the lesser crime of being in possession of arms, ammunition, or bombs, the sentence could be life. One could also be given a life sentence for belonging to the same club as someone found guilty of this crime.

There were many gradations in the 150 paragraphs of the regulations. Taken together, they provided the framework, now that Hitler's Reich was destroyed, for the most ruthless police state in the world.

The British had by any civilized political standard or legal system long forfeited the right to rule Palestine. Their presence, buttressed by 80,000 soldiers, was merely that of a regime of occupation maintaining itself by brute force. Quite apart from the implications of Jewish restoration and its betrayal by Britain, it was a moral imperative to overthrow such a regime. Such were my thoughts as I traveled toward Palestine. I knew too, that within a few days or weeks I would, merely by rejoining the Irgun, be liable to be hanged. Still, I was happier than I had been for a long time.

Part Two

THE STRUGGLE
FOR A STATE

10

Begin Commands the Irgun

In Jerusalem I was overwhelmed by self-pitying nostalgia. The physical surroundings in which I worked were a daily reminder of the collapse of the world of my youth. I took over a desk in the office of the Revisionist Party and looked around for living quarters. Aryeh Possek, who worked in the office, told me of a British official in the Light Industries Department named Messer who was about to go on long leave to England and was therefore anxious to sublet his home for four months. The house was in the heart of Katamon, a suburb where there were few Jews and many British officials and police officers. One of the tenants was a young British army officer and among Messer's near neighbors were Mr. Webster, the government Treasurer, and Mr. Giles, head of the CID, the adjoining apartment houses being occupied exclusively by British policemen and their families.

I did not know to what extent and in what way I would be working against this select company, but I was attracted by the prospect of quietly doing so under their very noses. I accepted Mr. Messer's terms, but it was a full week before he informed my wife that we could move in. The date of Messer's departure was postponed at the last moment, and we lived together for some days. One evening he told me why he had delayed the consummation of our arrangement. He had thought it necessary to inquire at the CID if there was any objection to my coming to live in this imperial neighborhood. I had been given a "clean bill." Apart from my being an active Revisionist, he was told, there was nothing known against me.

The implications of this information were interesting, but I decided to test them with the unconscious help of one of the neighbors, Major Lukyn, the Assistant Custodian of Enemy Property who, after the Messers had left for England, dropped in frequently for an evening drink and chat. In my discussions with him, I was emphatic in my denunciations of British policy and in justifying the activities of the underground movements. Whatever reports Lukyn passed on to the CID, they could hardly fail to emphasize the absence of any camouflage on my part.

It was a fortnight before the line of communication to the Irgun was opened. At a meeting in Tel Aviv, I was told by Yaacov Rubin, who had succeeded Isaac Remba as editor of the Revisionist daily *Hamashkif,* that "the boys" wanted to see me. He gave me a time, a place, and a password. My contact was waiting for me at the Tamar Cafe—Israel Epstein, a gentle intellectual who, between a variety of propaganda and liaison duties for the high command of the Irgun, taught at a primary school. I was given my first comprehensive briefing on the salient events of the preceding years.

We left the cafe casually and strolled beyond the Habimah Theatre. Sitting on a bench in the boulevard was a dark girl of about nineteen, to whom Epstein spoke. Then turning to me he said abruptly, "Ruhama will take you to the Commander. *Lehitraot.*" On the outskirts of the built-up area, on the edge of the open fields, we came to a building flanked by trees, where Ruhama rang the bell of a ground-floor flat. The name on the door was Oppenheimer. A woman opened the door and led us into a little room, where Menahem Begin was seated at the table, peacefully writing an article for the next issue of the underground *Herut* newspaper. Ruhama took his papers and a number of messages and left us alone.

Menahem Begin's place in history is assured by the success of the Irgun's struggle against the British. My own subsequent disagreements with him as a party leader in Israel have etched even more clearly in my mind the rare quality of his leadership in the underground. He was incontestably a brilliant underground political strategist.

Begin became the commander of the Irgun in 1943, when it was an organization held together only by the faith of its members. Some of its members had fought in the Palestine contingent in the British Army, in the belief that as long as there was danger of a British defeat there were good reasons for the "truce" with Britain that Raziel and his colleagues had proclaimed in 1939. But the British Government had recognized no truce and had acknowledged no Jewish partnership in the war. Their policies in Palestine underwent no change.

With the danger of German victory eliminated after their defeats in North Africa, and the beginning of German retreat in Russia, both the leaders of the Irgun and the rank and file realized that the hour of revolt had again struck. There was a frustrating interim while the Irgun looked to the Revisionist Party for political guidance. Dr. Altman developed the concept that the role of the Irgun was that of a military arm for the party, a threat to hold over the heads of the British administration when the time came to negotiate with them. But during 1943, Yaacov Meridor, Raziel's successor, and his colleagues in the Irgun Command became increasingly restive.

It was probably with a sense of relief that Meridor agreed to hand over his post to Menahem Begin, then newly arrived in the country, and to serve as his deputy.

Begin at once severed the connection with the Revisionist Party and announced that Irgun was to be its own political organization, using force as occasion required.

In January 1944, Begin, buttressed by a new High Command, issued a declaration of war and a call to arms. The first large-scale commando-style attacks were launched on British civil installations. In three rounds of simultaneous assault the offices of the Immigration Department, the Income Tax offices and the CID headquarters throughout the country were blown up. One limiting decision was taken. As long as Britain fought Hitler, the Army was not to be touched.

An intensive campaign of enlightenment accompanied the military operations: citizens going to their work in the morning found, posted up on the walls and shop windows in the towns, communiqués on the previous night's operations, analyses of the political situation and exhortations for support. A radio transmitter began regular broadcasts.

The British reacted with intensive searches for suspects, for printing presses, for the radio transmitter, large-scale arrests of suspects, and heavy sentences for those who could be brought to trial.

The sharpest opposition to the Irgun attacks, however, actually came from the official Jewish organizations. The violence of their attack in their newspapers was matched by the imaginative catalogue of their charges. Nihilists, maniacs, charlatans, Fascists, murderers, bandits were the familiar terms used in the spate of speeches, articles, and resolutions that poured out throughout 1944 against the Irgun and the Lehi. The Revisionist *Hamashkif* itself openly proclaimed opposition to the underground, heaping contempt on its pretensions, affirming its belief in the "partnership" with Britain, and in the exclusive efficacy of political negotiation. It even manifested a measure of co-operation with the British by meekly publishing—along with the Agency newspapers—the CID photographs of "wanted terrorists."

The propaganda was effective, especially in the rural areas where Irgun literature did not penetrate. Many accepted the image of the Irgun (and the Lehi) as a band of "criminals" and "Fascists" consciously "stabbing Zionism in the back" by aiming at the overthrow of *Jewish* authority.

There was even more direct pressure. The leader of the Haganah, Eliahu Golomb, accompanied by his deputy Moshe Sneh, met Begin to persuade him that he was wrong in his reading of the political situation, that in fact British policy would change after the war, that British public figures had actually so promised. They ended by threatening to liquidate Irgun altogether.

This threat was not an idle one. Eliahu Lankin, a member of the Irgun High Command who had taken part in the conversation with Golomb and Sneh, was handed over to the British in Jerusalem. Other denunciations and arrests followed. In October, 251 men, held as suspected Irgun and Lehi members in the Latrun and other detention camps, were deported by the British and flown in precious RAF planes to exile in Eritrea.

The Jewish Agency's campaign against the Irgun reached full flood the next month when Lord Moyne, the British Resident Minister in Cairo, was assassinated by Hakim and Beth-Tsoury, two Lehi members.

Lord Moyne was a remote figure whose hostility to measures for saving Europe's Jews was at the time not well known, and his assassination evoked almost universal condemnation. The Jewish Agency exploited this public feeling and to the full. In a speech to the Histadrut Conference on November 20, 1944 Mr. Ben-Gurion outlined his plan for liquidating the underground.[1]

Members of the underground, when discovered, were to be driven from their places of work or expelled from high schools. There was to be no sentimental hesitation about handing them over to the

British. Mr. Ben-Gurion emphasized that for the Jews in Palestine, there was a "common interest with the British."

The whole machinery of the Jewish Agency's security forces were now organized to wage war against the Irgun. The Haganah and the Palmach[2] were sent into action. Hundreds of members of the latter were drafted into the towns from their kibbutzim. Expulsions from schools, dismissals from places of work, kidnapings, beatings, torture, direct denunciations to the British, became the sole occupation of the action-hungry soldiers of the Haganah and the Palmach. In instinctive identification with the British overlord, they borrowed, from the tradition of the hunt, the term to describe this operation: it was called "the season."

When Mr. Ben-Gurion proclaimed the "common interest" with the British in crushing the rebels against their rule, he knew of an even greater betrayal by British statesmen than any of us imagined. Its background was Hungary that very year, when the Germans, on the retreat on all fronts, yet pursued with unabated ferocity the mass murder of Jews. In a memorandum prepared by Dr. Weizmann after the war he told of a proposal made by the Jewish Agency early in 1944 to parachute some hundreds of Jewish volunteers into Hungary. The plan had been approved by all the British military authorities concerned, who believed that it might save many Jews from extermination and could be of direct military value to the Allies. The Foreign and Colonial Offices intervened and called for immediate abandonment of this plan on political grounds.

In the summer of that year, Joel Brand came out of Hungary to discuss a deal the Nazis had proposed to the Jewish leaders, to exchange trucks for Jewish lives. Although Mr. Shertok was promised by the British High Commissioner Macmichael that Brand would be allowed to return to Hungary, he was later arrested by the British and sent to detention in Cairo. Shertok claims he protested to Macmichael at this breach of faith. Macmichael angrily reminded Shertok that "there was a war on."[3]

On July 6, Dr. Weizmann and Mr. Shertok made a verbal appeal to Mr. Eden, the British Foreign Minister, to destroy by bombing the concentration camps and the railways carrying the doomed Jews from Hungary to the camps. It was fifty-seven days, on September 1, before the British Foreign Office sent its reply, a period during which the majority of the Jews of Hungary were exterminated.

The bombing, stated the Foreign Office, was impossible because of "the very great technical difficulties involved."

Other events that summer gave brutal emphasis to the motives of British policy. That very month of July 1944, the Polish rising against the Germans in Warsaw broke out. Churchill moved heaven and earth to persuade the Russians and the Americans to come to their aid. Finally, in desperation, he ordered the RAF to do so from their distant Italian base.[4] It was a forlorn hope. Yet 181 sorties were actually flown.[5] The appeal of the Jewish Agency leaders was far less exacting. The death camp at Auschwitz was 200 miles nearer than Warsaw to the base at Foggia. The railway line from Budapest and Budapest itself were within easy range.[6] It is not surprising that the then Chief of RAF Bomber Command, Air Chief Marshal Harris, when confronted with the Jewish Agency's revelation, in 1961, of the approach, denied that the operation was impossible. Only, he added, he had no recollection of his ever having been asked to carry it out.

The rejection by the Jewish Agency leaders of the thesis that the British regime was the enemy of the Jewish people stemmed not only from the promises by British politicians of a change of policy and their belief in the Labor leaders, but from a long-developed subservience to Britain, a sense of inexorable British mastery in Palestine. They were quite incapable of imagining themselves rebelling against British rule.

The fact that in later years these leaders have failed to explain their policy but have retrospectively simply adopted the language of the Irgun toward the long-departed British, only emphasizes their inability to understand the British purpose.

"The season," as Mr. Ben-Gurion and his colleagues knew, meant civil war. Yet there was no civil war—because Begin forbade all retaliation. Day after day Begin learned of new arrests of officers carried out by British hands and guided by information from Haganah. Within a few weeks all the members of Begin's High Command were in British hands, in African exile.

Begin explained to his followers why there must be no civil war. The Irgun's political prognostication was unshakable. Analysis of British policy showed there was no hope of a change. One day this fact would dawn on the Jewish Agency and the Haganah leaders, and the Haganah would then join the fight against Britain. The prospect of fighting in unity, with an accelerated march to freedom, demanded that the Irgun should now suffer and wait.

Sixteen years later, the poet Haim Guri, one of the few Palmach officers of the time who have had the courage to express public repentance for "the season," recounted how as a cultural officer in Yagur he was asked by the Haganah commander in his area to help effect the capture of an Irgun group about to carry out a sabotage operation. He demurred, but when told that the operation would result in the killing of women and children, he acquiesced, after obtaining a promise that the captives would not be handed over to the British. Afterward he visited the prisoners. They were trussed up like chickens. He found that they did not curse nor threaten vengeance, nor utter undying hatred. One of them, Nehushtan, today a lawyer in Jerusalem, said, "You will regret this. The day will come when you too will be fighting the British." Nehushtan and his comrades were actually handed over to the British and spent four years in the detention camps in Africa.

Not a single act of retaliation against the Haganah was carried out by the Irgun, although the ranks were depleted and operations against the British were all but suspended. By the end of "the season," however, there was a completely new High Command, and a deeper self-confidence.

Begin's prognosis was fulfilled to the letter. The newly elected Labor government in 1945 laid aside the whips of the Conservatives only to take up their own scorpions. It was then that the Jewish Agency leaders decided to resist British policy with violence. They turned to the Irgun with the proposal that Irgun members should join the Haganah ranks, ending Irgun as an independent force. Begin had no confidence in the Jewish Agency, feared their lack of staying power and refused to liquidate the Irgun. But in order to achieve unity he agreed, as he had always promised, to accept Haganah leadership in the coming fight. The Lehi followed suit.

The Command of the United Tenuat Hameri (Resistance Movement) that emerged from the three-cornered negotiations became in fact that of the Haganah. The Irgun and the Lehi agreed thenceforth to carry out only operations that received its approval. The limitations were blatant, but the great object had been achieved. The whole people was at war.

The official Zionist establishment split in disagreement. Weizmann, consistent to the last, was opposed to violence against the

British in any form, whatever the consequence of submission. He was supported by the left wing of the Histadrut, the Hashomer Hatzair, voluble enemies of British colonization everywhere in the world, who throughout the years of British rule still remained on the best of terms with their own rulers. In the ranks of the activists a strange debate went on as to the kind of violence that would be right and proper. One school of thought believed that the operations must be limited exclusively to the British anti-immigration apparatus. Violence against any branch of British administration that had some relation to the prevention of immigration was legitimate, but violence against the British administration as such was immoral. This group was determined to demonstrate that the acts of violence were designed rather as a nuisance and not as an attempt to overthrow British rule. This theory of operation prevailed. Its opponents had to engage in long, hairsplitting discussions to prove the degree of relationship between this that or the other British installation and the immigration restrictions.

The scope and power of the decision of Tenuat Hameri was circumscribed and action considerably decelerated by this eccentric debate. There was also a tendency, at least on the part of the Agency political leaders, to test British reactions after each operation: "Maybe we can stop now, maybe they have had enough." Nevertheless the operations of all three organizations were massive. Radar stations, the Mobile Police installations, railways and bridges throughout the country were attacked by the Haganah. Railway workshops and an aerodrome were attacked by the Lehi. Railway stations and police stations were destroyed by the Irgun, and its attacks on aerodromes resulted in the destruction of a score of British aircraft.

The Lehi and its relations with the Irgun had followed a checkered pattern from the day in February 1942 when Avraham Stern was killed until, in November 1945, the two groups joined with the Haganah in the United Resistance Movement. Leaderless, hunted from pillar to post, their ranks thinned and thinning, the faithful remnant of Stern's followers, by dint of a desperate determination, kept together a nucleus of the organization. They continued to ignore the war against the Nazis, but disseminated vigorously their understanding of the British design in Palestine. Within eighteen months of Stern's death, Lehi, still small, but resolute in its purpose, had become an important force. Its literature bore the imprint of the intellectual capacity of its leaders—Nathan Friedman-Yellin, Yisrael Scheib, and Yitshak Izernitsky,[7] all disciples of Stern in prewar Poland.

They analyzed British policy and criticized the Jewish Agency leaders. They censured the Irgun for insisting on priority for the war against Hitler.

In this period the Lehi built up the great tradition of the courtroom. The trials of its members before the British military courts became sounding boards for the exposure of the British and for the doctrine of Jewish independence.

Lehi military operations were few, limited to attacks on personnel, especially the British detective force. Early in 1944, when the Irgun under Begin decided that the circumstances which had dictated a truce with the British were no longer valid and that the time had come to open the offensive, Lehi reaction was equivocal. They were gratified to see the end of their isolation, at the increase in volume and scope of the struggle and what seemed to them the acceptance of their policy by the parent organization. But they also nourished an understandable resentment at the scope of Irgun operations, which in proportion to Lehi and in numerical strength seems to have been about six to one.

Soon after the Irgun launched its campaign, the Lehi leaders adopted its tactical method, and directed attacks increasingly at the British Establishment as a whole. The restraints self-imposed by the Irgun to avoid human casualties were never accepted by Lehi. The Irgun had forbidden its members to carry personal weapons except on operations. Lehi members, after the death of Stern, were ordered to carry personal weapons. As a result there were repeated clashes with British soldiers and police, clashes which in some measure delayed the Lehi effort to build up an effective fighting organization. However, once the two groups started co-operating, the Lehi, on Begin's advice, abandoned the policy of carrying arms.

The united struggle of the Irgun, Lehi, and the Haganah had been in progress for seven months when I sat with Begin for the first time in his underground office in the flat of "Mr. and Mrs. Oppenheimer." He now wore a bushy mustache and beard, and the natural pallor of his face was deepened by the two years and more he had spent indoors. There was no other visible change in his appearance since my meeting with him in Warsaw eight years earlier.

We talked mainly of Britain. I had the advantage of my closer and more personal knowledge of the situation in London, but I soon discovered that, except for the details I was able to add, he had a complete picture of the strengths and weaknesses of the British. I found him less optimistic than I on the possible duration of the struggle. My calculation was a simple one: if the full force of the united onslaught was maintained for six months longer, Britain's growing economic difficulties in the winter would force her to cut her overseas commitments and, under the pressure of public opinion in Britain, agree to the inevitable withdrawal from Palestine. Begin, sobered by bitter experience, was dubious about my first premise: he was much less certain of his allies than I was. The Haganah had indeed a few days earlier blown up a number of bridges, a major operation which must bring home to Britain the grave possibilities of an all-out war. Nevertheless knowing the internal stresses in the Haganah, Begin was uneasy.

We talked for many hours and that day I re-enlisted for service. I was committed to the Revisionist Party until its world conference, due to be held in the autumn or winter, but until then I would be available for any specific duties that might arise and would help in the preparation of propaganda in English.

11

The King David Hotel

Begin was right. There were troubles with the Haganah. The agreement on which the United Resistance Movement was based contained a provision for one kind of independent operation by the Irgun: the capture of arms from the British. The Irgun's resources had never kept pace with its ever-increasing need of arms, ammunition, and explosives. Some of its most daring operations, involving elaborate planning and bold stratagems, had been to capture arms. One such attack was against the great British Army camp at Sarafand. There, disguised as British soldiers, an Irgun unit had raided the armory and carried off a substantial number of rifles and machine guns. In the withdrawal, however, two men, Michael Ashbel and Yosef Simhon, had been wounded and captured. They were tried by a British military court under the "emergency regulations" and sentenced to death.

The Irgun's demand that its captured men be treated as prisoners-of-war under the Geneva Convention was disregarded by the British. The organization announced that gallows would be countered by gallows and promptly kidnaped six British officers in retaliation. The British immediately clamped down a curfew and launched a country-wide hunt with house-to-house searches. They were given gratuitous encouragement by the Jewish Establishment. Because the kidnaping was unrelated to the Resistance agreement, the Jewish Agency press and the Haganah radio began a campaign of denunciation against the Irgun.

The sentence on Ashbel and Simhon was confirmed by the British G.O.C., Sir Evelyn Barker. One of the captured British officers escaped, and now the Irgun High Command released two other captives to tell their superior officers of the intended fate of their three comrades.

To the disgust of the Irgun leaders, the Haganah radio broadcast a completely mendacious announcement that it was as a result of their pressure that the Irgun had released the captives. The Irgun denied this in a public statement.

A tense inaction followed while a shoal of appeals by Jewish groups and individuals were sent to the High Commissioner to remit the death sentences. Through Israel Rokach, the mayor of Tel Aviv, the British at last signified they were ready to make a deal. An agreement was reached. Some days later the High Commissioner announced the remission of the sentences on Ashbel and Simhon to life imprisonment, and the next day the British officers were released.

Now the British struck at the Jewish Agency, the Haganah, and the Palmach. The operation started early in the morning of Saturday, June 29. All the available members of the Jewish Agency Executive except Dr. Weizmann were arrested and summarily sent to the Latrun Detention Camp. Four thousand members of the Haganah and Palmach throughout the country were rounded up and sent to a monster detention camp at Rafah on the Egyptian border. Searches for arms, executed with considerable brutality and pointedly described by Mr. Ben-Gurion as a "pogrom," were carried out in a number of kibbutzim. The Haganah was taken completely by surprise. Its will to resist collapsed. A few months earlier the Haganah had announced, "We shall never surrender. The Yishuv will not rest until it has won the right to its own country, the right to set up its own State . . . Resistance to the Government's policy is inflexible and determined, and is waged by responsible elements. Undoubtedly the Government can win in a trial of strength since the Jews have no tanks or planes . . . But our intention is to wage a prolonged struggle; the longer it lasts the brighter our prospects."

This brave declaration now proved false; with this first serious British reprisal, the Jewish Agency surrendered. Except for two minor operations in August, and again in July 1947, *the Haganah took no further part in the armed struggle against the British.*

This surrender was made in stages, with some initial token defiance. The Haganah announced that there would be no contact between the Jewish Agency and the British until their leaders were released and until the 100,000 Jews in the European camps were allowed to enter Palestine. The thousands of imprisoned Haganah and Palmach members were ordered to refuse to identify themselves to their captors. But the British Government insisted on unconditional surrender, an end to the resistance, and renewed co-operation by the Jewish Agency in crushing the Irgun. Within four months they had achieved their main objective. Early in November the British Government was able to announce that "in view of the condemnation of terrorism (by) the Inner Zionist Council, which is accepted as an earnest of the intention of the Jewish Agency and of representative Jewish institutions in Palestine to dissociate themselves entirely from the campaign of violence and to do their utmost to root out this evil, his Majesty's Government have concurred in the release of the detained Jewish leaders."

In the weeks immediately following the twenty-ninth of June, there was no change in the relations between the three resistance groups. The United Resistance leadership continued to function, and concentrated on planning a massive reply to the British onslaught. The appropriate measure chosen was the destruction of British Government and Military Headquarters, the very center of British rule, quartered in the south wing of the King David Hotel in Jerusalem. It was an operation which, when previously proposed by the Irgun, had not received the Resistance Movement's approval. Now, with general concurrence, the plan was prepared and discussed by the Irgun Operations Chief "Giddy" (Amihai Paglin) and the Palmach leader Yitshak Sadeh. On July 22, the south wing of the King David Hotel was blown up and completely destroyed. It was a brilliantly conceived operation, elaborately planned and executed with skill and courage. It was accompanied, however, by unplanned and unexpected tragedy: eighty lives were lost, among them senior members of the British Establishment, Jewish officials, and casual callers at the administration offices.

The reason for this loss of life has never been made entirely clear. One of the basic rules of Irgun operations was to avoid bloodshed wherever possible. This was fundamental to the timing and tactic of every operation which was directed at government or army objectives.

Although some clashes were inevitable, sometimes resulting in casualties, British personnel were not, except in a few specific instances, the target of Irgun attack. This was not a manifestation

of superior virtue or of half-heartedness, but the rational tactics
for a resistance movement facing a power infinitely superior in
numbers and firepower. Indeed, in the four fierce years of Irgun
resistance the number of casualties inflicted on British personnel was
amazingly small. There were some eighty to one hundred thousand
British troops in Palestine at the height of the campaign, yet the
total number of British personnel killed was little over two hundred.[1] This included casualties inflicted by the Lehi (who recognized
no restriction) and, in the seven months of its resistance, by the
Haganah.

The time chosen for the bombing of the King David Hotel was
before lunch hour, when the cafe on the ground floor of the wing
to be destroyed was empty. Specific precautions were then taken
to assure that the whole wing, and indeed the whole area, should
be evacuated.

A small preliminary explosive charge was set off in the street
opposite the hotel to frighten off passers-by—and the street was
cleared. The Arab workers in the kitchen were told by the attackers
to run for their lives, and they did. A warning of the impending
explosion was telephoned to the government secretariat twenty-five
minutes before the charge exploded. That warning went unheeded.
The British at first denied that such a warning had ever been received. Adina, the Irgun soldier who warned the hotel, also telephoned the nearby French consulate to open their windows against
the effects of possible blast. At the same time she telephoned the
Palestine Post editorial offices, whose switchboard operator telephoned the police. The news spread so quickly that by the time the
explosion occurred several newspapermen had arrived in the neighborhood and were eyewitnesses of the event.

Why did the warning to the British go unheeded? The Haganah
radio later broadcast a report that on receiving the warning Sir John
Shaw, the Chief Secretary of the British administration, had said:
"I give orders here. I don't take orders from Jews," and that he had
insisted that nobody leave the building. This version may be dismissed. It probably developed from the fact that while some of
Shaw's close colleagues and subordinates were killed, he himself
went unscathed, and gained credence when Shaw was transferred
from Palestine a month later.

A more likely explanation is that the British did not take the
warning seriously. They did not believe that the Irgun could pos-

sibly penetrate their well-guarded military headquarters or that, if they did, they would not be repelled. An alert was in fact conveyed to the guards on the ground floor of the building. The Irgun unit, disguised as Arabs delivering the hotel's supply of milk, came into the hotel unhindered, but were fired on as they left. They suffered two casualties, one of them fatal.

I met Begin the day after the attack on the King David Hotel and found him saddened and angered by the British for bringing about the unnecessary loss of life. He told me then that among the Jews killed were some sympathizers of the Irgun—one of them being Julius Jacobs, an assistant to the Chief Secretary.

The effects of the damaging blow we had dealt the British were overshadowed by the tragedy. This was understandable. Equally understandable, though not excusable, was the immediate race for cover by the Haganah leaders. Contrary to the terms of the inter-group agreement, under which all operations were to be credited to the resistance movement as a whole, the Irgun was asked to an-nounce its exclusive responsibility for the attack on the King David Hotel. The Irgun did so without equivocation. At first the Haganah propaganda joined the Jewish Agency Press in attacking us. Only after protests from the Irgun did the Haganah publicly concede that the British had had ample warning.

A few days later, the Haganah recovered enough composure to discuss further operations to be carried out by the United Resistance Movement. Haganah commander Moshe Sneh left Palestine quietly to take part in the meetings of the Jewish Agency Executive in Paris, there to press for the continuance of resistance.

The debate in Paris was prolonged, ending in Sneh's defeat. Weizmann pointed to the violence of British reactions as proof of the justice of his policy of submission and demanded surrender,[2] a policy in which Ben-Gurion concurred.

Ben-Gurion, in the months that followed, developed in public a new, though patently misleading, explanation of policy of surrender: "We shall have neither Vichy nor Massada"—neither surrender nor suicide. In his own mind, however, he could have had no illusion about the implications of the abandonment of resistance. On August 23, 1946 at the conclusion of the historic Executive meeting and under the immediate impact of its decisions, Mr. Ben-Gurion wrote a letter to his party in Palestine in which he set out with approval the political conclusions reached at the meeting:

The British, he said, could not or would not fulfill the Mandate; this deprived their rule in Palestine of all legal or moral basis. But—

> It sometimes happens that the weak have to submit to the strong —even when law and justice are not on the side of the strong—but this surrender is only from compulsion and not out of acquiescence or out of "Christian morality."

Nothing could more succinctly define the philosophy of Vichy, or indeed of any surrender in history. This letter was not released to the public.[3]

Meanwhile, the British Army continued to terrorize the kibbutzim in their searches for arms. In addition, a major campaign was launched against the survivors of Hitler's concentration camps daring to make their way to Palestine.

The Mediterranean fleet was sent into action to apply the tactics employed four years earlier in the campaign against Nazi ships which then carried supplies to Rommel's Army in North Africa. In a vigorous diplomatic offensive the British Foreign Office called Europe to her aid. France, Italy, Belgium, and Holland in the West, Soviet Russia, Poland, Romania, and Czechoslovakia in the East, were asked to deny exit or transit to prospective escapees. On August 14 a boatload of immigrants was trapped in the Mediterranean by a British naval vessel and conducted into Haifa. The immigrants were deported to the island of Cyprus.

By the subtle workings of chance, this refinement of Ernest Bevin's policy provided the Haganah with an alternative to armed resistance. Their political leaders, having finally decided within days of the new deportation policy to stop all resistance in Palestine, the Haganah concentrated on Aliyah B operations, and thus transferred the full burden of resistance to the immigrants themselves.

On August 14 and the few days following, the Haganah announced on the radio that it would answer the deportations with resistance and indeed sabotaged two British deportation ships in Haifa Port. After the Paris decision, instructions to resist were flashed by radio from Tel Aviv to the ships making their way to Palestine. When their little ships were boarded by British naval vessels the immigrants resisted with whatever came to hand—sticks, bottles, fists. Many of them were wounded before they reached Cyprus. Here and there a body fell overboard or a British bullet put an end to a life.

On shore, in Haifa, the Haganah organized public demonstrations which resulted in more Jewish casualties.

The pattern emerged. The Haganah organized the escape of inmates from the DP camps, cared for them in transit centers, brought them to embarkation ports, and sent them sailing into the Mediterranean. From time to time a ship evaded the British patrols but the great majority were stopped and taken to Haifa port and their passengers packed off to Cyprus.

Aliyah B performed one great and useful function in the struggle with Britain. It emphasized the problem of Jewish homelessness, dramatizing in human terms the perfidy of British policy, and making clear the moral drive of the underground's resistance in Palestine.

After its Paris decision to abandon resistance, the Jewish Agency campaign against the fighting underground was resumed. A new theory was developed, that the underground was helping the British in that the real intention was to overthrow the Zionist leadership. There was, too, a return to the old theme that the Irgun and the Lehi were insanely desperate, and threats were renewed to "take all possible measures against the underground."

The dilemma of the Haganah chiefs after the Jewish Agency had ordered them to abandon the armed struggle was a poignant one. To their rank and file they continued to promise resistance of their own in addition to the resistance by remote proxy on the Aliyah B ships. On the other hand, they had to keep in line with their political leaders and, for the benefit of the British, denounce the activities of the Irgun and the Lehi. In June the blowing up of bridges or railway lines were essential operations against the enemy. In September, they were unforgivable acts of terrorism. Had they depended on the power of logical persuasion alone, their troops might have deserted them. Strong appeals to discipline were made. The dominating principle of official Zionist education, deeply ingrained in the idealistic youth who filled the Haganah ranks, had always been that thinking was the responsibility and prerogative of the leaders. The positive virtue of discipline was elevated without much difficulty to the cult of intellectual abdication by the individual. The ranks were not happy; they grumbled; but except for some defections to the Irgun and the Lehi, they accepted the situation. Many of the more thoughtful quieted their qualms with the delusion that this reversal of policy by their leaders was a major act of camouflage, calculated to ensure the continued "legality" of the Jewish Agency, and that it had been effected as part of a cunning agreement for a new "division" of labor with the fighting underground.[4]

Indeed, many private citizens found in this wishful rationalization the solution to the otherwise unbearable paradox of a political leadership laying down its arms in the face of an implacable enemy, leaving the contest to a comparatively small "dissident" group, retiring to the sidelines and from there jeering at both sides.

The British, certain of their victory over the "official" forces, now prepared a shattering attack on the Irgun and the Lehi. It was delivered as a riposte to the blowing up of the King David headquarters. They were determined to crush the underground. They suspected rightly that the heart of resistance was in Tel Aviv, on which early one morning in August they made a sudden swoop, with twenty thousand troops—infantry, supported by tanks. The town was occupied. Its approaches were sealed off. A continuous curfew, which lasted for four days, was imposed.

Life in Tel Aviv was brought to a halt. Every house and apartment was searched. The adult male population was led in groups to screening centers set up throughout the town. CID officers armed with lists and photographs identified more than a hundred thousand people. Among them were almost all the leaders and staff of the Irgun and the Lehi, and the total Tel Aviv manpower of both organizations. Nearly eight hundred people were indeed led away to detention, and a British communiqué claimed the capture of many important terrorists.

In fact, the British operation was a fiasco. The total haul of "important terrorists" was precisely two: Yitshak Izernitsky, a member of the Lehi commanding triumvirate and Zusia Kromiers, an Irgun officer.

Begin, alone of the underground leaders, evaded the face-to-face screening. He hid in a concealed cupboard in his apartment, constructed for brief emergencies. When the searchers came, they were told by Mrs. Begin that Dr. Koenigshoffer (Begin's current pseudonym) had gone to Jerusalem. She did not dare open the cupboard to give him water or food, a platoon of British soldiers having chosen to camp out in the garden of the house, under the very windows of Begin's ground-floor apartment. She could not take the risk of the children's reactions, or of a Tommy walking in—as happened from time to time—to ask for a drink of water or a box of matches. Begin remained in this cupboard, in a space just large enough to hold him, without food or water, for four days in the heat of the summer.

12

The Irgun in Europe

I was now a member of the inner world of the Irgun. I saw Begin from time to time, as well as Avraham,[1] the indefatigable Chief of Staff, who was administrator and co-ordinator of the auxiliary arms of the Irgun and in charge of relations with other Jewish groups. Avraham was in fact the linchpin of the whole organization. His day began at dawn and often ended at midnight. He was in constant movement. He supervised the officers distributed throughout the town. He supervised the creation of Irgun literature and its distribution. He co-ordinated the work of the members of the High Command and of the executive staff. He briefed the emissaries to whom, in some part, the transmission of letters and instructions to the Irgun branches and supporters abroad was entrusted. He laboriously coded and decoded the correspondence to be sent by mail. He kept his diary in the fold of the long stockings he wore with his always immaculate khaki shorts. This consisted of a long strip of paper covered with minute writing. Avraham had no home life; his wife and infant were in Haifa, where the CID kept a close watch on them. Once or twice a year they came to Tel Aviv to spend a few hurried hours with him. There was no tension or strain apparent in Avraham's speech or his manner. He always seemed fresh and even-tempered. It was dangerous to concentrate so much authority in one man, but fortunately he was never arrested, nor were there any serious bottlenecks.

Meetings and talks with Begin and Avraham in Tel Aviv throughout that eventful summer gave me an education in the secret history of the Irgun and its relations with the world above ground. I soon decided that it would be a waste of effort to try to convert the Revisionist Party to the belief that, to be true to itself, it also must go underground. Many of its members were in any case active in the Irgun or the Lehi, some of them using the party as a cover.

I had expected that once the preparations for the Revisionist conference were made, and after the election of the delegates, I would merely hold the fort until a new executive committee was elected. But Dr. Altman asked me to go to Paris and Basel, and make the financial and organizational arrangements for the conference. Although I did not relish a task for which I had no experience or background, I agreed to leave for Europe early in October.

I was also given a mission for the Irgun: to deliver a number of messages from the Irgun High Command to two of its representatives, Elhanan (Dr. Shmuel Ariel), the Irgun representative in France, and Pesach, the responsible officer for Europe, who would be coming to Paris from Rome. After delivery of the messages I was to maintain contact with Pesach.

On the eve of my departure, Avraham, consulting his hieroglyphic diary, read out a number of instructions on a variety of subjects which I was to deliver to Pesach. I noted them down in my address book, converting each message into a private code of my own to decipher next day in the plane. Avraham spent half an hour teaching me the code I was to use in correspondence, if the need arose, and then presented me with a handsome pair of shoes, which I was to wear until I reached Paris, where I was to give them to Pesach.

From my talks with Pesach in Paris, I learned of the Irgun's activities outside Palestine and of European sympathy for the Irgun. The name, used by most Europeans to refer to all Jewish resistance in Palestine, had become part of the vocabulary of Europe and symbolic of the Jewish people in dramatic struggle. The newspapers featured the fighting in Palestine and frequently published friendly reports and surveys on the resistance. The callousness of the British Government toward the battered survivors of Hitler's death camps made the issue clear. The image of a dauntless group fighting against the might of an Empire and, moreover dealing it impressive blows, evoked a natural partisanship. Memories of their own underground experience under the Nazi regime inspired a sense, however passive, of comradeship with the Palestine underground. It was enough to identify oneself to any Frenchman (or Italian) as a Jew from Palestine to be met by a sympathetic, sometimes well-informed panegyric of the "Irgoun."

The warm feelings of the population were heartening, but Irgun officers and emissaries had still to work in strict conspiracy. In the centers of greatest activity, Italy and France, the authorities were thoroughly aware of the activities of the Palestine resistance movements, and tolerated them only as long as there was no flagrant breach of the law.

France was the central base of Irgun activity. When Ariel, the Irgun representative in France, came to Paris he began to try to win the support of the French Government for our political objectives.

By the autumn of 1946, when I arrived in Paris, Ariel had established excellent relations on several levels with the French authorities. His wide knowledge of French literature and politics and his easy identification with the French way of life provided excellent personal credentials. He was greatly helped in his task by Madame Claire Vayda, an ex-French Resistance fighter, who directed an organization to aid Jewish refugees. Madame Vayda had easy entré in many quarters, and although she never officially joined the Irgun, she gave Ariel useful initial contacts which he developed.

It was understood by Ariel and the French authorities that the Irgun could work freely, if discreetly, in France, as long as the Irgun did not carry out any direct anti-British action on French soil.

There was little mobilization of Irgun members in France. A comparatively small number of young people, French-born, and newcomers from Eastern Europe, were organized as a Betar movement trained clandestinely in the use of small arms, and served in auxiliary capacities. It was through these young people that Ariel had contact with the impressionistic rank-and-file of the organization in Paris. It was because of these young people that I carried instructions to suspend Ariel from his post.

Ariel had adopted a standard and a mode of living far removed from the very modest regulations laid down by the Irgun. It was difficult for him to maintain a sense of discipline among the young people in the local organization who were in contact with him. The Irgun to them meant self-sacrifice and denial and they could not understand the sybaritic way of life of the man they knew as a senior representative of the embattled Irgun.

Reports had come to the High Command in Palestine that Ariel was living "like a lord." Indeed, along with the order for his suspension there was an order for an inquiry into the source of his finances. This inquiry established conclusively that, far from squandering Irgun money, Ariel was living entirely at his own expense. He had found lucrative employment of his own, work which did not interfere with his activities for the Irgun. The suspension, however, remained in force.

At our first meeting Ariel defended his way of life vigorously. The work he was doing could be done only if he could meet French personalities on equal social terms. That meant a good address, lavish entertainment on a natural and permanent scale. I disagreed. I could not believe that the political significance of the Irgun's struggle could be heightened in anybody's eyes by a display of insouciant lavishness. Nevertheless, I believed it was quite wrong to dismiss him. As a diplomat he was irreplaceable.

Ariel was not employed by the Irgun for any work of significance for more than a year. He maintained his contacts—and his good humor. He was to make a dramatic return.

Pesach (later known as Eliezer and finally as Eli), who was in command of the Irgun in Italy, gradually took charge of mobilization and organization for the whole of Europe.[2] He held a degree in philosophy at the Hebrew University, but he had devoted his post-graduate life to service in the Irgun, and had risen to be head of its Intelligence Department in Palestine. During "the season" he had been kidnaped, incarcerated, and tortured by the Haganah. He was still, after six months, in Haganah hands when the negotiations for the United Resistance Movement opened in the autumn of 1945. Begin had refused to conclude the negotiations till he was released. Eli was smuggled out of the country and made his way to Italy.

In Italy he had built up an effective organization. Almost all his recruits came from the Displaced Persons' transit camps, survivors of the concentration camps and ex-partisans from Eastern Europe. Eli was responsible for the substantial volume of propaganda and information disseminated in Italy. He was responsible, too, for the training of hundreds of prospective Irgun fighters and inculcated in them a strong sense of identification with the struggle in Palestine.

He was waiting eagerly for authority to launch operations in Europe and was overjoyed to discover the authorization in the contents of the shoe I brought him. A few days after our first meeting he returned to Italy to organize the first attack.

For the next two months I divided my time between preparing

the Revisionist conference and a variety of self-imposed errands for the Irgun. The work for the conference was in the main formal, though complicated by financial difficulties and, as I had expected, by my own lack of experience. Fortunately I was helped out in the final stages in Basel by my old friend Dr. David Bukspan, whose experience stood me in good stead. I took only a formal part in the proceedings of the conference, and quietly brought my active association with the Revisionist Party to a close.

In Rome, Eli worked speedily. He aimed directly at the center of the British operations against immigration: the embassy in Rome. On the night of October 29 the embassy was blown up. An Irgun communiqué in Italy announced the opening of a new front in the struggle for Jewish independence which would now be extended to Britain itself.

I at once took the train to London, not indeed to extend operations there, but to study the climate of public feeling on Palestine. The explosion in Rome and the Irgun communiqué had a tumultuous effect in London, far exceeding my most sanguine expectations. For all the contumely poured upon it by British official sources, by the British press, and by the Jewish Agency, the Irgun had achieved, in Britain as throughout the world, a reputation for daring, bravery, and reliability. It carried out both promises and threats. Its attacks had become more ambitious and more effective. The Irgun had already delivered two sharp shocks to British public opinion. In the spring, its fighters had destroyed twenty-two RAF planes on the ground at the Kastina airfield. In the summer, the King David headquarters had been bombed. The Irgun had achieved a hostile but real and growing respect. The news from Rome, proving its capacity to operate beyond the bounds of its home territory, shocked the man in the street into the realization that there was "a war on."

I could hardly believe what I saw and heard in London in the three days I spent there. The Irgun's bald declaration of forthcoming operations in Britain was translated into a threat of immediate action. The less responsible but widely circulated newspapers vied with one another in manufacturing vivid reports of Irgun plans. On the day of my arrival, as I traveled down Regent Street by bus, I saw the headline of the day chalked on a blackboard: IRGUN THREATENS LONDON. It was a fair reflection of what the *Evening News* had reported under a page-spread banner headline. The

Jewish terrorists were planning to blow up government buildings, to kill public figures, to sabotage industrial installations, big hotels, communications, and postal services.

The newspaper also reported that Irgun (and "Stern Group") agents had already infiltrated into Britain, and the diplomatic correspondent of the *Evening News* offered specific information that the Irgun and the Lehi had established a combined General Staff for operations in Britain. They had, he asserted, drawn up a "death list" which included General Barker (the G.O.C. in Palestine), Sir John Shaw (the recently transferred Chief Secretary of the Palestine Government) and Viscount Hall (the former Colonial Secretary) and even certain unnamed Jewish public figures. The newspapers featured statements by the Irgun in Palestine that no precautions would prevent the carrying out of operations in Britain, and by Samuel Merlin, in charge of the newly opened Paris office of the Hebrew Committee of National Liberation, that if "Irgun men wanted to get into England they would do so, without anybody recognizing them." The *Evening Standard's* Jerusalem correspondent had a colorful story on the ingenuity of Irgun and Lehi disguises. In London too, he suggested, "that typical British officer might be a member of the Stern gang."

For days the popular newspapers carried hysterical stories about Irgun operations. The authorities took more sober steps against possible attacks.

The ports and airports were watched. Passengers on ships were carefully scrutinized. Three companies of troops were given "stand-by" orders in London. Cabinet Ministers were provided with special guards. The gates of Scotland Yard were closed at night and, for the first time since the World War, its Press Bureau was closed altogether.

The new session of Parliament was about to open. Unprecedented precautions, according to the newspapers, were taken to guard the King and Queen on their way to the opening ceremony. Armed detectives mingled with thousands of police in the crowds. The vaults of the House of Commons were searched with "unusual thoroughness."

The War Office portentously announced that "no information is being given for publication about the engagements of Field-Marshal Montgomery." Special guards were sent to the embassy in Lisbon, visitors to the embassy in Paris were subjected to search. Mr. Bevin on a visit to New York was heavily guarded.

These precautions suggested a complete lack of understanding of the Irgun's strategy; but their general effect was highly satisfactory. The climate in Britain had changed recognizably in the six months since I had left London in May. The British public was fully aware at last of what was going on in Palestine.

In fact, there was no ground for British fears. I was the only Irgun agent to visit England for the next several months. Until the spring of 1947 there was not even any specific plan for operations there, nor anyone in England who could carry it out. In the whole of Britain there was only one accredited representative of the Irgun— Leo Bella, a businessman whose Irgun pseudonym was Weiss—and his activities were confined to disseminating Irgun literature and raising funds. I discussed with Weiss a plan to build up an active "branch" to prepare for physical operations. The membership would be "individual": each recruit would know only Weiss.

It was difficult to maintain such secrecy. The group of fervent young people under Tuvia Preschel who produced the *Jewish Struggle,* a journal which courageously reproduced large quantities of Irgun and Lehi literature, had to be eliminated as recruits because they were under constant surveillance by Scotland Yard. So presumably were the leaders of the Jewish Legion, an organization of ex-servicemen who openly espoused the cause of the Irgun. Bella proceeded to seek recruits elsewhere.

I went to Rome to confer with Eli. The Italian police, spurred on by the British, were hunting for suspects in the bombing of the embassy in Rome. Many were arrested. One was Israel Epstein, who had been sent by the Irgun High Command to take up Ariel's duties in Paris and had stopped over in Rome on his way. He arrived there at the time the embassy was bombed. Whether his arrival seemed significant to the Italian investigators, or whether they had more specific information about him, we do not know.

At first, I had some difficulty in finding Eli, who kept moving, believing that the Italian police were on his track. Several of his subordinates were in jail. When I did find him, we met three or four times at short intervals and at different cafes or street corners, so that Eli should not have to spend more than fifteen or twenty minutes at any one spot.

We discussed at length the prospects for further operations in Europe. I believed that it was impossible to conduct a campaign of great intensity against British installations on the Continent, where one had to consider governments and people not involved in the problems of Palestine. I held that each operation should be planned with an eye to major effects and to this end we should make Britain itself our central objective. Eli did not disagree with me, but argued that as we could not do more immediately to prepare operations in England, we should consider closer targets, for which some of his men could be deployed. France was the most obvious choice for an operation but was ruled out by our gentlemen's agreement with the French authorities. In the circumstances, he suggested that we examine possibilities in Switzerland.

We had little knowledge of the country, but I planned to spend the next fortnight there during the Revisionist Conference and World Zionist Congress, and could survey the ground. I could call for assistance on the Irgun representative in Switzerland—Rammy, a medical student at Geneva, who after active service in 1944, had been spirited out of Palestine during "the season."[3] Another Irgun member, Reuben Hecht, was in Basel.

We decided that I would visit Geneva on my way to Basel for the Revisionist conference, apprise Rammy of our intentions, and co-ordinate a plan of reconnaissance. Should we find a target, I would signal Eli or, if he had been arrested, his replacement. Two of the soldiers who had carried out the Rome attack would then be sent to Rammy in Geneva for instructions.

Eli was arrested a fortnight later. Though the Italian police may have had their suspicions, they were unable to prove his connection with the embassy attack. He spent three months in the Regina Coeli Prison.

In the end, the plan to attack British installations in Switzerland was abandoned. My own discussions with Rammy, a survey of conditions in Geneva and Basel, a two-day investigation in Berne by Hecht, convinced me that any operation there would be too complicated and hazardous.

The Zionist Congress at Basel, meeting for the first time in seven years, was a meeting of heavy hearts. In the interval, one third of the Jewish people had been destroyed. There was much to

trouble the conscience of the delegates as well. The one great warning voice that had pleaded with the Jews of Eastern Europe to
evacuate Eastern Europe had not been heeded, and it was the
Zionist leaders who had most vociferously urged the Jews to
shut their ears to his warning. This subject was however hardly
mentioned at the congress.

More depressing was the speed with which the congress divested
itself of a sense of immediate realities. The British Government, in
logical execution of its policy was pursuing its offensive, against
the immigrants physically and by a world-wide diplomatic and
propaganda campaign. Moreover it had now published a "new" plan
for Palestine—called the Morrison Plan, after Herbert Morrison, who
was temporarily acting for Bevin—which was only the old, old plan
but naked and unashamed: the virtual annexation of the country
by Britain, with local autonomy for Arabs in most of the country and
for Jews along the coastal strip. Yet the congress spent days dis-
cussing whether they should accept a British invitation to new talks
in London.

That many of the delegates sincerely hoped for the resumption
of the United Resistance Movement only heightened the unreality
of the debate. The congress had opened in the tense expectation
that Dr. Sneh, and Dr. Silver with his powerful United States delegation, would succeed at least in making their demand for resistance the dominant theme. They were frustrated and defeated by
Ben-Gurion, who led the Mapai delegation. In spite of heated argument with Weizmann, Ben-Gurion opposed resistance and favored
negotiations with the British. Characteristically, the congress ended
with bold words and no action.

"We shall not discuss the Morrison Plan with the British Government," said Mr. Ben-Gurion in his public speech, "and we shall not
propose a partition plan. If we negotiate with the British Government, we must insist on our full rights in the whole country. And
if they propose a reasonable compromise—it will have to be considered and decided upon by the authoritative institutions of the
movement."[4]

Long before the congress was over the resisters were discovered
to be resisting only the British invitation to the London conference.

It was inconceivable that the voice of the Irgun should not be
heard to thrust upon the distracted attentions of the delegates, the
truly simple realities of the situation. On the eve of the congress I

received from Tel Aviv a bulky booklet, with Begin's analysis of the current phase of the struggle, for translation and distribution. I soon discovered that this simple task was a major operation. In its execution I discovered that the hall porter at my hotel was a police informer who was impressed enough by the comings and goings in my room to report me as a gold smuggler to the customs authorities; that the Swiss police, briefed by the congress authorities, had warned all printers and duplicating offices against accepting foreign political material; and that the congress hall itself was guarded and all packages brought there examined by a platoon of husky young men brought from Palestine for the purpose. Nevertheless, on the fourth or fifth day, every delegate found facing him on his desk a neatly duplicated booklet embellished by the familiar Irgun emblem. The really difficult part of the operation—bringing several hundred booklets into the congress hall—was carried out by a group of delegates from the D.P. camps, with the aid of an innocent-looking girl from London—Thelma Levan.

In Paris I met Smertenko. He had virtually been expelled from England for his vigorous attacks on Ernest Bevin. He was on his way to Rome on behalf of the Hebrew Committee for National Liberation to try to secure the release of the arrested Irgunists. His first efforts there were executed for Israel Epstein, who had now spent two months in prison without even being questioned. There was not the slightest indication of how long he might yet be kept there. He had grown restive and impatient, and pleaded that he should be helped to escape. When Smertenko's representations in Rome failed to elicit a response, the Irgun officers worked out a plan.

Something went wrong. Epstein came out of his cell and onto the prison wall. He came into the sight of a guard. Perhaps the guard called out to him, and Epstein, believing that this was part of the plan, went on, unheeding. The guard fired, and Epstein died there in the prison yard.

That very weekend, Britain's prestige suffered a blow of incalculable effect at the hands of the Irgun. A seventeen-year-old Irgun soldier, Binyamin Kimchi, tried by a military court for carrying arms, had been sentenced to eighteen years' imprisonment. Eighteen lashes were added to the sentence.

The Irgun warned the British not to carry out the flogging, that if Irgun soldiers were whipped there would be retaliation in kind. The warning was flashed around the world by newspaper correspondents. On the eve of the Sabbath, Kimchi was flogged.

Two days later, Irgun groups captured two British officers in Tel Aviv, one in Natanya and one in Rishon-Le-Zion. Each was given eighteen lashes and sent back to his unit.

This simple physical and symbolic act made manifest the significance and implications of British rule in Palestine and the essence of the Jewish revolt. Even in Britain chagrin was mingled with wry understanding of the Irgun reprisal.

Its tangible effects were immediate. A sentence of lashes passed on a second Irgun boy was hastily canceled. Within a fortnight, flogging was also abolished by the British Raj in rebellious India.[5]

The British, enraged, carried out countrywide searches. Hundreds of young men were arrested. Now too the shadow of the gallows reappeared. On the first of January a British military court sentenced Dov Gruner to death. Gruner had been wounded and captured nine months earlier in an attack on a police armory at Ramat Gan. The sentence was soon confirmed by the G.O.C., General Barker, and the execution set for January 28.

The High Commissioner, together with General Barker, was called urgently to London to confer with the Cabinet and with the Chief of the General Staff, Field Marshal Montgomery. Unofficial reports of this conference indicated decisions to "crush the terror once and for all." The British press in Palestine told of the condign punishment that would be visited on the Jewish community if it did not help destroy the terrorists: martial law would be imposed. Meantime, the British troops were ordered not to visit cafes, bars or places of entertainment and to move in pairs.

I spent many hours with Begin in the little room in the Oppenheimer apartment. I told him of what I had seen and heard and done in Europe, of the repercussions and undertones in London after the Rome attack.

Together we examined and analyzed the show of British power and its weaknesses. These were becoming more sharply defined. Our task was clear: to intensify the struggle, increase its scope. It was essential to bring home to the British people the strength of our purpose, to expose the growing and ultimately crippling price they would have to pay, in prestige, in material, and in human resources for their continued alien presence in Palestine. The struggle for them was senseless. The fiercer our onslaught, the faster would this understanding be achieved.

To the threats of martial law we published and broadcast a laconic response:

"We have a simple reply to the threats of the British terrorists. You will not frighten us . . . Even in the most difficult circumstances we shall find ways of hitting at the enemy."

These words were backed by the knowledge of the plans even then being made to broaden the immediate scope of operations. They sprang from the constant weighing of the contending forces in the struggle and from the concepts central to the Irgun's strategy from the outset: that the ending of British rule *was* within our power, that the British *could* be forced to leave Palestine.

Of course the British could physically crush the Jewish population of Palestine. But we knew something far more important: that there were limits of oppression beyond which the British Government dared not go. She could not apply the full force of her power against us. Palestine was not a remote hill village in Afghanistan which could be bombed into submission. Palestine was a glass house watched with intent interest by the rest of the world. The British Government had discovered in 1945 that their behavior toward the Jews was an important factor in American attitudes and policies. American good will and American economic aid were vital to Britain's hopes and plans for revival from the ravages of the war and for the social reforms of the Labor Government.

The countries of Europe, still reeking of the gas chambers, were also a potential restraining influence. Europe, beginning to recover from the nightmare of German Occupation, would see excesses against the Jews as a British resumption of Hitler's work. Such a hostility might be of little practical significance; but it could not be disregarded by the British Government.

Less obvious but of a certain and, as we saw it, ultimately decisive force, was the climate of opinion in Britain itself. Only a deep and violent hatred could tolerate the kind of war their government would have to wage in order to crush the Jews. No such hatred existed.

The British had not been outraged by their government's efforts to liquidate Zionism and to subject the Jews of Palestine to its will. Foreign policy altogether was an area in which it was generally assumed that the government of the day knew best what it was about.[6] If they had been convinced that it was a vital national interest they might even have tolerated and accepted, with distaste and some protest, severe military measures in Palestine. But they had no such conviction. On the contrary: for a generation they had been told that Britain's task in Palestine was one of mediation and supervision, that she was fulfilling an altruistic role: ensuring justice, holding the peace, keeping Jews and Arabs from each other's throats. The elimination of the Jews "for the benefit of the Arabs," in a military campaign which could not be brief and which no censorship could conceal, was not a policy which could appeal to the British people.

The Irgun was now concentrating on attacking British military transport. It forced the suspension of railway traffic. Day after day roads were mined; jeeps, trucks, and armored cars were blown up. A new type of mine and a flame-thrower, both the products of the ingenious brain of the Chief of Operations, Amihai Paglin ("Giddy"), were used with great effect.

In those January days the difference between our outlook and that of the Jewish Agency was clear. The Weizmann school of frank defeatism had indeed been rejected at the Zionist Congress, and Dr. Weizmann had been forced into retirement. Weizmann honestly believed that to fight Britain was inconceivable; Ben-Gurion spoke of "resistance" but believed it was impossible, we were too weak, the British too strong. His view, expressed at the Zionist Congress in December, was that "we must not overestimate our strength."

In late January and early February, he and his colleagues, ostensibly barred by the Zionist Congress from attending the London Conference, were nevertheless negotiating with the British Government. A series of "private and informal" conversations were in progress in London. Ben-Gurion, Shertok, Locker, Nahum Goldman, flanked by senior officials, were meeting with British and Colonial ministers as though nothing but differences in policy separated them. During those weeks the dispatch of immigrant ships was suspended. But the British statesmen would concede nothing and were in fact at that very time calling a Conference in Paris with the United States and with France to secure their collaboration in the campaign against the immigrants.

In the midst of these conversations Ben-Gurion paid a flying visit to Palestine to set in motion a new campaign against the under-ground. After a meeting of the Vaad Leumi (the National Council of Palestine Jews) he succeeded in extracting a resolution reiterating the call to discipline and promising that "the Yishuv would defend itself with force against acts of coercion and intimidation aimed at extorting money, coercion of teachers, students, policemen and drivers, etc." The catalogue of specifications reflected what we knew of the divided purpose in the Jewish Agency and, what was more important, of the temper of the people, among whom the members of the Irgun lived and worked. They would not tolerate the renewal of physical attacks on us. Nor was there any enthusiasm in the Haganah for a new "season." Nevertheless the Irgun published warning after warning of the grave consequences of internal conflict and for the next several months this uneasy twilight of peace between the two bodies continued.

There were other problems. Of the 3000 members of Irgun, the total full-time staff—the High Command, district commanders, instructors, storekeepers, and secretaries—numbered only about fifty. They were paid hardly enough for subsistence. War however is an expensive undertaking. We needed arms, explosives, and raw materials for their manufacture. We needed printing facilities. No institutions subsidized us. There were no existing public funds to draw on and it was impossible to conduct large-scale campaigns for support.

Money collected in Palestine required an individual approach, which was in itself a breach of the law of conspiracy. There was pitifully little help from abroad. We had no fund-raising organization in Europe. In the United States the Hebrew Committee of National Liberation raised large sums but applied them to purposes they had set themselves. Throughout the struggle the Committee had sent to Palestine no more than ten thousand dollars.

The only country from which regular aid arrived was South Africa. There the Revisionist Party branch launched periodic campaigns for the party in Palestine on the understanding that a proportion of the proceeds would be diverted to the Irgun. There too from time to time a group of young sympathizers, headed by Raphael Kotlowitz, working directly with the Irgun made separate efforts to raise funds. Indeed at this time my wife, on a visit to her family, was engaged in a clandestine appeal for funds.

Sometimes a public figure, like Professor Joseph Klausner or Mr. Abraham Krinizi, the mayor of Ramat Gan, would act as a channel for a cautious donor from abroad. There were always great gaps in the Irgun budget. Planned operations were delayed, there had even been short periods of complete suspension of action, because of this lack of funds.

It was a problem we had to resolve. It was inconceivable that the decisive struggle for the independence of our people should be paralyzed, or dangerously decelerated, for the lack of money. In dangerous daylight raids, Irgun units, often dressed in British army uniform and armed with forged papers, led by officers whose English was at least passable, penetrated British army camps and raided the armory, or with some inside co-operation attacked a police arms store. There were losses in casualties and prisoners. It was during one of these attacks that Dov Gruner was wounded and captured.

Once a British army pay train was held up, enriching the Irgun by £30,000. A number of raids were carried out on banks, although here the results were meager and casualties high. Goods held by Jewish merchants, usually textiles or diamonds, were confiscated, their losses being covered by British insurance companies.

The Irgun had very little transport of its own. From time to time a British vehicle was captured and for specific actions Jewish vehicles had to be temporarily confiscated. The procedure became standard. A truck or taxi driver would report to the police that he had been held up by armed men, his vehicle taken from him and he himself left tied up for some hours in a wood or field before being released. In the vast majority of cases—but not all—the driver was himself a member of the Irgun or selected from its panel of volunteer helpers.

Sometimes a wealthy merchant who had been recommended to the Irgun as a sympathizer and potential contributor to its funds, proved to be quite unco-operative. There were cases where such merchants were intimidated into making contributions. In only one single case, as far as I am aware, was force actually employed—not on an unco-operative merchant but one who had actually expressed his sympathy for the cause. He made an excuse to arrange a second visit by the Irgun agent, but the latter cautiously sent a scout on ahead. The scout discovered British police in the store.

Few as the cases of coercion were they provided the motif for considerable vilification of the underground. In those January days they were the main burden of a lurid propaganda campaign by the Jewish Agency.

Even some of our well-wishers were disturbed by the possible implications. In the spring of 1947 Mrs. Rebecca Sieff, the WIZO[7] leader—who, with characteristic independence of spirit, gave financial aid to the Irgun—told me, in an underground conversation, that she was concerned at the possible influence of their terrorist activities on the future behavior of the young men who carried out raids on banks or other forms of confiscation. I told her of the intense and continuous education to which the young members of the Irgun were exposed, and the high moral purpose which informed them. I was not certain that I convinced her. In the event, I believe that since the State was established not a single former Irgun member has been involved in any crime of violence.

The Irgun in Palestine was a tightly knit organization in all its departments. With a high level of discipline and responsibility the leadership was able to maintain control over every activity. In Europe however its embryo organization was in a state of disarray. It had been left leaderless with its most pressing problem still unsolved: its relations with its friends. This had been the main reason for the ill-fated dispatch of Israel Epstein. Begin believed that the respect in which he was held by the Betar leaders in Europe would help him to induce a sense of perspective in them.

Except for tiny groups here and there in the settled Jewish communities in Europe, the only substantial reservoir of Betar strength was in the Displaced Persons camps, in the Betarim who had survived the catastrophe. The vast majority of these saw the Irgun as the only instrument of national redemption, and they were a natural source of manpower for the Irgun. Moreover Betar provided an ideal "front" as a legal organization. For these very reasons the Betar leaders decided that the Irgun in Europe should be subject to their control, and to their prewar ideas on running a youth organization.

Both Eli and Ariel were in constant conflict with the Betar leaders—as they were with representatives of the Revisionist Party. Begin could have severed the Irgun from the Betar, but he preferred to seek a compromise. In early 1946 Begin had agreed to set up a triumvirate in Europe—of Revisionist, Betar and Irgun representatives—to co-ordinate activities. This division of authority filtered down to the local level, so that each local Betar leader was, in effect, a censor of Irgun activity and there was sometimes friction over "spheres of authority."

Begin now sought a new compromise. He evolved the idea of a collective "representation of the Irgun" with its headquarters in Paris. In his list he included representatives of the Revisionists, Betar, and the Hebrew Committee of National Liberation. By giving this body auxiliary functions, including the collection of funds, he hoped to assure a free hand for the Irgun in recruiting, training and the execution of operations.

He asked me to return to Europe at once to establish such a group. I had been appointed a member of the Irgun High Command and could act with authority. I was not enthusiastic about the scheme. I did not believe that the Irgun should accommodate itself to other interests. I feared, moreover, that this semi-civilian body would engage in endless debates. Yet Begin's view, strongly supported by Avraham, was that because of our need for speed the elimination of friction with our friends might be the best means of furthering our aims. In spite of my disappointment at having to leave the country at this crucial stage, I obeyed Begin's request.

13

Plots and Counterplots

In Paris I had a pleasant surprise. Eliahu Lankin, a member of Begin's original High Command, had arrived there four days earlier after an incredible odyssey of escape from the British internment camp in East Africa. One of the Haganah's first victims in "the season" in the autumn of 1944, he had spent only a year in internment before breaking out of the camp with three comrades. The others were recaptured. For fourteen months Lankin had lived the life of a hunted fugitive, with a price on his head, first in Abyssinia, later in French Djibouti. Finally, the French authorities, pretending ignorance of his identity, gave him permission to enter France.[1] I carried with me his contingent appointment as commander of the Irgun in the Diaspora and he took up his duties immediately.

Lankin was hostile to the plan for a "Representation" in which Revisionists would be included. To him the Revisionists were the obstructors of 1944, who had all but co-operated in the hounding of the Irgun in its most desperate days. He was against the call of expediency, especially as he did not believe that the Revisionist Party could make any great contribution to the struggle. He could not see why they should not simply place themselves at the disposal of the Irgun as individuals. His attitude, in short, was similar to my own.

However, I obeyed my instructions and the "Representation" was set up. Very little came of it; it never functioned as a coherent body; but in the end it did reduce the friction with the Betar.

Lankin and I met in Samuel Merlin's suite in the Hotel Lutetia, which served as the office of the Hebrew Committee of National Liberation. During Lankin's first months in Paris, the Hebrew Committee provided most of his income. This gesture was quite out of keeping with their resolute denial of financial help to the Irgun in Palestine.

The Hebrew Committee had succeeded brilliantly in mobilizing a body of support for the Jewish renaissance such as America had probably never seen. In the early days of the revolt against Britain, they had provided the American public with information on its background and purposes. But now the need for an expensive machine to report and explain the revolt had been greatly reduced. A body of American newspapermen in Palestine were doing this seriously and, on the whole, objectively.

The result was a painful paradox. Although sympathy for the Irgun was widespread in the United States the Irgun received practically no help from American Jews.

The committee, flushed with their remarkable success in gaining support for the Emergency Committee to Save the Jewish People of Europe, failed to realize that once the struggle with Britain was joined in Palestine, their role must become an auxiliary one. They failed to grasp the vital importance of tight central control to an insurrectionary organization. They sent occasional messages of loyalty to Begin, but they refused to bow to Irgun discipline or even to accept the Irgun's decision on priorities.

They did not realize they were being overtaken by events. They clung to the theory that it was essential to set up a provisional-government-in-exile of the Hebrew people. Yet only the Irgun could provide the political backing in Palestine for this step. Such a sponsorship would have forced on the Irgun a bitter struggle with the Jewish Agency, a full-scale civil war. From beginning to end, the Irgun exerted itself to avoid such a conflict.

The Hebrew Committee accused the Irgun of being a "shooting-agency" for the Jewish Agency, paving the way to power in a Jewish state for Ben-Gurion and his friends. We were perfectly aware of this ironic possibility which, in the end, became historic fact. But the alternative was a fraternal bloodbath which might destroy the hope of any Jewish state at all. But as long as the Jewish Agency simply clung to its official authority and its power in the Jewish community, as long as the Haganah contented itself with threats and with verbal kowtowing to the British, we resigned ourselves to their reaping the political fruits of our struggle.

The Hebrew Committee made a faulty assessment of the internal situation, the delicate balance of forces, in Palestine. They were chained to a doctrinaire concept of revolution which bore no relation to the specific reality within which the Irgun lived and fought.

A second, more pragmatic, divergence between the Irgun and the Hebrew Committee arose from their repatriation activities. This had more immediate repercussions. The Hebrew Committee had long planned the organization of Aliyah B shipments. After 1945, however, all Jewish parties were agreed on the policy of Aliyah B; and the Jewish Agency, through the Haganah, had built up machinery for this purpose. This remained their only act of defiance of the British. Now the Haganah was doing the job, there was no need to add Aliyah B to our burdens.

The Hebrew Committee had played a major role, in the years of Zionist desolation in the United States, in awakening the public conscience to the problem of Jewish homelessness and the plight of the homeless. Where they had sown, the Jewish Agency and Haganah later reaped. Now it was difficult for them to suppress their emotions, readjust their public attitudes and leave the field of immigration to the Jewish Agency and the Haganah. They avoided the crucial question as to the justification in diverting money from the revolt—on which all else hung—in order to add another ship or two to the many sent by the Haganah.

Later there was a change in policy, but at this time the Hebrew Committee refused to accept its role as an arm of the Irgun. In their accounts for 1946, they recorded an expenditure of $386,000 (52 per cent of their total expenditure) on repatriation activities; on pro-resistance activity (political and propaganda) they spent $19,-973 (2 per cent of the total).[2]

With Lankin installed in Paris, and his immediate plans for organization laid, I made my way to London.

I came to a Britain deep in crisis. A wild and cruel winter was wreaking havoc with an already straitened economy. Living and traveling conditions were appalling. The government published a White Paper—Economic Survey for 1947—which painted a grim picture. It detailed a chronic shortage of coal and power, of steel and timber and food, of labor in crucial places, the permanent loss of overseas income, the load of overseas debt. It summarized the situation laconically: "The central fact of 1947 is that we have not enough resources to do all that we want to do." Parliament called for sacrifices by the British people.

I sent a full description to Tel Aviv. I expressed the opinion that the ravages of this terrible winter were a providential ally for us in speeding the relaxation of the British hold on Palestine. The dramatic tensions in Palestine and the now incessant attacks of the Irgun were brought to the attention of the British along with the coal crisis, the snow, the cold, the gloom, and the deprivation.

I paid social calls on a number of old friends, giving a publishing project as the explanation of my presence in England. Through one of them I had a surprise visit one morning from a young South African named Boris Senior. I had last seen him years earlier as a small boy at his home in Johannesburg, where I used to have heated discussions with his father, Woolf Senior, a prominent Zionist, and a stout supporter of Dr. Weizmann, fiercely opposed to all I stood for. Boris told me that he was studying at the London School of Economics, but was restless and frustrated at being inactive while the battle for Jewish independence was being waged. He had been a pilot in the South African Air Force during World War II, and was certain that he could be of some service. Surely I could help him get in touch with the Irgun.

I was taken aback and tried to dissuade him. His elder brother, Leon, had been killed in the war. Knowing, moreover, his father's extreme antipathy to the Irgun, would it be fair to take the risk of bringing more sorrow down on his head?

Boris was firm. He had risked his life for South Africa. He had the right to risk his life for the Jews.

"I appreciate your concern," he said, "but I don't think that you have the right to prevent me. If you have the information I need it's your duty to give it to me."

I promised to do as he asked. He told me he had a friend from Palestine, a fellow student at the London School of Economics, a World War II air veteran, who shared his feelings and wanted to join the Irgun. His name was Ezer Weizmann, a nephew of the Zionist leader. I hesitated even longer about him, but decided finally that Dr. Weizmann's relations had as much right as anybody to be rebels. I made arrangements for them to report to Lankin in Paris.

They both became part of the select band of volunteers who, innocent of previous "suspect" associations and exercising extreme care, never came under the notice of a vigilant and active Scotland Yard.

In the group was yet a third air veteran of World War II: Paul Homeski, of the Free French Forces, a son of Benzion Homeski who had shared imprisonment at Acre with Jabotinsky for taking part in the defense of Jerusalem in 1920.[3]

When I returned to Paris, Lankin told me of a plan to bring one Irgun veteran into England. It was Yoel, who had taken part in the blowing up of the British embassy in Rome. Once in England, Yoel was to pass as a Briton. I was dubious about this. He had indeed served in the British Army and had no doubt picked up some English, but hardly adequate enough to help him pass as British. I spent an "English half-hour" with him and was dumbfounded to find that, though his vocabulary was not extensive, he spoke English with a Welsh accent and intonation that would have passed in Portmadoc or Merthyr Tydfil. He had an unusually sharp ear, he was a gregarious soul and his close friends in the army had been Welshmen.

Lankin's plan was carried out on a spring day some weeks later. A young couple apparently absorbed in one another sat in a car in a lane by a Surrey field. The sound of an aircraft losing height was heard. The young man, Ezer Weizmann, jumped out of the car and waved. Piloted by Boris Senior, the plane landed in the field, disembarked Yoel, then took off again. Weizmann and his companion, Deborah Landman, took Yoel to London, where he was supplied with an identity card. The group now concentrated on carrying out one of the specific orders given by Lankin—the execution of the death sentence passed by the Irgun in Palestine on the recently replaced G.O.C. British forces in Palestine, General Evelyn Barker.

The British Government believed that the Irgun was interested in assassinating a wide range of British personalities, from the Royal Family downward: the press, with its sensational stories of "death-lists," fostered this fantastic nonsense. The only case in which they guessed correctly was that of Barker, whose racist proclivities had been publicly exposed the previous summer when a copy of a secret order he had issued to his troops, ordering them to refrain from all contact with Jews and infused with a primitive anti-Semitism, had been secured by Irgun Intelligence.[4]

Time after time reports had reached the Irgun (and apparently Haganah and Lehi) of Barker's anti-Semitic outbursts in the presence of subordinates and civilian colleagues. He had announced his intention of hanging a terrorist from every lamppost in Palestine. The brutalities and disregard of Jewish life manifested by some of his troops could be traced directly to General Barker's hatred of the Jews. Before he left the country in mid-February, as a valedictory gesture to the Jews of Palestine he signed the death sentence passed by a British military court two days earlier on the three Irgun soldiers captured on the night of the floggings—Alkochi, Kashani, and Rosenbaum.[5]

After Yoel's arrival in London, Irgun patrols kept watch near Barker's headquarters and other haunts. The general, whose elaborate measures of self-protection in Palestine had become a byword, presumably took even more elaborate precautions in England. The Irgun watchers did not even catch a glimpse of him.[6]

Scotland Yard was now continuously watching Weiss, who was in charge of Irgun operations in England. One morning, as he was about to drive off to Oxford on business, Weiss went up to the car in which his shadowers were sitting and suggested that they save petrol (still rationed) by joining him in his car, an offer which was declined.

This close attention to Weiss was Yoel's undoing. Impatient at his enforced inaction for several weeks, he visited Weiss and was detained by the detectives. As they soon discovered that he was no Welshman, he adopted the role of a refugee seeking asylum in England. He was charged with illegal entry, spent several months in jail and was then deported to Germany.

No other agents came to England, although the European headquarters developed a far-flung organization throughout the Continent.

In London, that freezing fortnight, I turned my attention to another plan for a major operation. One of the best organized groups of Irgun supporters was the Shanghai branch of Betar. Its leader was Judith Hasser, an attractive young woman who was an executive of a large import-export firm. I had met her in Basel, and in Paris we had discussed the possibility of sinking British merchant vessels in Shanghai Harbor. She and her group were now asked to work out the details of this plan. As soon as it was ready, we would issue a statement to the world press. I prepared a rough draft. After explaining that at sea too there would be no one-sided wars, the statement warned that from a given date "any British vessel wherever it may be will be regarded as a legitimate target for attack. We warn prospective passengers on British ships to transfer to ships of other nations. We warn traders to send their goods by other ships." A fortnight later we would sink a British cargo vessel in Shanghai.

A still more daring plan came to me from a former officer in the

Royal Navy, an erstwhile supporter of the Labor Party. Shaken by
the British betrayal in Palestine and ashamed of the Royal Navy's
part in hounding the survivors of the death camps, he had sought a
way to make contact with the Irgun. We happened to have a common
friend at whose house we met. He felt that the Jews needed to
deliver at least one retaliatory blow at the Navy. He developed a
plan whereby we were to blow up a British destroyer when it put
in for repairs at Portsmouth. As he explained it to me, the operational plan, given the correct timing, was a simple one. He drew me
a sketch plan of the port area, with the berthing arrangements and
the location of the watchman, and promised to provide the men to
help him. From the Irgun he required explosives, to be delivered to
his specifications.

I accepted this offer, but the execution would need time.

In the House of Commons, at the height of the coal crisis, Winston Churchill warned that Britain could not sustain, morally or
materially, a long campaign in Palestine. He pointed to the expenditure of eighty million pounds in two years to maintain 100,000
soldiers there. She had no such interests in Palestine as to justify
such an effort. Mr. Bevin's determination to fight seemed unshaken.
He had grounds for optimism.

In continued public contempt of the Zionist Congress, which had
forbidden them in the existing circumstances to negotiate, the
Jewish Agency executive entered into negotiations with the British
Government. Throughout weeks of talks in London, the only change
in the status quo suggested to them was collaboration for the destruction of the Irgun and the Lehi. The Agency leaders—Ben-Gurion,
Moshe Shertok, and Golda Meirson—agreed that the underground
should be destroyed, and solemnly announced that they could not
accept the suggestion of active collaboration because the British had
made no real concessions to them!

Though Bevin's Intelligence reports from Palestine must have
made clear to him that there was little hope of a renewed "season,"
continued pressure on the Jewish Agency achieved repeated assurances from them that they at least intended no armed resistance.
Thus reassured, Bevin and his colleagues prepared what they believed to be the final and decisive campaign against the rebels.

All wives and children of British officials and police, and other
civilians, were ordered out of the country. By the end of January

this had been achieved. In each of the major cities—Jerusalem, Tel Aviv, Haifa—central built-up areas were taken over to provide the British Power with concentrated areas as bases for headquarters. These were called "security zones" and enclosed by permanently guarded high fences or walls. Into these security zones, at once nicknamed Bevingrads, none might enter without a special permit.

These preparations made, and with an intensive propaganda campaign in progress on the horrors of martial law, Bevin was ready for a political master-stroke. On February 19 in the House of Commons he announced that he would submit the Palestine problem to the United Nations.

Ernest Bevin was crippled in his handling of the Palestine problem by two grave weaknesses. He had no understanding of Jewish nationalism and indeed denied its existence. He was encouraged in his ignorance by the Prime Minister and by his Chief Adviser at the Foreign Office, Harold Beeley. His friendly biographer, Francis Williams, writes in bald understatement:

"Like most men self-educated by experience, Bevin tended to underestimate what his own experience did not make intelligible. Hence his underestimation of the real force and violence of Jewish national feeling in Palestine."

He was certain that the Jews, ungrateful as they were for the status of a protected minority which he offered them, would yet, by their lack of national character, be betrayed into submission. He reasoned that a good dose of martial law, with its disruption of economic life, with its paralysis of public services, its thousand daily hardships for every man, woman, and child, its hovering hint of violence personified in the ubiquitous British soldiery, would extinguish the spirit of the Jews and force them to appeal for terms. The underground would then be isolated. For the underground there was too the additional weapon of the gallows.

With Palestine thus "pacified," the displaced persons in Europe would resign themselves to the prospect that only a fraction would be allowed there, while the majority were sent to America or remained in Europe. Bevin calculated that once he neutralized the underground in Palestine, public hostility to his policy in the United States would evaporate. Then would be the time to secure American co-operation in, and international sanction for, the British solution.

It was logical to assume that it would not be long before the United States recognized the importance to Western interests of the retention of British control of her remaining bastion in Palestine. When that day came the United States would surely relax her pressure on Britain and help her achieve the sanction of the United Nations for a reasonably free hand in Palestine.

This was not a fantasy. What Bevin needed for its achievement was time—sufficient time to demonstrate that Britain was indeed in effective and undisputed control of the country.

The timing of his announcement to the House of Commons was well calculated. The next meeting of the United Nations was still seven months away—in September 1947. The proceedings then must inevitably give birth to a committee of investigation which would report back to the following session in September 1948. This period gave Bevin eighteen months or more, first for applying adequate measures to bring the Jews to heel, then for maneuvering and negotiation.

Bevin's decision to submit the Palestine question to the United Nations, while designed to appease the growing concern in Britain itself, was essential to his program for Palestine. His statement in the House of Commons was couched in suitably vague terms: he did not reveal precisely what the United Nations was to be asked to do. What was clear was that he was in no hurry. A week later, on February 26, pressed by the opposition, Mr. Creech-Jones the Colonial Secretary, was much more explicit: there was no question of relinquishing Palestine, he said:

> We are not going to the United Nations to surrender the Mandate. We are going to the United Nations to ask for advice on how the Mandate can be administered. If it cannot be administered in its present form, we are asking how it can be amended.

There is in retrospect a certain Chaplinesque quality about Mr. Bevin's actions at this crisis. One may imagine him lighting a match on the sole of his boot, lighting a cigar and throwing the match nonchalantly over his shoulder into an unsuspected powder barrel. Within a month his strategy was blown to fragments.

14

The Irgun's War

The specter of martial law had assumed monstrous proportions in Palestine. The Jewish Agency in Jerusalem dealt from a position of weakness. Mrs. Meirson appealed to the British Government not to impose martial law, while other members of the establishment demanded that the Irgun and the Lehi should desist from their provocation of the British.

Aware of British preparations for a drastic step in Palestine and of the implications of Bevin's announcement in the House of Commons, the Irgun made its dispositions. The storm broke on March 1. It was a Sabbath, a day on which the British believed they were entitled to the benefits of a one-sided truce, and they were taken completely by surprise. Sixteen separate operations were carried out. Four British camps—three in the north, one in the south—were stormed by mortar and machine-gun fire. British military vehicles were attacked throughout the country. The most devastating operation of the day was the frontal assault on the British Officers Club at Goldschmidt House in the center of Jerusalem. An Irgun unit overcame the resistance of the patrols and guards and blew up the building. British casualties in killed and wounded that day numbered more than eighty. A score of armored vehicles were destroyed.

In Britain there was an angry reaction. A headline in the *Sunday Express* read: GOVERN OR GET OUT. Bevin proceeded with his plans. When the people in Palestine turned on their radio for the early morning news next day, they learned that in the area containing Tel Aviv, Ramat Gan, and Petah Tikva and a part of Jerusalem, martial law was already in operation.

All government services were suspended. There was no postal delivery, and all but a few telephones were inoperative. There were no trains, no buses, no taxis, no motor transport at all. The civil courts were suspended and a special military court was set up. Food was to be distributed only by the army.

No movement was allowed in or out of the zones. A British army cordon sealed off all the approaches to each zone. Every soldier was given the authority of a policeman. Anyone disobeying any order by a soldier was liable to be shot. Two people were killed almost immediately—no one ever learned what order they had disobeyed, especially as one of them was a four-year-old girl. The objective of martial law was clear—the Jews were to be terrorized into betraying the underground.

General Gale, Commander of the operation in Tel Aviv (solemnly named Operation Elephant), explained breezily to newspaper correspondents that the restrictions were designed to lighten the army's task of unearthing the terrorists, known to be concentrated in these areas. Martial law would continue until the terrorists had been run to earth.

Within a fortnight martial law collapsed ignominiously. First the Irgun and the Lehi demonstrated that they existed outside the martial law zones. British transport and installations were attacked in the north and the south outside the periphery of Elephant and of Hippopotamus (the latter name given to the operation in Jerusalem).

On the seventh night, a number of operations were carried out simultaneously in the heart of the Tel Aviv area, including one on the "Bevingrad" centered on Citrus House. Thereafter, in utter disregard of the British cordons, both the Irgun and the Lehi switched their attacks in and out of the zones at will. In all, by British army count, sixty-eight assaults were carried out.

The most damaging blow was delivered on the eleventh night. The British fortified zone centered on the Schneller Buildings in Jerusalem was subjected to a meticulously executed frontal assault. The major part of the Jerusalem garrison was stationed there and it was heavily defended. The Irgun unit broke through the peripheral fortifications, blew up the high wall and tore through the barbed-wire defenses on the inside. Overcoming resistance in close fighting, they penetrated the buildings and blew them up. British armored reinforcements summoned to the scene were held off by the covering fire of supporting units. The Irgun force, commanded by a brilliant young officer named Yehoshua Goldschmid, withdrew safely. On March 16, four days after the Schneller attack, martial law was lifted.

Dramatic as were the events in Palestine of that fortnight, their political repercussions in Britain were even more spectacular. Bevin had flown to a Four-Power Conference in Moscow. He had every reason to believe that it would fail to bring understanding with the Soviet Union and that in consequence the United States would be drawn closer to Britain. He was right. He also believed, presumably, that by the time he returned the army would have crushed the resistance in Palestine and dammed the flow of opposition in Britain to his policy. The devastating failure of martial law, the striking demonstration of the power and scope of the Palestine underground, turned the tide of opposition into a swelling flood which demanded his immediate retreat. Each blow delivered in Palestine had its immediate echo in the House of Commons.

Winston Churchill was now convinced that the government could not hope to crush the Jews. He did not mince words.

"One hundred thousand Englishmen," he said, "are being kept away from their homes and work for a senseless squalid war with the Jews. We are getting ourselves hated and mocked by the world at a cost of eighty millions."

Before the Irgun offensive opened on March 1, Churchill had insisted that the approach to the United Nations be turned into a demand for urgent action. On the day after the Irgun's punishing commando attack in Jerusalem, he extracted from the government a request for the United Nations to meet in a special session on the Palestine problem.

Except, perhaps, for the swift revelation in Prague in March 1939 of the hollowness of Chamberlain's policy at Munich six months earlier, it is difficult to find in current history a more dramatic illumination of political truth than in the events that followed the imposition of martial law in Palestine in March 1947. The vulnerability and ineffectiveness of British strength, when faced by an intelligent, resourceful and courageous resistance; the immediate and sharp impact of Jewish resistance first on British public opinion and then on the political strategy of the British Government was clear—the Irgun thesis had been put to a severe test and, as though providentially, had been vindicated.

A week after the British declaration of martial law, I made my way back to Palestine. At Lydda Airport the Immigration officer directed me to a little room, where I found a detective brooding over my luggage. He went through my bag and my attaché-case with great care, then very politely asked me to empty my pockets, which were bulging. To the collection of fictitious letters to publishers, which gave me a respectable aura, I had added two "genuine" letters in the same spirit. One had been obtained in Paris by David Knout, the poet, from the *Centre de Documentation Juive*. It proposed to appoint me its representative in Palestine. The other I got from an American publisher associated with the Hebrew Committee. I dutifully laid them all on the table, together with several snapshots and personal letters. The only written material in my pockets that could have interested the detective was coded into my address book. As I would be needing this for my report to Begin, I thought it better to leave it in my pocket.

The detective formed a pile of the papers and began reading. As he was a slow reader, when he had done two or three of the letters, I decided to take a seat. He put one hand over the pile and said impatiently:

"We'll keep these. We'll let you know when you can have them back."

I was glad to leave his office. Our Intelligence Service had told us that the British CID had compiled a list of "suspicious characters" for its officers at the airport. It contained three categories: A, B and C. The A's were to be questioned about the purpose of their journey, and a report on their movements was to be sent to CID Headquarters. The B's were to be searched as well as questioned. The C's were to be arrested on sight. I had obviously been promoted to List B. Armed with a resident's permit for entering the martial law zone I nevertheless did not go there directly. I traveled first to Haifa, spent the night at my brother-in-law's home, and only next morning went back to Tel Aviv.

There was an incongruously festive air in the streets of Tel Aviv. Deprived of their regular transport services, the people had unearthed the most unlikely conveyances. Horse-drawn carts, some of them looking as though they had been thrown together from old pieces of wood, plied for hire. Here and there one could see an animal conjured into renewed youthfulness by a bright red ribbon at his ears. Cartloads of children drawn by donkeys and mules sang gleefully above the clatter of hoofs. The town's full complement of three generations of bicycles tinkled in rustic abandon along the unencumbered streets.

Although fear and doubt lodged in the hearts of the people, outwardly they displayed a cheerful, even bantering defiance which grew more pronounced with each counterblow of the underground.

Underground headquarters were effectively decentralized, its departments scattered over the town in offices and storerooms hired under various descriptions, and in the offices of members or sympathizers who carried on their business in one room even as members of the Irgun staff worked in another; there were also private apartments, made available at an hour's notice for meetings with visitors from the "outside." Brief business meetings were held by Irgun agents with each other or with regular contacts from outside in cafes and street corners.

I worked in a large building in Allenby Road in the center of the city, my office cluttered with the empty wooden trays of a diamond merchant I never saw. I had a desk with a double top for concealing documents and, for half a day each day, a typist highly efficient in several languages, a bright redhead whom I called Sima and who called me Karni and whose real name I do not know to this day.

I never saw more than three or four of the other "full-time" offices and never more than once or twice. I would be taken by Avraham for some quick consultation with Yoel,[1] the head of the ramified Intelligence Department which also maintained the day-to-day contact with the press; or with Yitshak,[2] who presided over the central staff office, where foreign-language propaganda material was duplicated and dispatched. Sometimes I went to Avraham's own tiny cubbyhole tucked away under a roof in Tschernichowsky Street. In the five months I used it I had no more than a dozen visitors at my office. Indeed, except for Avraham, whose job included knowing everything and everyone, none of us met anyone or went anywhere or even asked questions not essential for his task.

There were no guards at any Irgun establishment. Each member of the full-time staff developed the personal camouflage most suitable for his circumstances. Begin lived "deep" in the underground under assumed names, most of the time at his own or the "Oppenheimer" apartment, occasionally moving briefly elsewhere though always in Tel Aviv. He never went out of doors by day. Suspected as I was by the CID merely of being sympathetic to the movement, I lived under my own name but outside Tel Aviv, using a selection of pseudonyms for my Irgun colleagues and for the various outside contacts I now established.

Begin presided directly over the Irgun's central sphere: the political department, with its arms of propaganda, of information, of exhortation to the people at large and to the world outside, its psychological warfare directed at the British Army and their people; its stimulation of education and discussion within the ranks of the Irgun. I was responsible for disseminating information in English about the Irgun. I published a monthly bulletin called *Irgunpress* and wrote booklets on the background and purposes of the Irgun struggle; I also translated the Irgun broadcasts into English and provided the pattern for our propaganda in French, Italian, Greek, Bulgarian.

I became the spokesman of the High Command to foreign correspondents. As it became known that certain newspapermen had personal contacts with the Irgun, they were subjected to some surveillance by the British, but our Intelligence took elaborate precautions to throw possible watchers off the scent when they brought the journalist to the place of meeting. In most cases I felt a casual manner the best safeguard. I would meet Lucien Frank, the correspondent of the *Agence France Presse,* over a cup of coffee at the home of his Jewish colleague, Nathan Gordos. The journalists must sometimes have been confused. The correspondent of the Associated Press of America, Carter Davidson, who in time established frequent contact with us, was, for his first interview, driven through the streets of Tel Aviv and then, in darkness, made to climb three flights of stairs to the apartment where Avraham and I awaited him. On other occasions, with Intelligence permission, I met him in daylight in a cafe.

The journalists also had their disappointments. I met Ruth Gruber, of the New York *Herald Tribune,* at the home of Moshe Brilliant, the local correspondent of the New York *Times.* She afterwards expressed her disappointment in me to Moshe. She had presumably expected a "real" terrorist, no doubt armed to the teeth, dressed like a mountain brigand, flanked by moustachioed guards. Moshe, she complained, had presented her with a "salon terrorist." Carter Davidson himself, whose comprehensive writing on the unfolding scene was marked by a manifestly serious study of all its facets, expressed surprise in his account of his first interview, that the men he met could have been taken for bank clerks.

No dramatic aura surrounded the full meetings of the High Command. Its members would slip in one by one to Begin's current headquarters, usually his own apartment in quiet Rosenbaum Street, near the Habimah Theatre, giving only a code ring at the doorbell to announce themselves. There were neither arms nor guards, the carrying of arms except on operations being forbidden to all Irgun members. Full meetings concentrated on the tactical conduct of the struggle with the British, the detail and timing and political impact of major operations, on the guidance and acceleration of the interacting process of attack and counterattack. Decisions were usually by consensus, now and again by majority vote. Such meetings were infrequent and irregular. None lasted more than three hours laid down by Begin as the salutary maximum for fruitful conclave. More often they were held sequentially. Begin would sound out each member, as he came to report or consult, on the problem of the hour. If an emergency decision had to be made, one member of the High Command would speed around the city for consultation with his scattered colleagues. Not every contingency could be foreseen or forestalled. In the spring of 1947, the struggle was entering a period of agony.

15

Heroes and Martyrs

The British hanged Dov Gruner, Mordekhai Alkochi, Yehiel Drezner, and Eliezer Kashani two hours after midnight on April 16, 1947. From his prison cell in the hundred days after their military court had sentenced him to death, Dov Gruner, a quiet, gentle-eyed intellectual dramatized the struggle between the Hebrew underground and British power. Even in Britain the contrast struck home. In the heated debate at the end of January, Winston Churchill and other members forced upon the attention of the House of Commons Gruner's nobility of spirit, the boldness of his comrades in their efforts to prevent his execution, and the pusillanimity and mendacity of his captors.

Dov Gruner had served for five years as a volunteer in the British army in the war against Hitler, in the African, Italian, and Western Front campaigns. He was wounded twice, and was thirty-four when he was demobilized. Within weeks, he rejoined the Irgun in which he had served briefly in the quiescent days of 1940. In his first operation—the attack on the armory of the Ramat Gan Police Station —he was wounded and captured. For eight months he lay in hospital, undergoing several operations on a smashed jaw. Almost immediately after his release from the hospital, he was hauled before the military court. He refused to recognize the right of the court to try him and took no further part in the proceedings, reacting without emotion to the sentence of death.

Gruner had no intention of appealing and so involving himself in a judicial process which might lend a semblance of legality to the British decision to hang him. Denied the rights of a prisoner of war, he knew that the Privy Council could not reverse the decision of the military court without destroying the very fabric of the occupation regime. He dismissed contemptuously as a surrender of all he was fighting for the suggestion that by the very act of submitting an appeal he would soften the hearts of his captors. He regarded death calmly: "Of course I want to live. Who does not?" he wrote in a letter to Begin that was smuggled out of the death-cell. "I could use sonorous phrases like *Dulce et decorum est pro patria mori*. But at this moment it seems to me that such phrases sound cheap." He expressed his clarity of purpose in cool words: "This should be the way of the Jewish people in these days: to stand up for what is ours and be ready for battle even if in some cases it leads to the scaffold."

He knew there was no turning back: "I write these lines forty-eight hours before the time fixed by our oppressors to carry out their murder, and at such moments one does not lie. I swear that if I had the choice of starting again I would choose the same road, regardless of the possible consequences to me."

There were other forces at work to divert Gruner from his purpose. The Jewish Agency was in a panic. Summoned by the High Commissioner when Major Collins and District Court Judge Ralph Windham were captured by the Irgun as hostages, its representatives were warned of the proclamation of martial law. Terrified by this prospect, the Agency launched a campaign of pressure, urging the Irgun to release the hostages. The Irgun stood its ground. The British backed down and postponed Gruner's execution, announcing that an appeal to the Privy Council was pending. No such appeal had been filed, but the Agency tried to persuade Gruner to sign one. When he declined, the Agency urged one of the Irgun lawyers to submit an appeal based on a general power of attorney Gruner had given him. When the attorney refused to act against Gruner's wishes, they prevailed upon another lawyer, Asher Levitsky, who from time to time still appeared for arrested underground fighters, to convince Gruner of the vital need for an appeal.

Levitsky visited Gruner many times and finally broke him down by persuading him that it was the Irgun's wish that he sign the appeal. This was not true. The Irgun gave no orders to men condemned to death. It was prepared to go to extreme length to save their lives but left decisions of that nature to the condemned man. Gruner knew this but, bewildered by the apparent change in Irgun policy, he signed the paper for the appeal. He did, however, make his signature conditional on the countersignature of Kritzman, his own lawyer. A day later Gruner, learning that he had been deceived, rescinded his signature.

A year later, in Jerusalem, Levitsky assured me that he had indeed been given authority by an Irgun officer to obtain Gruner's signature and that he would not have abused Gruner's confidence and conscience by a lie. I had a high respect for Levitsky's integrity, but the internal inquiry in the Irgun proved nothing.

A month passed without any move by the British. They professed to be waiting for the outcome of an appeal by Gruner's uncle.[1] The execution of Alkochi, Drezner, and Kashani was also stayed, and during March 1947 the British imposed martial law. When it was lifted, the four young men were left face to face with their executioners.

Appeals to the British to annul the death sentence poured in from all over the world. The strange contest of wills was followed with passionate interest in many countries.

We do not know what was discussed at the conferences and consultations that were held in those weeks between Colonial Office and Foreign Office and its chief, Ernest Bevin, still involved in the Four Power negotiation in Moscow. At some point toward the end of March, after martial law had broken down, Bevin was given sanction by a Cabinet wearily preoccupied with Britain's economic troubles to renew the order for the hanging of Gruner and his associates.

We did not know of this decision, but after some doubt came to the conclusion that the British did indeed intend to use the gallows as a weapon. We decided that if they did so, we would retaliate in kind.

Meantime, we sought ways of saving the lives of the condemned men. They had been joined by a fifth man, Moshe Barazani, a Lehi member who had been sentenced to death for carrying a grenade in his pocket.

Giddy brought forth an ingenious plan which the High Command approved. A British police armored car would be captured at a spot remote from Jerusalem, driven to Jerusalem by Irgun men dressed as police, with a "prisoner" to be delivered to the jail. At the hour of the daily afternoon exercise of the prisoners, the car would drive into the courtyard. At a prearranged signal, the condemned men would run to the armored car and seize arms prepared for them, and the car would rush the guards at the gate.

However, the Irgun detail of veterans failed to capture an armored car, at the right time of day, in spite of several attempts.

The British acted suddenly and in secrecy. Gruner was suffering extreme pain and his doctor, Shalit, decided that a further operation on his jaw was necessary. The prison authorities invented a series of excuses for delaying his transfer to the hospital. Finally, on the thirteenth of April, they assured the doctor that "in a day or two" he could move Gruner.

Early the next day Gruner and his three Irgun comrades were moved under heavy guard to the Acre Jail. The government information officer called a press conference to assure the correspondents that there was no real significance in the transfer. There was still the mayor of Tel Aviv's appeal pending at the Privy Council, he told them, without mentioning the fact that the British had that day secretly "enacted" a regulation retroactively abolishing the right of appeal from a military court judgment. The "regulation" was published only after Gruner's death.

Gruner's lawyer's urgent inquiries at Acre were met by the promise that he would be allowed to continue visiting his client. Gruner's sister, who had come from the United States, visited him in the Jerusalem jail and was informed that she too could continue visiting her brother at Acre.

On the second morning after the transfer, the British solemnly announced that the four prisoners had been executed during the night.[2]

All we could learn of their last moments came from the report of an Arab official in the jail. He told the Jewish inmates that the men were not given enough time to change their clothes. When the sentence of death was read out by the hangman, Gruner was ordered to stand up. In a last defiant gesture, he refused. He was dragged forcibly to his feet. As he was marched the few yards to the scaffold, he sang. Each of the others, the Arab said, sang his way to death.

Men like Gruner and the others went to their death as heroes of our time. They were moved to risk their freedom and their lives by their belief in a cause. Blind chance alone singled them out for capture and for martyrdom. Helpless in the hands of their captors and executioners, each one in his own way suffered in gentle fortitude, defied the enemy with strength and calm, comforted by their friends and loved ones. These brave men were unshakeable in their loyalty to their creed and love of their people. Some were more articulate, some less. The force of circumstances and the mystery of personality have given Dov Gruner's name to the world as their spokesman and their symbol.

Fifteen years later an Israeli newspaper editor, Noah Moses, on a visit to Nigeria was sought out by a Major Donnelly, the man who wounded Gruner during the attack on the Ramat Gan police station. Donnelly told how the wounded Gruner was carried into the station. There Donnelly and his wife tried to stop the flow of blood with the handkerchief of their six-year-old child.

"Gruner was almost fainting," Donnelly told Moses, "but he managed to twist his shattered jaw into a kind of smile and to say in English: 'Thanks.' "

Months later, when Gruner was brought to trial, Donnelly appeared as a witness. Gruner smiled at him. "At the luncheon interval, I was told not to leave the Court for fear that the Irgun would kidnap me. So I remained there with Gruner and his four guards.

"We talked . . . Gruner was cool and composed. I had to remind myself time and again that here was a man in the shadow of the gallows.

"I was the one who started the conversation—to this day I do not know why. Maybe I wanted to apologize for appearing as a witness against him.

"I said: 'In your attack you endangered the lives of my wife and child.'

" 'We had strict orders,' he replied, 'not to hurt anybody, only to capture arms. I am sorry about the Arab policeman who was killed.'

"Then he said, 'I know that you British policemen only carry out orders. But you are not in the right.'

"He told me of his life in the little Hungarian village; of the fate of his family, most of whom were destroyed by the Nazis; he told me all about the terrible things the Nazis did to the Jews. I had a vague idea about it, but I'd never interested myself in the details. Now, listening to this terrible account flowing so quietly from the lips of a man over whose head hung the death sentence and who yet showed not the least concern for his own fate, speaking only of others—of those who had been killed in Europe and of those waiting in despair in the refugee camps for the opening of the gates of Palestine—I was shaken to the core.

"I can still hear the words he spoke at the end, as the Court began to fill up again:

" 'If these things had happened to you, to your people, to your families, you would do exactly what we are doing.'

"At that moment I agreed with him."

When the death sentence had been pronounced, Gruner was taken out to an armored car and back to the prison.

Later that day Donnelly went to the prison on routine business. There, to his surprise, the commandant, Charlton, told him that Gruner had asked for him. He went with Charlton to the cell.

"Gruner, who was lying on the mat on the ground, got up as I came in.

" 'Mr. Donnelly,' he said, his scarred mouth twisting into a smile, 'will you shake hands with a Jewish terrorist?'

"I gave him my hand through the bars. Charlton went off with a snort.

"Gruner took my hand in both his and squeezed it.

" 'In other circumstances,' he said, 'we could have been friends.'

"I did not restrain myself. I burst into tears.

"He, the man who was going to die, put out his hand, patted my shoulder encouragingly and said with that wonderful calm: 'Don't worry. It'll be alright . . .'

". . . I have heard that you have put up a monument to him. I would like to put a wreath on it, to the bravest man I ever met, to a friend."[3]

The killing of the captives brought no glory to Britain, although obviously here was the source from which Bevin hoped to draw strength for his position at the special session of the United Nations a fortnight later. Two more underground fighters were in British hands, available for hanging before the session opened. Moshe Barazani of the Lehi was still in the death cell at Jerusalem. Another, Meir Feinstein, was captured after an Irgun attack on the Jerusalem Railway Station. The four men at Acre had hardly been buried when the date of the new executions was announced for April 21.

This time there were no delays or postponements. Here imperial resolve was to be manifest. Yet the two young men marred British victory. Through the underground communication's service they sent notes to their comrades outside, asking for hand grenades, which they intended to use to kill themselves and their executioners on their way to the gallows. A grenade was smuggled into their cell concealed in a scooped-out orange.

They were compelled to abandon part of this plan. On the eve of the execution Rabbi Goldman spent several consolatory hours with them. On leaving he told them he would return at dawn to be with them in their last moments. He would not be dissuaded from this and they could not endanger his life. In their cell, in the early morning, shortly before the hour set for the execution, they embraced each other with the grenade squeezed between their bodies, released the pin, and blew themselves up.

In the days which followed the executions, routine Irgun operations were pursued with vigor, but the essential objective was not achieved. Irgun patrols throughout the country had field courts attached to their units to try captives, preferably officers. There were special groups to carry out death sentences. That was the only way to ensure that there would be no more hangings of our men. The British knew this as well as we did. They issued strict orders—some of which fell into our hands—to reduce exposure of their forces to a minimum and our patrols were unsuccessful.

But we had a powerful plan in preparation, and in those days awaited impatiently Giddy's meticulous reports on each of its complicated details. Meantime, however, the United Nations Special Session opened at Lake Success.

16

UN Considers Palestine

The United Nations debate on Palestine was a retreat for Britain, but to a prepared position. Britain wanted the stamp of international authority for her policy in Palestine. The American State Department was concerned primarily with American oil interests in the Arab states, which they naïvely believed to be jeopardized by a pro-Jewish policy, and supported the British approach.[1]

But many Americans were sympathetic to the Jewish cause in Palestine. In a message to a Zionist Conference at this time Dean Alfange, the Chairman of the Christian Committee for Palestine in New York, wrote:

> The brave men and women of the Resistance Movement in Palestine are no more extremists than the American colonists who staged the Boston Tea Party or the Irish rebels of the 1920's. These militants are the heroes of tomorrow's history. Moreover they are doing more than anyone else to eradicate anti-semitism by portraying the Jew to the Christian world as a fighter for national freedom. We respectfully submit that the resistance against British tyranny in Palestine be continued with the same spirit—and in greater strength—in the difficult days that lie ahead. We believe that Americans, as descendents of the heroic colonists of 1776, will rally to the support of the Jewish patriots in Palestine at this critical time.

Many American intellectuals and public figures, led by such men as Senator Gillette and the author and dramatist Ben Hecht, had rallied to the call of the Hebrew Committee of National Liberation. When British Ambassador Lord Inverchapel officially protested at the ferocity of the contents of a full-page advertisement, under Ben Hecht's signature, published in the New York *Times* after the hanging of Gruner and his comrades, the State Department was reported to have promised its sympathetic attention. But it could do little to counteract the emotions aroused among Americans, apparently including Harry Truman, at the events in Palestine. Only the crushing of the resistance there could silence its echoes abroad.

On the eve of the United Nations session, the meeting of Foreign Ministers in Moscow had ended in loudly acknowledged failure. The blocs were taking shape; and America and Britain were lining up to march as brothers-in-arms.

Bevin's tactic at the United Nations session was disarmingly simple. All debate on the merits of the Palestine situation was to be avoided. The session was to appoint an inquiry commission, whose objectivity would be presumed by its being recruited from the representatives of the smaller nations. The inquiry would be held in Palestine while Britain sought the formula of American co-operation in an "agreed policy." Given American consent to the major theme of perpetual British rule, Bevin would willingly make some concessions on Jewish immigration, at one stroke eliminating the pressure of the Jewish Agency, quieting the doubts of President Truman and, by corollary, appeasing the conscience of public opinion in the United States and Europe.

It soon became evident during the session that, in spite of everything that had gone before, the policy of the Jewish Agency might still be accommodated within the broad outline of Britain's plan.

The Jewish Agency was now given its first opportunity to speak for the Jewish people in an international tribune. Here was a forum in which to set forth the determination of the Jews to achieve liberation and independence. The Agency could have impressed upon this international gathering of realists that their deliberations could be worthwhile only if they realized that there was no peaceful alternative to British evacuation.

Instead, the chief spokesman of the Jewish Agency, the presumed militant Rabbi Abba Hillel Silver, proclaimed with incongruous pathos the Agency's readiness to accept continued British rule if only Britain would fulfill the Mandate and abrogate the immigration and land restrictions.

British relief at this generous forbearance was expressed in a few complimentary and certainly sincere words of appreciation by her senior representative, Sir Alexander Cadogan.

In other speeches and in private conversations, the Agency spokesmen did suggest the alternative of a partition state. Yet even then they tried to ingratiate themselves with Britain's current rulers. In one such private conversation with Richard Crossman, M.P. —which Crossman promptly published—Mr. Ben-Gurion held out the prospect of a Jewish state in an undefined portion of Palestine at once making two major contributions to the Labor government's peace of mind: it would convert the Arab world to socialism, and would serve as a bastion against the inroads of Soviet Russia in the Middle East.

Backed by the United States delegation, the British mobilized a large majority for appointing a committee and postponing the discussion to the next ordinary session in the autumn. True, the breathing-space was short. Instead of the eighteen months Bevin had originally hoped for in February, there were now only six. But since February the Americans had been drawn into the Mediterranean zone, taking over responsibility for the defense of Turkey and Greece; and the split with Russia had become a complete breach. The Americans in the UN were therefore now manifestly more co-operative and eager to help Britain.

Discussions were interrupted by shattering news. On the morning of May 5 the Irgun delivered its most powerful blow.

The Acre fortress had been breached. Situated in the heart of an almost exclusively Arab town, the fortress was remote from the traditional centers of Irgun action. It was covered by a cordon of British army camps. It was historically impregnable, having resisted Napoleon's artillery. Yet a large Irgun contingent, in broad daylight, penetrated the British defenses, stormed the fortress, and blew it open. Forty-one Irgun and Lehi prisoners escaped.

The apparently brilliant political timing of the Acre operation was in fact almost fortuitous. It had been planned for weeks. Its objective was not primarily to attack the fortress, but to secure the release of at least some of the hundreds of underground fighting-men condemned for months and years to frustrating and wasteful idleness. As the days of its consummation approached, we were mindful of its possible impact on the attention of the world's statesmen assembled at Lake Success.

The success of the Acre attack depended not only on the skill of the planners and the determination of the attackers but on the close co-ordination achieved with the men inside the fortress.

The underground had always maintained excellent communication with their comrades in jail. In spite of the vigilance of the cap-

tors, coded letters were received by the prisoners in pieces of soap
or cake, fruit, or articles of clothing. The co-operation of visiting
rabbis or doctors or lawyers supplemented the system. The prisoners
were kept informed of events and—in case of senior officers—of
major decisions. There was a continuous flow and counterflow of
schemes for escape.

The Acre plan involved a difficult military operation from without.
Its timing and minute-by-minute execution were perfected by the
escape committee within the jail, led by Eitan Livni, a member of the
high command and Giddy's predecessor as chief of operations. The
organization and timing of the withdrawal set limits to the number
that could be freed. Of the 150 Irgun and Lehi prisoners then in
Acre, 41 were selected for freedom. In the confusion that overwhelmed the British guards, 214 Arab prisoners were able to escape.
The Jewish prisoners who had not been selected remained in the jail
so as not to endanger the operation.

The attack was mounted with utter precision. As the correspondent
of the New York *Herald Tribune,* Homer Bigart, reported: "Their
execution of perhaps the most ambitious and difficult single mission
yet undertaken was perfect." Though a sharp machine-gun battle
developed with the guards on the watchtower, the precious load of
liberated and liberators withdrew without mishap at the moment
and in the order planned by Giddy.

It was after the attack that disaster struck. It was a Sunday
afternoon and three parties of British soldiers had gone bathing in
the sea south of Acre. As always, they carried their unit arms. At
the sound of the explosion they hastily dressed and rushed to the
road in time to surprise and intercept the convoy of liberated prisoners, five of whom were killed or mortally wounded. Among them
was Michael Ashbel who, a year earlier, had with Yosef Simhon
been saved from the gallows by the kidnaping of British officers—a
remarkable young man who had written the Irgun's rousing battle
song, "On the Barricades." Four of the liberators were killed, one
of them the commander of the operation, Dov Cohen, called Shimshon, who had won fame in the Second World War as a commando
officer in the British army. Seven of the released prisoners were
recaptured.

Through a failure of signals a group of five of the attackers was
left behind in the withdrawal. They were captured and sent to take
the place of those they had freed. Three of them, Avshalom Haviv,

Meir Nakar and Yaacov Weiss were to pay with their lives on the scaffold.

British newspapers, strangely uncommunicative on the deliberations at Lake Success, devoted their front pages to the attack. British military experts described the operation as a masterpiece. From Jerusalem, the Reuters Agency reported the confusion of the authorities at the escape of so many arch-terrorists, with months of work, of searches, arrests, trials and investigations thrown away. In the House of Commons an M.P. cried: "There has never been anything like it in the history of the British Empire." Beyond the storm of anger came the increasingly louder chorus of voices proclaiming: "We must get out of Palestine."

There was still another sensation during this session of the UN. Andrei Gromyko, the delegate from Soviet Russia, proclaimed to the astonished delegates that his country now favored the establishment of a Jewish state.

For thirty years the Soviet regime had treated Zionism as a major heresy and Zionists as dangerous criminals serving the interests of British imperialism. Prison, exile and slow death were their lot. During World War II, with the Soviet annexation of eastern Poland, large numbers of Zionists, including many who had fled to the Soviet zone from the advancing Nazi armies in Western Poland, were summarily arrested, interrogated, and exiled. Among them was Menahem Begin who, charged with being an agent of British imperialism, had spent two years in the Soviet far north.

There was an element of ironic truth in the Soviet charge that Zionists were working for the aims of the British. It was Britain's original alliance with Zionism that gave her the key to Palestine. On the Zionist side there was a conscious identification with British interests. Weizmann believed the link unbreakable. Jabotinsky had offered Britain a strategic alliance in exchange for Jewish independent statehood. If furthering British interests was a crime, Zionists generally were certainly accessories. Soviet Russia's own interest in the Levant, though in the interwar period not very active, was concentrated on the Arab national movements which, however fitfully and impotently, promised British expulsion. During the Second World War and up to 1947, there was nothing in official Zionist attitudes to suggest a capacity to break with Britain.

The Soviet authorities had, however, been following the struggle of the Hebrew underground, with its demands for an end to British rule and its fierce and daring campaign to achieve that end. For the first time they saw in a Jewish national movement the possibility of the waning of British influence in the Middle East.

We knew of the change that was taking place in the Soviet outlook. In Europe representatives of one of the Soviet satellite countries had established contact with Irgun headquarters, offering help in exchange for Intelligence services. Our spokesman refused. The Irgun was prepared to receive help. We believed that any struggle for national liberation deserved help on its merits, but we were not prepared to buy support at the price of involving ourselves in other peoples' affairs. The contact was broken. One of the Irgun officers who escaped from British internment in Africa held long conversations with a Soviet ambassador, who revealed that in the special Soviet classification of political movements the Irgun was a "true national liberation movement." We monitored the Moscow radio, and were conscious of the sympathetic treatment of our activities.

At the UN session, the Polish delegate had delivered a blistering speech against the British, largely based on the memorandum we had prepared and, through the Hebrew Committee in New York, circulated among all but the British delegates at the United Nations session. He demanded that the British release political prisoners, abolish the death sentences, and cease deporting immigrants. Andrei Gromyko's speech, like that of the Pole before him, was made in defiance of the agreement to avoid discussion of the Palestine issue itself. He spoke bluntly about the events that had led up to the session.

"It is well-known," he said, "that bloody events have been occurring in Palestine. These events are becoming more and more frequent. That is why in ever-increasing measure, they are claiming the attention of the peoples of the world and above all of the United Nations Organization. It is because of this result, of the bankruptcy of the Mandate in Palestine, that the question has been brought before the General Assembly.

"The very fact that the Mandate Government has itself brought the problem to the General Assembly for discussion can be interpreted only as an acknowledgment that the continuation of the present situation in Palestine is inconceivable."

Gromyko proposed that independence should be granted in a presumably bi-national state. Yet he concluded that if this solution was not practical, the Jews should be accorded statehood in a part of the country.

In the spring of 1947, Ernest Bevin could still have gained a respite in the battle with the Jewish resistance. He could have won time for his generally intelligent political prognostications by relaxing immigration restrictions and increasing "legal" immigration to the 100,000 demanded by the Anglo-American Commission and by the American President. Then the Jewish Agency would have suspended "illegal" immigration, the ugly blockade could have been called off, and the hostile attitude of the other nations at the UN changed.

This would have given him the outright collaboration of the Jewish Agency in its effort to destroy the underground; and the Agency did in fact continue to offer him such collaboration.

In August 1946, Ben-Gurion in Paris had summarized the conclusions of the Jewish Agency: Britain would not or could not fulfill the Mandate and thereby forfeited the right to her presence in Palestine.

Six months later, Ben-Gurion, heading the Jewish Agency delegation at the "unofficial" and unauthorized talks with Bevin and Creech-Jones in London, was saying:

"I understand from the Foreign Secretary that the Mandatory Power will have to remain a few years. We would welcome that. We have not always been happy with the Administration. But as long as the Mandatory Government remained, the Jews should have full rights in the whole country."[2]

The context of this statement is fascinating. At that moment the Irgun revolt was destroying the effectiveness of British rule. Bevin was evacuating British civilians from Palestine, setting up his "security zones" and making plans for martial law.

Nothing that Bevin said, neither his repeated assertions that he did not intend to return to the Mandate, nor his declarations that Palestine in fact belonged to the Arabs, persuaded Ben-Gurion and his colleagues of the futility of their urgings. They explained to Bevin that the Mandate had envisaged a Jewish state—but they were prepared to leave that question open, as again Mr. Ben-Gurion remarked:[3]

When we say that Palestine should be a Jewish State we mean that there should be large-scale immigration and settlement leading to a Jewish majority. *But if such a decision cannot now be taken we should be willing to accept the Mandate as it was before the 1939 White Paper* without raising the question of the ultimate aim. If Britain is unwilling to continue the Mandate (as the Foreign Minister suggested) and is also unwilling to take a decision, then we shall be *willing to consider* the establishment of a Jewish State in a divided Palestine.

Mr. Creech-Jones, the Colonial Secretary, pursued the matter further. "Assuming," he said, "that the White Paper were wiped out—if that should be possible—was it the Jewish demand that Jewish immigration should be completely free? The Jews talked about economic absorptive capacity but were they prepared to have the High Commissioner determine that?"

The minutes of the meeting do not hint at even a slight pause, a hesitation, a nervous cough, a reddening of Ben-Gurion's cheeks. They simply continue:

"Mr. Ben-Gurion said that in their view there should be finality about the Palestine question.

"The fact that no-one knew what would happen in the future made for unrest. The decision should be made clear from the beginning, and policy conducted in accordance with it. If such a decision were taken, immigration should be controlled by the Agency; but if a decision were impossible *then the practice of 1937 should be restored under which the High Commissioner determined the Labour Schedule.*"

In April 1947 at the Special Session of the United Nations, they reiterated their plea for a return to the Mandate. Fourteen days after that Ben-Gurion described the plea for a return to the Mandate as "dangerous and destructive of Zionism." At that point he decided to work for partition: "a viable Jewish State in a part of the country."[4]

This raises a crucial question. How did the Jewish Agency leaders envisage a Jewish state even in a part of the country unless the British evacuated? Even if they did not grasp the British Government's larger purpose, they must certainly have realized that the British would not leave unless they were forced out. Against our efforts to force them out, the Agency fought tooth and claw. How then did they expect a Jewish state would come about? This question has never been answered. The accounts of the history of the period simply omit any analysis of the Agency's policy. There is no mention of surrender in 1946, or proposals to Bevin to return to the Mandate in 1947. There is a vague generalization about the "struggle" with Britain. An easy disregard of dates hints at a prolonged three-year struggle. The pathetic unequal battles of the unarmed passengers of the immigrant ships are somehow made to appear part of a larger battle presided over by the Jewish Agency.

There is a key to these strange phenomena. The leaders in 1947 were the same as those of 1937, and the mainsprings of their behavior had not changed. Now ten years older and in uninterrupted control of the affairs of Zionism, they were certain of their own indispensability and the continuation of their power had become an end in itself, nullifying other considerations.

The obsession with power was the motif of their unrelenting drive against the underground, and in Ben-Gurion at least it was sharpened by his own frustrated longings for militancy. By the spring of 1947 the public evidence of the vindication of the underground was crowding in thick and fast, and the Agency leaders found it incredible that the great power should even consider evacuation because of this underground pressure. They were angered during their meetings with Bevin in February, when he ignored their fervent assurances that they wanted nothing better than the perpetuation of British Mandatory rule. When Bevin said, "Some Jews have declared war on us," one of the Agency representatives burst out: "I am surprised to hear that."[5] At that very meeting, moreover, Bevin "made it quite clear" that the "British people would not stand for keeping troops in Palestine fighting."

Perhaps in their anger the Agency leaders did not grasp the very real fact that the underground was forcing on the British the desirability of pulling out of Palestine. One of the most frequent charges the Agency made against us was that we were blackening the name of the Jewish people in the eyes of the gentiles.

Yet only one delegate at the UN meeting in April criticized our methods and he was an Indian. The only other "neutral" delegates who mentioned the subject were Federkiewicz of Poland, who demanded that the British release terrorists from illegal detention and stop hanging them, and Gromyko of the Soviet Union who, even before his sensational speech, had urged that the right to appear before the Assembly be granted not only to the official Jewish Agency but also to "other representatives of the population."

By this time sympathy for Jewish resistance, whatever its motives, was a fact which no Agency propaganda could becloud. But the Agency leaders saw the vindication of the Irgun methods as a threat to their own power. Moshe Shertok, head of the Political Department of the Jewish Agency, at a press conference on June 11, appealed to the foreign correspondents in Palestine: "not to report the activities of the underground so much in terms of glorification" which "encourage the terrorists and undermine the efforts of the responsible Jewish institutions to isolate them and to deny them the sympathy of the public."[6]

17

Jew Against Jew

The intensity and scope of the Jewish Agency's campaign against us in Palestine grew in direct proportion to the volume of evidence indicating that the British Government was retreating under the Irgun's onslaught. The note of desperation became clearer as the bitter and reckless campaign against us progressed. Fantastic stories were concocted and broadcast.

When, in the course of an Irgun operation in the north of the country, a water pipe at Kiryat Hayim was accidentally damaged—without even, as it happened, any interruption of the supply of water to the village—the Jewish Agency press spread the news throughout the country that we had deliberately blown up the water supply of Kiryat Hayim.

Another time, a Jewish policeman, Berger, was brutally beaten in a Tel Aviv street by a Haganah group. According to our Intelligence reports their purpose was to injure but not to kill him. Nevertheless he died. The Haganah reported that Irgun had killed him.

At Petah Tikva a violent dispute broke out over the distribution of work between workers belonging to the General Histadrut and the National Labor Union. The country rang with the news that Jewish workers had been attacked by an Irgun "gang."

We learned from our Intelligence service inside the Haganah that a rumor was being circulated that an Irgun plot to murder the Zionist leaders had been uncovered.

The Agency leaders made great efforts to get their people to spy on us, in order to frustrate any specific Irgun operation "without cooperating with the British." Indoctrination in this spirit was now the main preoccupation of the Haganah.

Three circumstances combined to nullify their efforts. First, the vast majority of the people were with us, however passively, and little co-operation could be expected from them. Second, the Irgun and Lehi members had developed a great capacity for conspiracy. Finally, to be effective, lies must be believed. We had an unblemished reputation for truthfulness. One American foreign correspondent had told me bluntly: "Our instructions are: Irgun statements of fact may be treated as fact; Haganah statements must be checked first." For the majority of the population the Haganah fabrications lived only the day or two before our rebuttals were published.

Yet there were large areas in which their propaganda was effective. It was difficult for us to influence the kibbutzim, which were heavily guarded against external influences. The Irgun's message never got through to them. In the kibbutzim, the image of the Irgun presented to them by their leaders was similar to the image of Trotsky built up by Stalin.

Moreover, the Haganah, a large and amorphous organization, was not composed of political analysts. Many of its younger members believed blindly in the wisdom of their leaders and carried out even distasteful orders.

In the light of the fierce, uninhibited campaign which the Jewish Agency and the Haganah leaders developed against us that year, it is remarkable that they accomplished so little. Yet they had their successes, for which we—and they—paid the price.

Those months brought a new intensity and growth of scope to our work. The international political front made pressing demands on our attention. The Jewish Agency campaign against us demanded a new alertness, the conscious planning of countermeasures against the chance that the Agency might succeed in leading some of their followers into head-on conflict with us. The Irgun's manpower grew from day to day. The intake of volunteers rose steeply, enhanced by a steady trickle of transfers from the Haganah and the Palmach. Other Haganah members, resolved on helping us at least to resist civil war, placed themselves at the disposal of our Intelligence service.

New Intelligence contacts were made in the civilian population. Each of our departments expanded, pressed and strained our resources, against the limits of sheer human capacity of those who directed and controlled the intricate underground machine.

It was a grueling time for all of us. The only adjustment in our division of labor that I remember was the occasional transfer to me from Avraham of the political briefing of our Intelligence staff.

My pattern of conspiracy had its nagging drawbacks. In the small and friendly housing estate where my wife and I lived it was essential to present a face of normality and to maintain a minimal observance of social amenities. To dissimulate in social intercourse was not difficult. What was more difficult was to find time for social occasions. After the most wearing days of crisis, of tense discussion and hard decision, I would race to Ramat Gan in the evening so as to be in time to take a leisurely stroll through the *shikun*[1] for tea with the X's, or to receive, in apparent insouciant relaxation, a visit from the Y's. The strain on my wife was very great. She was never certain when I would come home or indeed if I would come home at all.

The High Command operated in an atmosphere of constant emergency. The British Military Court in Jerusalem met on June 2 to go through the formal preliminaries for the hanging of the prisoners taken after the Acre operation. We decided not to wait for the end of the trial. Once again we tried to capture British officers, a difficult operation, as army and police personnel, in obedience to orders, appeared only in groups. After much reconnaissance two policemen were caught at the Galei Gil swimming pool at Ramat Gan, but within forty-eight hours the British had located them in a house near Herzlia and freed them. By coincidence, as if indicating collaboration, three days later the British, as part of the official rejoicing on the King's birthday, magnanimously released thirty-two Haganah members, sentenced at various times for concealing arms.

Though the trial of the Acre prisoners dragged on for two weeks, at its conclusion we still had no hostages. But by this time we had evolved a new plan for a major operation.

The local "Bevingrad" lay in the heart of Tel Aviv, centered in Citrus House, which now housed the six hundred members of the British Area Military H.Q. It was surrounded by the regulation high fences, topped by barbed wire, heavily guarded, and seemed impregnable. One day a middle-aged, balding, gregarious gentleman called Oppenheimer came to that neighborhood. He spoke only German and sought a small storeroom for his wholesale business in potatoes. After some searching he finally found a suitable cellar directly opposite Citrus House. He rented it, and thereafter day after day a truck would arrive loaded with bags of potatoes and later return to carry them away again. Mr. Oppenheimer was a member of the Irgun staff, and some of the bags were, on their return journey, filled with earth from a tunnel which was to lead into the foundations of Citrus House.

The plan was simple but difficult to execute. When the tunnel reached the appropriate point under the building, an explosive with a time mechanism, contrived and tested by Giddy, was to be planted. The tunnel would then be sealed off. The Irgun radio would warn that in forty-eight hours' time an attack was to be launched on *all* the Bevingrads throughout the country. The nature of the attack would not be disclosed. We had no doubt that the warning would be taken seriously. Every Irgun warning since the King David Hotel explosion had been promptly acted upon. In these weeks indeed the efficacy of our warnings was again proved in attacks on the railway stations at Ramleh and Athlit. In each case we telephoned a warning forty-five minutes before the explosion and the stations were evacuated, with no casualties.

Though the quantity of explosives for the Citrus House operation was carefully calculated to destroy the building and do no more than blast damage in the vicinity, we had drafted a warning to the residents in the neighborhood to get out. A detail of men would, at the appointed time, hustle any stragglers away from the scene.

Our comprehensive warning, we calculated, would smoke the British forces out of every one of their regional military headquarters. The destruction after public warning of one of their strongholds would undermine their faith in all of them. The blow to British prestige would be incalculable.

By this time, too, the United Nations Commission had arrived in the country. The attack would impress on the committee Jewish determination to bring British rule to an end. We believed that this operation might well prove the decisive blow of the revolt.

Each day we received reports of the progress of the tunnel. A meter, two meters, three meters. By the eighteenth of June the diggers had reached a point midway under the road, only a few yards from the British guard post. To establish the tunnel's security a small explosive charge was left at its farthest point.

On June 20, all of the British press, except for the London *Times,* ran approximately the same story: the Haganah had saved the British. A young Jew had blown himself up foiling a terrorist plot which the police said would "probably have caused the biggest catastrophe in the history of Palestine."

The Haganah leadership had discovered the Irgun plan. They acted swiftly and with reckless stupidity. According to their own statement, a group of their members, headed by Zeev Werba, was sent to frustrate the plan. Werba went into the tunnel and set off the explosive. He was killed instantly.

The British understood the message of the tunnel. Their gratitude to the Haganah was spontaneous and uninhibited. It seemed to them, moreover, that at last, without having relaxed their oppressions in the slightest degree, they were to have renewed Jewish collaboration in this crucial round of their war on the Jews. The Haganah gave Werba a magnificent funeral as though he had engineered a great victory. In the funeral procession official representatives of the British power marched side by side with Haganah officers. After the funeral, a British general announced that he would be glad to invite the Haganah leaders for a drink.

18

The Arab Question

We did not believe that the direct influence of the United Nations Special Committee on Palestine would be very high. International attitudes would be determined by the interaction of the interests of the Great Powers, primarily of the United States and the Soviet Union. During the days of the committee's sessions in Palestine, the fissure between East and West widened, and thus brought the United States closer to Britain. At a new conference in Paris the Soviet Union set its face against the plan for aid to Europe originated by the United States Secretary of State, George C. Marshall, and the Russians forced on their satellites (including an unwilling Czechoslovakia) a rejection of the plan's benefits.

In London, the British declared that they would have no hesitation in flouting a decision of the United Nations—which could urge and recommend but could not dictate acceptance of its resolutions.

The Irgun prepared a comprehensive memorandum for the United Nations Committee in which we set out the historic background of our rights to Palestine, of the ties to Palestine that bound Jews scattered all over the world, of the British responsibility for the distortion of Palestine's reconstruction. We described the methods by which the British had deprived us of the country, the repressive police state she had built up, and our determination to force her evacuation.

We also explained our attitude to the Arabs, on which perhaps more nonsense had been written by our enemies than on any other subject.

Jabotinsky, and later the Irgun, had been accused of being the enemy of the Arabs. The truth was that we felt it unfortunate that we were forced into a clash with them. Our claim to the country was absolute. We had not deviated from the purpose of establishing a Jewish majority. We had rejected outright the suggestion—made by the British Labor Party before it came to power—that the Arab population be transferred elsewhere. We saw no reason why we could not live at peace with the Arabs within the framework of a Jewish state.

Enmity to Zionism derived from one central argument: that the Arabs had lived in the country for thirteen centuries and that they were consequently its lawful owners. In fact, the Arabs had ruled Palestine for only a small fraction of that period. For centuries the country had been part of the vast Turkish Empire, and the handful of Arabs who lived in Palestine were a small minority of the whole people. They had never attempted to achieve independence. They had not even taken part in the few forays against the Turks organized by T. E. Lawrence.

To the Jewish people, however, Palestine was the unchanging and unchangeable homeland. We had ruled the country and been driven from it by force, but had never relinquished our claim to it. Throughout the ages, moreover, Jewish life in Palestine had never been completely suspended: there was always a Jewish community in the country.

For the Jews life in Palestine was a passionate necessity; for the Arabs an accident of birth. The Jews saw themselves as the trustees and the forerunners of the national Return. Time after time, throughout the centuries, movements sprang up in the Diaspora to hasten or even to organize this Return. The impulse, and the movements and the writings to which it gave inspiration, are a part of the history and literature of Western civilization. In our generation, a vast influx of Jews had been prevented by British power from emigrating to Palestine.

At the end of the First World War, the Arab leaders did not regard our striving for the revival of our state with hostile eyes. King Feisal found nothing inimical to Arab interests in the famous agreement he made (in the presence of Colonel Lawrence) with Weizmann. There he gave his blessing to the movement to reestablish the Jewish state. His father, Hussein, the Sheikh of the Hedjaz, had earlier urged his people to welcome the returning Jews.

The enemies of Zionism described Zionism as an injustice to the Arabs; but why? Out of the thirty million Arabs about to achieve their independence, one small segment, numbering in 1919 some four hundred thousand and even in 1947 still less than a million, would remain a minority, guaranteed economic, political and cultural freedom.

The grim historic truth was that Jewish statelessness in our own generation cost us the lives of six million people. The prospect of minority status for the Arabs in a Jewish state meant that in a country surrounded by seven Arab states they would have to put up with the inconvenience of having a Jewish Prime Minister. They could have their share in a free Jewish state of judges, teachers, officials, ministers.

Jabotinsky had sung of the future state:

> There in plenty and joy shall flourish
> Arab's son, Nazareth's and my own.

We believed that this was a prospect that the overwhelming majority of Arabs in Palestine would sooner or later accept. In spite of a generation of British incitement, of terrorization by British-backed feudal politicians, the urge in them to co-operate with the Jews was still strong.

The recurring outbreaks of Arab violence were patently the contrivance of British imperial rule, executed by a minority. The "Revolt" of 1936–39 had been fought mainly by mercenaries imported from Syria and Iraq. Throughout the years of our struggle with the British, the Arabs, though incited by the British to attack us, had remained inactive. Returning from operations through Arab villages, our fighters were often welcomed and always given what aid they required. The Irgun had a file of letters from Arabs who wished us well and in some cases asked for the opportunity to help in the struggle against the common enemy. Only a few months earlier Arabs from the village of Abu Ghosh had risked and forfeited their freedom in order to organize and execute the escape from British imprisonment of Geulah Cohen, a Lehi radio announcer.

A few weeks before that, after several clashes between Arab and Jewish prisoners at Acre Prison, they had joined together, and the Arabs had told their British jailers that any act of brutality toward Jewish political prisoners would be met by Arab retaliation.

Once the Arabs were liberated from the British-imposed leadership of the Mufti group, and integrated into a democratic and progressive society, we believed that the state, under predominantly Jewish rule could, within a reasonable time, produce a co-operative bi-national society.

In our memorandum we made a secondary argument which projects a fascinating illustration of the clash of policies and aims in Palestine. It had to do with statistics. For the British, statistics were a sharp and eloquent weapon, used with great effect throughout the years. By some magic chemical process the Arab population was, by British figures, in a perpetual process of fantastic multiplication. They claimed that the Arabs outnumbered the Jews by about two to one.

We pointed out to the committee that the Arab figures had been consistently inflated. For decades, for the purposes of British statistics, no Arab—certainly no rural Arab—had died. Begin, Yohanan Bader, and I, who prepared the memorandum, calculated that the Arabs of Palestine numbered no more than 900,000. Instead of a ratio of 12 to 6 we advised the committee to assume a ratio of 9 to 7.[1]

Overall, we were against partition, against the division of the country into two separate states for which the Jewish Agency was pressing. We had often examined the idea of partition and the specific proposals put forward for its implementation, for the impulse to partition existed in many quarters friendly to our people, persuaded to think that this was the way to achieve Jewish independence.

The Zionist leaders professed that they were ready to accept partition because—as Weizmann told the committee publicly—they believed it was a solution to which the Arabs would reconcile themselves; in short, that it would bring peace.

We did not agree and stated:

> Either there will be peace between Hebrews and Arabs, in which case, once the British have left, it will reign in the whole country; or peace is impossible, in which case it will be disrupted equally in the part of the country assigned to the Jewish State and in which the Arabs form a substantial part of the population.

It was clear to us that partition would leave unsolved all the problems it was supposed to avoid and create new ones. The area envisaged in the Zionist proposals as adequate to set up a "viable" Jewish state would contain a large Arab population, about one half of the total. If it was impossible for a million Arabs to live at peace with the Jews in a Jewish state in the whole of Palestine, why could half a million Arabs live peacefully with the Jews in a dwarf state? If it was impossible in principle to "subject" a million Arabs to minority status in a Jewish state, what made it possible to "subject" five hundred thousand?

What could partition bring with it? The Jewish state would be crowded, filled to capacity in the narrow coastal strip, its large empty areas requiring generations to develop. Partition would give us a long frontier difficult to control, the narrow strip at its waist dominated by the hill country—to be allocated, by the Agency plan, to the Arabs —a severe strategic problem, a palpable temptation to aggression.

The division in the Zionist Organization on this subject was sharp. The minority parties threatened to have their say separately, if partition was officially proposed to the committee. Under this pressure Ben-Gurion stated the Jewish Agency demand for a Jewish state ostensibly in the whole of western Palestine, but reminded the committee that they had already—in earlier statements—expressed their willingness to accept statehood in a smaller area.

19

A Secret Meeting

The first session of the UN Committee in Palestine opened on the afternoon of June 16. Two hours earlier the Jerusalem Military Court had sentenced Haviv, Nakar, and Weiss, who had been captured in the Acre attack, to death by hanging.[1] The prisoners had refused to recognize the court and had responded to the sentence by singing "Hatikvah," joined by all the spectators in the court.

We tried to involve the UN Committee in our efforts to prevent the executions, and, after a long and heated debate in which the Guatemalan Jorge García Granados, the Uruguayan Enrico Fabregat and the Yugoslav Josha Brilej, argued tirelessly for intervention, it was decided by the vote of the Swedish chairman, Emil Sandstrom, to take action. They cabled the Secretary General of the UN, Trygve Lie, expressing their concern at such a sentence passed on the very day of their first session. Trygve Lie transmitted the appeal to the British Government.

The committee received an angry reply by Sir Henry Gurney, the British Chief Secretary. He denied that there was any connection between the timing of the sentence and the opening of the session.

We made a direct approach to the committee. The prisoners had been beaten and tortured. Haviv, although unhurt when he was captured, had nevertheless spent two weeks in the prison hospital. The wounded were given no medical attention. We asked the committee to call Haviv, Nakar and Weiss to testify to their experiences.

We were unsuccessful, despite the fact that we were able to press our request verbally. For the next night we met, in secret, with a delegation from the United Nations Committee.

Setting up such a meeting proved complicated. The decision to meet us was taken by Sandstrom, the chairman. Fearing that his colleagues might not maintain the secrecy and thus endanger us, he decided not to inform them of the proposed meeting until after it had taken place. Only the secretary, Dr. Victor Hoo (of China), and the American assistant secretary, Dr. Ralph Bunche, were in his confidence. He was aware that Carter Davidson, the Associated Press correspondent, was in contact with the Irgun and asked him to arrange the meeting. Davidson told me of the proposal in a crowded cafe. I agreed to the meeting and to Davidson's request to be present. As the committee was due to tour the coastal area, visiting Jaffa on June 24 and Tel Aviv the following day, we set the evening of June 24 for the meeting.

Watched closely both by British agents and by newspaper correspondents, the committee's hour-by-hour timetable published in advance, Sandstrom and Davidson had to take great care even in talking to each other. Indeed Davidson was able to tell Sandstrom of our security instructions only by meeting him in the washroom of the British Sporting Club in Jaffa where the committee had lunch.

After their tour of Jaffa was over, Sandstrom, Hoo, and Bunche took rooms at the Park Hotel in Tel Aviv. It was still daylight. They took a rest, had a leisurely dinner, and at eight o'clock, as darkness fell, strolled out of the hotel. A few yards away Yoel and Davidson awaited them in a car. The three men were driven to the apartment of the poet Yaacov Cahan in Bialik Street.

Begin, Avraham and I awaited them there. For over three hours we told them of Irgun ideals and its determination to bring British rule to an end. Their questions were searching and far-ranging.

We had previously heard that Sandstrom, a former judge under the British in Egypt, was still subject to British influence, but this was not evident from his questions. At the end of the meeting he expressed his regret that the other members of the committee could not be present to hear what we had said. Dr. Bunche made notes of the discussion at a furious pace. These notes formed the basis of the comprehensive official report on the meeting. He contrived to put questions of his own and from time to time to whisper suggestions to Sandstrom. At the door, as they were leaving Bunche said: "I can understand you. I am also the member of a persecuted minority."

Yet the only hint of a political judgment came from the impassive Dr. Hoo, a diplomat and the son of a diplomat. During the evening he had asked a provocative question. Palestine, even on both sides of the Jordan, he said, was a small country. If we introduced millions of people a population problem would be created. What would happen in three hundred years?" I turned the question back to him: "What do you think," I asked, "will happen in three hundred years' time in, say, China?" Now, in taking his farewell, he exclaimed: "Au revoir in an independent Palestine."

It was close to midnight before they returned to their hotel. One of them found some need for relaxation and went to the neighboring Pilz Cafe for a drink. In a forgetful moment, in breach of our understanding that the news of their meeting with the underground would not be published until the committee had left the country, he informed one of the newspapermen that he and his colleagues had met the Irgun leaders. This news was flashed around the world. The only agency which failed to carry the story was the Associated Press. Carter Davidson, assured of his scoop, had returned to his room to write it up at leisure for release at the appropriate time.

Sandstrom issued an emphatic denial, but nobody believed him. We could not help poor Davidson, being bound by our agreement. Bunche sent us the draft of his report for our confirmation within two days of the meeting. We published it only after the committee had arrived in Geneva. Our reactions to the meeting were contained in a brief, internal report issued to the Irgun ranks—where secrets were inviolate.

"A meeting has taken place," we wrote, "between official representatives of the United Nations Special Committee and representatives of the Irgun. We are not misled by the cordial atmosphere created in the course of the conversation and we are not blinded by the 'impression' our words made. Indeed the atmosphere was truly cordial . . . Yet there is a great difference between getting a good impression and forming a correct opinion. We know this and we therefore have no illusions about the practical political value of the meeting, just as we have no illusions about the value of the committee's work altogether.

"Nevertheless the meeting is not without significance. The fact that the Irgun was the only body to whom the committee took the initiative in proposing a statement of its views, indicates the importance attached to the Irgun, and its struggle, by the international institutions."

Two other members of the committee found their way to us. Jorge García Granados of Guatemala and Enrico Fabregat of Uruguay were angry when they learned of the meeting to which they had not been invited and sought to make their own contact with us. A few days before the departure of the committee we arranged one with them, at the apartment of Israel Waks.

Avraham did not attend. His replacement was Alex, whose real name is Marek Cahan, a genial older member of the Irgun staff and formerly a lawyer in Warsaw, who under various guises served as a kind of head of the Irgun "household." He was the Mr. Oppenheimer who had played such an important role in our abortive plan to blow up one of the Bevingrads.

We were captivated by our guests, both of whom had been rebels in their own countries. Both had a clear-eyed understanding of British policy. There was no judicious probing of our background and our objectives, for they had come as friends and not to conduct an inquiry. Fabregat spoke no English, and Granados had to translate all our conversation into Spanish. When Begin revealed his name, Granados exclaimed excitedly, "So you are the man!" while Fabregat impulsively threw his arms around Begin and hugged him.

We learned from Fabregat and Granados that, in spite of the inevitable distaste of several members of the committee for a decision which would embarrass Britain, the unrelenting character of our struggle caused everyone to realize that continued British rule was impossible. They believed that a recommendation to end British rule was certain, but that there was a good chance that a majority would propose partition.

We pressed them to urge the creation of a Jewish state for the whole of the country.

"We would willingly do it," said Granados, "but we cannot be more extreme than the Jewish Agency. The members of the committee see the Jewish Agency proposal for partition as a compromise between your demands and those of the Arabs. There is no chance of a decision to give more than the official Jewish representatives demand."

"At least," we replied, "you can issue a minority report for a Jewish State in the undivided country. This will make clear that partition far from being a 'concession' to the Jews is in fact a compromise proposal, and a compromise that creates more problems than it solves. Such a report could be of great historic importance."

Granados was regretful but firm. He and Fabregat had calculated these chances, but if they withdrew their two votes from the possible eight or nine that might be achieved for partition, less enthusiastic members might default.

The significance of the approach by the committee to the Irgun was not lost on the Jewish Agency. They saw in our meeting with the United Nations representatives a further blow to their own prestige and at once sharpened their campaign against us. They began one of the most confusing chapters in the whole sad story of their efforts to frustrate the underground. A new, anonymous group calling itself "Trustees of the Community," but whose inspiration was obvious called for renewed violence against the Irgun.

A number of our younger Irgun members were caught in their homes in Tel Aviv and brutally beaten. Although most of the men were members of the Irgun, some were unknown to us and victims of faulty Haganah Intelligence. In Haifa, several families were "sentenced to exile" because of their alleged sympathy for the Irgun, ordered to leave Haifa, and beaten when they refused.

In a meeting of the Irgun High Command we made an assessment of the situation. We concluded that only a section of the Haganah had been cajoled into direct action against us. Second, we reaffirmed our decision to retaliate in kind. Third, even if we had to retaliate against the Haganah, we would not relax operations against the British.

This minor "season" came to an abrupt end when it became obvious that the majority of people were outraged by these attacks. This attitude was reflected inside the Jewish Agency, among the minority parties, and within the Haganah itself. Our own swift counteraction was effective. Our Intelligence having identified the Haganah officers responsible for the attacks, they were each given a retributory thrashing.

Meantime crisis had piled on crisis. Our efforts to save Haviv, Nakar, and Weiss, were complicated by an excruciating difficulty with Lehi.

A sixteen-year-old member of the Lehi, named Rubowitz, had disappeared, feared murdered by British police. The failure of the British authorities to bring to trial Major Farran, the man positively identified as the officer seen hustling Rubowitz into a car, moved the Lehi to carry out reprisals against the British army and police.

We appealed to the Lehi leaders to postpone such activities. Their first effect would be to frighten British personnel away from

Jewish areas and our chances of capturing British officers, clearly the only possible means of preventing the threatened hangings, would be reduced to a minimum. After much argument the Lehi leaders consented to wait a week, at the end of which, despite our appeals for delay, groups of British soldiers and policemen were shot in a Tel Aviv street and a Haifa cafe.

On July 8, the British G.O.C. confirmed the death sentences. We had no illusions about British intention to carry out the hangings. We thereupon repeated our warnings that such executions of captives would be met by similar executions on our part. On the night of July 11 one of our units in Natanya captured two sergeants of British Army Intelligence. They were imprisoned in a specially constructed cellar in a house in the little town.

The British launched what must certainly have been one of the greatest manhunts in history. Martial law was clamped down on Natanya. A twenty-four-hour curfew was imposed. All transport and communications were suspended. Ingress and egress from the town by its fifteen thousand inhabitants was prohibited. A cordon of two thousand soldiers kept guard on its landward sides and every building in the town was searched by a party of soldiers, and every adult in it was interrogated. The very building in which the prison for the captured British sergeants had been constructed was searched several times, the searchers separated from our prisoners by only the floor on which they stood. Yet they were not found. The country was in a turmoil. We were determined that the British should not execute our men.

20

Exodus 1947:
Fifty-five Days of Hell

Other news strengthened our resolve to hold firm—news of the immigration ship *Exodus 1947,* which was carrying 3000 men and women, 600 teenagers and 950 children and infants to Palestine. On July 17 *Exodus 1947* was intercepted in the open sea, seventeen miles from Haifa, by the British cruiser *Ajax* and five destroyers, a force nearly as large as the British naval forces in the first battle of Narvik. The ship was rammed seven times by two of the destroyers and a hole torn in its side below the water line.

A party of British sailors armed with studded truncheons, water hoses, oil hoses, tear-gas bombs, and automatic weapons tried to board the vessel but were repulsed by a shower of potatoes and food cans. Returning to the attack, they succeeded in going over the rail and opened fire on the crowded deck. Two men—one of them an American member of the crew—and a fifteen-year-old boy were killed. In the succeeding melee twenty-seven men, women, and children were injured. The captain surrendered. The *Exodus* was towed to Haifa. There the passengers were forcibly transferred to three British vessels.[1]

This naval action was the first evidence of a change in Bevin's tactics. He was in a highly optimistic mood. For some weeks now he had been assured of the weakening of American support for the Jewish cause. President Truman had been persuaded by the British Foreign Minister's allies in the State Department to issue an appeal to the American people not to give aid to "illegal activities" in Palestine. The Yugoslavs, whose ports could serve as transit centers for immigrants, had worked out a favorable trade agreement with the British Government in return for their agreement to deny facilities to the ships of Jewish immigrants. Italian naval vessels had blocked the departure for several weeks of one such ship, the *Exodus 1947,* then named the *President Garfield.*[2] Now on the twelfth and thirteenth of July, following the rejection by the Soviet Union of the Marshall Plan, Bevin and French Foreign Minister Bidault sponsored a conference of European nations to discuss and decide on the application of the plan to their countries. It was the first postwar conference to end in complete agreement, and heralded a new era of Anglo-American co-operation in the struggle against Communism.

In Palestine itself there was renewed collaboration by the Jewish Agency in Bevin's efforts to eliminate the underground resistance.

At the Paris Conference on July 13 Bevin received a report of the arrival at Port de Bouc, near Marseilles, of the ship *President Garfield.* He interrupted the proceedings to demand of the French Foreign Minister that the boat be prevented from leaving. Bidault, aware of the implications, replied diplomatically that the passengers had valid visas for a South American country, and that he consequently had no legal right to prevent their departure. Bevin exploded. It was, he said, an international scandal. Through his ambassador, Duff-Cooper, he brought pressure to bear on the French Premier, Ramadier. It was reported in the press that Ramadier had sent police to the port to hold the vessel, which, renamed *Exodus 1947,* had nevertheless sailed into the Mediterranean.

In London the next day (July 14) Bevin's decisions were swift and far-reaching. Within three days the naval operation against the vessel had been organized and executed and by July 22—after the three British vessels, with their human cargo, whom they had removed from the *Exodus* had left Haifa for the open sea—a British spokesman in London announced laconically that in future "illegal immigrants" would be returned to the country from which they had come.

Now the anger of the Jews in Palestine was absolute, "All faith in Britain," wrote the usually timid *Haaretz,* "has been lost." For a few days it seemed that the Haganah would resume at least the "restricted" attacks on the British they had so timidly abandoned a year earlier, for two attacks were carried out on radar stations near Haifa, and a British transshipment vessel, *The Empire Lifeguard,* was damaged by an explosion. But no more—except for words.

The Agency denounced the British Government and assured the heroic men, women, and children on the *Exodus* of the Yishuv's undying readiness to help them. That week the British official communiqué indiscriminately included the three Haganah outbursts of action in the schedule of fifty-one "terrorist attacks."

The three ships with the *Exodus* passengers sailed aimlessly in the Mediterranean while Bevin tried to persuade the French Government that it was their duty not only to receive the Jews on French soil but to use force to disembark them. The reactions of the French were voluble and emphatic. Not since the British had ousted them from Syria and Lebanon two years earlier had such a wave of anti-British feeling swept the French people. The government's reply to Bevin was diplomatic, but no less firm. The French would give asylum to the Jews, but they would not force them to land in France against their will. Foreign Minister Bidault announced that his government would not accept any share of responsibility in applying the White Paper of 1939, and the Zionist flag suddenly appeared on a number of French buildings in Paris.

In the early morning of July 29, after nine days at sea, the three boats were allowed to approach Port de Bouc, and anchored outside the port. The crowd assembled on the jetty, which included a host of newspapermen, a number of Jewish officials and the total population of the village, were warned not to go near the ships. Some of the journalists disregarded the order. On that day and the next they hired motorboats and ventured close enough to one or other of the vessels to see what was going on aboard.

The Reuters correspondent hailed the people on the deck of one of the ships: "Will you land?" The reply came in chorus: "No. We prefer to die of hunger."

A group of French officials headed by the prefect of the district went on board and read out their government's declaration, which offered the passengers asylum in France. He was interrupted by shouts of "We don't want declarations. Come below and see how we're living." The French officials accepted this invitation. There, as one reported later, they found two large cages. In each were some eight hundred men, women, and children lying huddled almost on top of one another. The odor was unbearable.

The London correspondent of *Haaretz,* Aryeh Gelblum, sent to Port de Bouc to cover the arrival, reported to his paper on his "visit" to the two other boats:[3]

On approaching the Ocean Vigour I witnessed the most terrible spectacle I have seen in my life. It was a spectacle I shall never forget. On the deck, in narrow, very high cages, worse than those in a Zoo, surrounded by barbed wire, were crowded together my brothers and sisters of all ages. There the sun had beaten down on their heads for eighteen days at sea. They had not even been able to lie down at night. Between the cages stood red-bereted guards isolating each cage. I called in Yiddish: "Will you leave the boat?" They answered in unanimous chorus "No." Then I called to them in Hebrew: "Shalom!" Again they answered in chorus: "Shalom!"

The Britons on the deck turned their arms on me and I had to retreat. As I drew away I heard calls from the boat "Lehitraot!" Then they sang *Hatikvah* while I, choking with tears, blew them kisses.

Meanwhile each of the passengers on the boats was asked individually by the French officials if he wished to land. There were altogether 4500 people, including the sick and pregnant women, but each refused, a refusal reinforced by a Haganah agent in a motorboat, who sped from ship to ship, urging the passengers not to land.

The next day Gelblum went out again, this time towards the third vessel, the *Runnymede Park,* in the company of a group of British and French newspapermen.

A pregnant woman, he wrote, who had presumably been persuaded to leave the ship, was being helped down the ladder by the British soldiers. Suddenly she changed her mind and climbed back to deck. The British journalists hung their heads. The French cheered.[4]

While the three boatloads of *Exodus* passengers were sailing into the harbor at Port de Bouc, at dawn on July 29, the British hanged Avshalom Haviv, Meir Nakar, and Yaacov Weiss in Acre Prison.

Thirty hours later an Irgun communiqué announced the execution by hanging of the two British sergeants who had been held as hostages.

The Agency press and some foreign newspapers later published reports that the decision to execute the sergeants had been accompanied by serious internal dissension in the Irgun, where a group had been opposed to the action. In fact there was neither dissension nor discussion. The decision to apply retaliation had been taken months earlier, after we had warned the British to observe the Prisoners-of-War Convention. We had warned them specifically, repeatedly, and in the clearest terms, that we would not tolerate execution of captives: that there would be retaliation in kind.

The decision of the conditions under which the war was to be fought lay entirely in British hands, and every British soldier was subject to those conditions. Only tactical failure had prevented the Irgun from carrying out its warning after the execution of Gruner and his three comrades. The capture of the British sergeants and their trial by a field-tribunal had been carried out under long-standing orders. No special meeting of the High Command took place after the execution of Haviv, Nakar and Weiss to consider what action to take. In the close contact maintained among its members there was no further discussion. We had made our position clear.

Vengeance had no part in it. We knew if we faltered now, the British rule would gain in strength and confidence, and a new dark night would descend on our people.

In *Irgunpress* I had written shortly before the hangings:

> We recognize no one-sided laws of war. If the British are determined that their way out of the country should be lined by an avenue of gallows and of weeping fathers, mothers, wives and sweethearts, we shall see to it that in this there is no racial discrimination. The gallows will not be all of one colour, the tears not all of one racial origin. If the British claim that this is unfair because Jewish blood and tears, having been more frequently shed, are cheaper, we shall prove to them that their age-long cheapness has come to an end. Their price will be paid in full.

There were no more executions in Palestine. The last weapon of terror in the British armory had been broken. The gallows at Natanya proved to be the culminating blow in the struggle to end British rule. Eight weeks later the British Government announced their intention to surrender the Mandate and to withdraw from Palestine.[5]

The immediate repercussions were violent. In the following three days groups of British soldiers ran amok several times, firing in crowded streets, shooting into Jewish buses and into Jewish cafes. Seven Jews were killed, a number wounded. In England, Fascist-inspired demonstrations took place, and Jewish shop windows were broken in Liverpool and Glasgow. But the limits of British terror had been reached. Of this the official British riposte, of August 5, provided startling demonstration.

Shortly after the hanging of the sergeants, I left for Geneva. At our meeting in June with Granados and Fabregat—the two members of the UN Committee—we had argued that it would be desirable to maintain contact in Geneva, where the committee was deliberating. Later, in the belief that circumstances might make possible the exercise of some influence on its deliberations, the Irgun high command decided to send a member to Geneva, and Begin proposed that I should go. My wife would accompany me as far as Geneva, and once I had established my conspiratorial routine in Geneva, she would go to London to assist in a secret campaign for funds for the Irgun.

I traveled to Jerusalem two days before the committee was due to leave Palestine, sought out Dr. Bunche and arranged to get in touch with him in Geneva.

The days of fevered activity at the end of July forced me twice to postpone my departure and I left a week later than I had intended—six days after the execution of the sergeants.

My wife and I arrived at Lydda at eight in the morning. After the Customs examination our bags were taken to the inevitable little room and searched by a frozen-faced detective, who asked me what the object of my trip was. I told him I was going to England on my publishing business and then might spend a holiday with my wife in Switzerland. I then rejoined my wife, who told me that all the other passengers had been passed through without question.

We boarded the plane, the door was shut, and we waited for the take-off. There came a banging at the door. The steward opened it. A British policeman walked in and announced, "All out." As we left the plane he took our passports away and we trooped back to the airport building. We sat down at a table away from the other passengers, and I briefed my wife, from memory, on the notes I had coded into my address book. If I was to be arrested she could at least convey the instructions and requests I was carrying for Paris and London. How much she absorbed I never knew, for we were both very agitated.

A young man walked past our table, whispered, "The police have telephoned to Jerusalem for instructions," and moved on. We sat there for nearly two hours. At last, at eleven o'clock, the stewardess announced our return to the plane. At the door, a detective held the pile of passports and called out each name. My wife was among the first, but she waited with me. Finally only my passport was left.

As I stretched out my hand for it, the officer said portentously: "I'll give you your passport on condition you give me your address in England." I gave him the address of our onetime doctor in London.

That night in Geneva we learnt that the CID had early that morning made fifty-two arrests, nearly all of well-known Revisionists. Added to them were the Irgunist lawyer Max Kritzman and the mayors of three towns: Israel Rokach of Tel Aviv, Oved Ben-Ami of Natanya, and Avraham Krinizi of Ramat Gan. Krinizi was the only one of this trio who was a constant friend of the underground.

I spent three weeks in Geneva, several hours with Bunche, and established frequent and friendly rapport with Granados, who told me he was certain that any thoughts lingering in the minds of some of the committee members as to the possibility of continued British rule had been erased by the swift retaliation for the hanging of our three comrades. All were agreed that Britain must go.

I was given unequivocal confirmation of our prognosis of Arab reactions. All the Arab states had made declarations of uncompromising resistance to the idea of a Jewish state. However, the spokesmen of the Christian minority in Lebanon had angered the Moslem leaders and startled the committee by calling for the establishment of a Jewish state in part of Palestine. An even more far-reaching proposal had come in a memorandum to the committee from the head of the Christian community in Lebanon, the Maronite Archbishop Moubarrak, for the establishment of a Jewish state in the whole of Palestine side by side with a Christian state in Lebanon. Granados told me that the Arab leaders were unanimously opposed to Jewish independence on any terms. Nevertheless, though partition might not be the best solution to the problem, it had the appeal of being a "compromise."

"Whatever we may feel about it," he said, "the Jewish Agency is pressing so hard for partition as the only solution, that our colleagues have begun to regard it as the maximum. Fabregat and I cannot be more Catholic than the Pope."

Three members of the committee would, he believed, present a minority proposal for a scheme of federation: the Yugoslav, the Indian and the Persian. I sought out the representative of the Belgrade *Borba* whom I had met clandestinely with Begin in Tel Aviv, and then Brilej, the alternate Yugoslav member of the committee.

They were very cordial, not overcommunicative, but clearly immovable.

Bevin's battle of attrition with the *Exodus* passengers continued in obstinate silent ferocity. The days of their incarceration lengthened into weeks. Eight days after the arrival of the vessels in Port de Bouc, journalists, to their surprise, were allowed to board the *Ocean Vigour*. Although they were refused permission to go below decks to view conditions in the floating prison, they could not be prevented from shouting questions down into the bowels of the ship or from hearing the replies that came up from the six hundred men, women and children who were living in suffocating congestion in a cage.

Ten days later the oppressive heat gave way to a violent storm. The hundred prisoners on the upper deck were transferred to the sheltered horror below, where they remained standing until the storm abated. Pregnant women who sought asylum in the sick bay were sent back to stand in the cages. Five children were born in that purgatory, thereby earning the privileges of British citizenship. Yet there was no surrender. In the third week the Jews clashed with their guards on all three ships. They declared a hunger strike in which all joined. To the United Nations, to the Jews of the world they sent passionate appeals to act to break the blockade on Palestine; and terse declarations of their own unaltered determination to reject all havens but that of Palestine.

On a brief trip to Paris I was startled by the bellicosity of French reactions to the treatment of the immigrants. Frenchmen seemed to have no other topic of conversation. No epithet seemed too strong for conveying their horror and disgust at the agonizing drama at Port de Bouc.

At my old hotel I was greeted with unusual warmth. The manager came up to my room to tell me what he thought of the British. "We are all with you," he said.

"Don't you think your government may give in," I asked, "and force the people to land from the boats?"

He was shocked. "Impossible!" he exclaimed. He snapped his fingers. "The government would fall—like that!"

In Britain that August, the government presented a comprehensive plan of economic concentration. A new "Battle of Britain" was announced by the Prime Minister. Labor, raw materials, and investments would henceforth be controlled and directed by the government. Imports would be severely restricted. The standard of living would be substantially reduced.

"This is a situation," said Mr. Attlee, "as serious as any that has faced us in our history. The plan means hardship for all—longer hours for some, changes of jobs for many, harder work for all."

While reports forecast imminent dollar bankruptcy, Mr. Attlee promised that savings would be effected in the military establishment: of 450,000 soldiers stationed abroad, 200,000 would be brought back to Britain. No mention was made of the 95,000 men in Palestine.

We heard that some of Mr. Bevin's advisers were urging him to send his 4500 *Exodus* victims to Kenya, already established as a prison for four hundred members of the Irgun and the Lehi. Mere exile however did not satisfy him. On August 22, after a six-hour ultimatum to the prisoners had met with no response, the boats left Port de Bouc and sailed for Hamburg in Germany. At Gibraltar, where they stopped to refuel, welders were brought aboard to strengthen the cages on the decks and in the holds.

The climax prepared at Hamburg, recalled to the passengers many of the sights and sounds of the Nazi horror they had survived. A thousand British troops awaited them on a dock lined with cages. They were armed with machine guns, rifles, tommy guns, tear gas, pistols, steel-tipped truncheons and high-pressure hose pipes. In the background were fifteen hundred German police, fifteen hundred more being in reserve. As the passengers came off the boats a loudspeaker began blaring out jazz music, the very accompaniment the Nazis had so often used for their transports to the death camps.

The passengers from one of the boats—the *Empire Rival*—came off peacefully, indeed hurriedly, having left a time bomb ticking in the hold. There was violent resistance on the two other boats. Men, women, and children at first threw bottles and cans and sticks cased in barbed wire; then they used their fists and their nails and their teeth and their feet. An American correspondent saw one small boy punching a soldier in the nose.

In the *Runnymede Park* the four hundred armed Britons were at one stage forced to retreat from the onslaught of the thousand five hundred Jews, but they returned to the attack. First, they used their water hoses to knock down the enemy or to flatten them against the wall, then their truncheons. Half-naked people, drenched and battered, came stumbling off the ships, some dragged off still struggling, others carried off unconscious.

The Germans were not entirely deprived of their share in the victory. In Hamburg center five hundred of them, led by a British colonel, broke up a crowd of 1300 displaced persons demonstrating in solidarity with the *Exodus*.

Two camps, at Amstau and a larger one at Poppendorf, had been prepared for the prisoners. As in Nazi concentration camps, they were surrounded by barbed wire and had the familiar watchtowers and searchlights. German police reinforced the British guards and German doctors attended the victims.[6]

The ordeal of the people of the *Exodus*—the fifty-five days of hell which Bevin ordained for them and to which the Jewish Agency, through Haganah, legitimately urged them to expose themselves— made not the slightest difference to the policy of surrender of their official leaders.

21

The Proclamation

The Jewish Agency leaders continued to make fiery speeches. When the boats left Port de Bouc they declared a day of fasting. When the boats arrived at Hamburg, they declared a day of mourning. But 40,000 members of the Haganah were forced by their leaders to hold their fire against the British and to direct their attention to crushing the Irgun. When Bevin once again proclaimed that there was a war in progress with the Jews, a Jewish Agency spokesman heatedly issued a denial. The only war, he said—on August 3 when the assault on the *Exodus* had been in progress for seventeen days —was between the British Foreign Office and the terrorists.

Yet the Haganah leaders, although in reality mere bystanders, added a pompous postscript to the tragedy. In a statement on August 22, they expressed their regret at not being "strong enough to land the European immigrants in Palestine. We shall do our best to return them to Palestine as soon as possible. The courageous stand of the immigrants and their hard and prolonged struggle will be inscribed in the glorious pages of Jewish history and of all humanity. The Jewish struggle for freedom will continue."

In Geneva, I found that the members of the UN Committee had just returned from their tour of the DP camps. Dr. Granados informed me of the unanimous decision of the committee to recommend the ending of the British Mandate in Palestine.

I had known from the beginning of August that the committee would make this recommendation, and so had the Jewish Agency. It was not long after the arrival of agency members in Geneva that intelligent forecasts began to appear in the press. The economic crisis in Britain, the reports of pressure in the British Cabinet against Bevin's intransigence on Palestine, the revelation by Attlee that his government *would* accept the recommendations of the United Nations, made it safe to wager that the end was in sight.

Now Ben-Gurion made three discoveries about which he hastened to tell the world. On August 8 he said to his party comrades in council:

"The time has come for us to object to the very existence of the British regime. It is not enough to reject the White Paper. *We must demand the liquidation of the British regime in Palestine—without any delay.* This regime has no legal basis nor political justification. It was not elected by us, nor by the Arabs . . . It was once the agent of the League of Nations and the conditions of its rule and authority were laid down in the Mandate. It broke the Mandate and thus destroyed the legal basis for its existence, and ever since it has rested on brute force alone."[1]

Nine days later he had discovered that Britain was conducting "a war on the Jews."[2]

And on August 26, he had a double message:

"Bevin," he said, "wishes to remain in Palestine at all costs . . . But there are historic forces stronger than Bevin—economic and political forces—which will force him to leave Palestine."[3]

He gave no reason for his past collaboration with the predatory power he now considered illegal. His speeches had their own purpose: to place on record, before it was too late, that he too had demanded that the British leave Palestine.

These speeches by Ben-Gurion were made at a time when he was making a new effort to bring about a full-scale Haganah attack on the Irgun. With the departure of the British, Begin and his comrades were obviously not to be allowed to reap the political rewards of the Irgun war on British rule. Ben-Gurion was to be acclaimed as the man who had forced the British to leave.

On August 31 the United Nations Committee published its recommendations, one of which was to end the Mandate for Palestine.

A majority of seven recommended partition into Arab and Jewish states, with Jerusalem under international control.

The Jewish state was to be composed of eastern Galilee and the Jezreel Valley, the narrow coastal strip from Haifa to a point north of Gaza and the major part of the Negev. The estimated Jewish population was 500,000 with a minority of 416,000 Arabs. There was to be economic union so that the Arab state should be subsidized by the Jewish state. During a transition period of two years the British would, on behalf of the United Nations, continue to govern and to prepare the ground for the independence of the two communities. During this period 150,000 Jews would be permitted to enter the country.

A minority of three, India, Iran, and Yugoslavia recommended a federal state, with the Jews given local autonomy. The impact of the committee's decision remained to be seen.

The Irgun Command in Paris was working at high pressure. Eitan, who four months earlier had organized the prisoners in Acre Prison for the breakout, had come from Palestine to train instructors. Branches now existed in many countries, and he traveled the length and breadth of Europe.

Eli performed wonders in conspiracy. He had no passport, yet he moved from country to country at will, using a Red Cross Identification card.

In August he organized four sabotage operations against the British, although only one was materially successful—the derailment of a British troop train near Melnik in the British Zone of Austria.

When I arrived in Paris on the last day of August, we discussed further ventures. We were unhappy about our lack of success in Britain itself, where Scotland Yard's vigilance had been heightened by several abortive Lehi attempts at operations.

The projected plan to blow up British ships in Shanghai had been hindered by problems with our letter code. The message I found awaiting me in Paris was quite incomprehensible.

I went on to London, having been away from Palestine six weeks, long enough, I thought, for Scotland Yard to have received at least routine details about me. I was not entirely calm when I landed at London Airport.

Yet nothing happened. No one questioned me about the purpose of my visit. In London I casually asked my friend Dr. Louis Sheldon, at whose house I relaxed over the weekend and whose address I had given to the policeman at Lydda, whether there had been any inquiry for me. There had been none.

There was an air of optimism among our people in London, who confirmed that Scotland Yard was indefatigably vigilant, our veterans being cheerfully aware of the personal attentions of its agents. We had meantime sent an operations chief, Yonah, from Palestine, and they were confident that he was unsuspected.

Dr. Israel Lifschitz, a dedicated South African Revisionist, had come to London to organize a fund-raising campaign. He had introduced some of the methods developed in the South African organization. In private homes the Irgun message was presented and often hotly debated. The official Zionist authorities, shocked into counteraction, had warned their followers against providing forums for this new subversion. Most often this had a contrary effect. My wife, Doris, who, after a short stay in Geneva, had gone to England to raise funds, had repeated her South African success, if on a smaller scale, in London and Manchester.[4]

There were also a number of new recruits, some of them British Jews and others Palestinian students whom Yonah, now already pursuing his duties with energy, saw as promising material for operations in England should these remain necessary.

The naval officer reported to me on the projected sabotage operation at Portsmouth. All personnel was ready, materials available, the intrinsic timetable calculated. He awaited only our permission and the arrival of a suitable target at the port.

It was now, however, September 23. In Britain the almost unanimous demands in the press for the evacuation of Palestine seemed to reflect the mood of the people. The British Cabinet had met two days earlier to make a firm decision, and on the day of my arrival Mr. Creech-Jones had flown off to New York armed with a statement of policy. Every knowledgeable source in London confidently reported that the government had decided on evacuation. On September 27 Mr. Creech-Jones proclaimed to the United Nations Assembly Britain's intention to leave Palestine.

This was certainly not the moment to launch any offensive operations in Britain, and I asked the naval officer to hold his plan in abeyance.

Creech-Jones proclaimed that his government would withdraw their troops and their administration from Palestine "as soon as possible." They rejected the inquiry committee's suggestion that they should administer the country in the interim period before the independent states were set up. They would not, said Mr. Creech-Jones, co-operate in applying a solution not acceptable to both Jews and Arabs. They would not use force to impose a solution, he said. On that very day, September 27, the British naval forces boarded yet another Jewish immigrant ship, the *Af-Al-Pi,* and forcibly transferred its passengers, one of whom was killed in the process.

The United Nations had no armed force to impose solutions, and no armed force could be established that would satisfy both the Soviet Union and the Western powers. The threats of Arab resistance resounded through the world. At Lake Success there were reports of troop concentrations in the neighboring Arab states. These reports increased on the eve of the United States declaration of policy at the United Nations.

The American State Department, desiring Britain to remain in Palestine, was in an acute dilemma. It was resolved by the pressures of public opinion in the United States. The events of the summer in Palestine and the brutality on the *Exodus* had evoked disgust and horror in that country, particularly when General Marshall revealed that he had advised Bevin against returning the *Exodus* passengers to Germany. The massive influence of the American oil companies on the State Department was neutralized, while Washington realized that for the United States to side with Britain at this moment would leave the Soviet Union the only defender of what the vast majority of the American people regarded as a just solution in Palestine.

On October 12 Herschel Johnson, the U.S. spokesman at the United Nations, announced American support for the partition plan. He suggested "only" a few territorial modifications to the proposal of the UN Committee, the most significant being the inclusion of Jaffa in the Arab state.

Two days later the Soviet delegate, Mr. Tsarapkin, made an almost impassioned plea for the creation of a Jewish state. The two-thirds majority in the Assembly seemed assured.

Bevin however had still a card to play. If the international decision could not be prevented, it might yet be frustrated. He, after all, still had his forces in Palestine. He played his card to the end.

I returned to Tel Aviv in mid-October, to find a state of high tension prevailing in the Irgun. We analyzed the forces now ranged in the international arena prepared to exercise their diverse pressures on the future of our people. The fact that the British Government had ostensibly submitted to the UN decision made little difference. In our judgment it seemed clear that Whitehall intended to frustrate the promise of British retreat.

We broadcast our analysis of British motives and purposes over our clandestine radio during October and November. We printed it in our wall posters and discussed it in interviews with foreign newspaper correspondents. We forecast the bloody events of the months that were to follow. There is no mystery about this prescience, for we never lost sight of the British purpose and policy. We were, it seems, the only ones.

The severities of this policy were not abated in the least. Within a week after the *Af-Al-Pi* had been subdued two more ships, *The Jewish State* and the *Geulah,* had been similarly disposed of by the British navy. Only, the immigrants were now sent to Cyprus and not to Germany.

In London, Mr. Bevin summoned the Minister for Panama and demanded that his government should take steps to prevent ships flying the Panamanian flag from carrying "illegal" immigrants to Palestine. In November he was still pressing the French to co-operate to the same end.

At Lake Success on October 17 Mr. Creech-Jones amplified his reiteration of Britain's determination to leave Palestine by an ominous explanation.

"We shall withdraw our forces and the Administration from Palestine," he said, "in order to show the Jews and the Arabs alike what will happen if they do not reach agreement."

In Palestine the High Commissioner warned that chaos, suffering and bloodshed would follow the departure of the British if the Jews and the Arabs did not reach agreement.

The date of Britain's departure was not mentioned. We published repeated warnings that there would be no early evacuation and that if the United Nations Assembly recommended partition, British forces would remain in the country to ensure as much protection as possible for Arab attackers. In the belief that we would be defeated by the Arabs, they would be available for us to beg them for help and to be forced to accept a "British solution" as the alternative to complete destruction.

To the Irgun a United Nations decision for a Jewish state was not a charter of independence but a recognition of our rights. If there was to be war, we would not surrender half of our already truncated country. The territory proposed for us had little room for a substantial increase in population.

Nevertheless on October 3 Rabbi Silver, on behalf of the Jewish Agency, had announced acceptance of the proposal of the United

Nations Committee—that is, of a state without western Galilee, without Jerusalem, with a population density in the narrow coastal strip higher than the average of industrial Western Europe. They had agreed to economic union with the projected Arab state and the subsidization by our people of that state. Now they were trapped into the negotiation of further "compromises," for the Americans proposed to hand Jaffa over to the Arab state, and then pressure was exerted for the Jews to give up Beersheba and parts of the Negev. Beginning with a brave-sounding declaration by Mr. Shertok that the Agency proposal was a "minimum," a defensive battle was fought which was lost from the outset. They finally accepted the excision of Jaffa, of Beersheba and a strip in the southern Negev to create a corridor between Egypt and Transjordan. The Arabs, the "partners" in this compromise, prepared for war.

The Agency leaders finally began to understand the British purpose. By October 29 Ben-Gurion had discovered that Bevin's aim had always been to perpetuate British control. Almost parenthetically Ben-Gurion consigned to the flames the very foundations of Agency policy. He now expressed a cautious suspicion of what for a month he had been reading in Irgun declarations: that Bevin was engaged in sabotaging the proposal for a Jewish state.[5] These however were no more than dim glimmerings of comprehension, for at the same time, Mr. Shertok at Lake Success, on behalf of the Agency, was appealing to the British to stay in Palestine in order to implement the partition proposal.

Immediately after Creech-Jones's first statement the Irgun renewed its call for the establishment of a provisional government which would press the British to implement their promise to leave and which would establish the machinery of statehood. At least here it seemed at first that Ben-Gurion was thinking along the same lines.

> England having announced that she will not implement any arrangement of the United Nations . . . [he said on October 2], we must inform the world, the United Nations, that we shall be the ones to implement. We ourselves. We want, we are prepared and are able to act as a Government immediately, from the beginning of the interim period, in place of the British Government which is leaving the country.[6]

In fact, though the British purpose became clear, no action that might be construed as defiant of the British Government was ever taken by Ben-Gurion. No provisional government was set up until the date finally set by the British for their departure.

We ourselves called for a national policy based on the possibility of gaining the whole country for a Jewish state and asked for the establishment of fighting unity among all the Jewish forces.[7] Ben-Gurion's reply was a renewed declaration of civil war. In mid-October, the Irgun was subjected to a vicious onslaught.

With every day Ben-Gurion's need to rid himself of the Irgun grew stronger. That autumn the danger we represented to his political ambitions must have occupied his mind more than ever.

In our broadcasts, in our wall posters, we laid bare the absurdity of the Jewish Agency's acceptance and pursuit of partition. We warned the people in terms that could be understood by any school-boy that the peace for which Ben-Gurion and his colleagues were willing to make a heavy sacrifice was a mirage and a delusion.

Haganah units launched attacks against the youngsters who pasted up our propaganda. At a number of centers throughout the country they were set upon and beaten. For the first time, too, the Haganah used firearms and two boys at Rishon-le-Zion were wounded.

They were not the only victims. Bands of Haganah members in-vaded the homes of suspected Irgunists, and some of our people were kidnaped and tortured for information. Here and there parents of the victims were beaten. Most of the attackers were young re-cruits who were carrying out their orders as good soldiers.

The reactions surprised the aggressors. The Jewish Agency was flooded with demands to put an end to the dangerous brutality. At a meeting of the Vaad Leumi, Yitshak Gruenbaum gave voice to what was certainly the feeling of the vast majority of the people. "I shall not be a party," he said, "to a union between Ben-Gurion and Bevin against Begin."

The first Haganah attacks had already taken place when I saw Begin on my return from Europe. I found him deeply disturbed. He still hoped that public opinion would quench the flames that Ben-Gurion had lit and issued repeated warnings of the inevitable conse-quences should such attacks continue. But as the days passed they spread, and after two weeks we retaliated. Punishment was meted out on the Haganah officers and members directly responsible. The young distributors of our propaganda were provided with armed guards. At Rehovot, they returned the fire of their attackers.

The Haganah leaders now proclaimed that we had launched civil war. Nevertheless, the campaign against us died down.

At Lake Success the debate continued. The United States contrived to press the Jewish Agency to make territorial concessions. Day after day Jamal Husseini, the spokesman of the Palestine Arabs, announced the utter rejection by the Arabs of any plan which included a Jewish state. At session after session Arab delegates gave notice of their intention to annihilate such a state. Yet the Jewish Agency spokesman succumbed to the State Department's importunities. The texture and spirit of their struggle is manifest in the context of a short speech made by Mr. Shertok on November 22.

> We wish to clarify one point. We have made a proposal which I see has not been adequately emphasized in the report of the subcommittee. We have proposed that the town of Beersheba and a certain area together comprising 300,000 dunams should be taken out of the Jewish State and added to the Arab State. We have agreed too that two million dunams in the southern Negev, adjoining the Egyptian border, should be joined to the Arab State and thus create a common frontier between the Arab State and Egypt. This is a considerable concession on our part in order to facilitate the establishment of the Jewish State. We ask you to remember that already in 1922 the first partition of Palestine was effected. We Jews have the right to settle in the whole of Palestine, but we believe that by our concession we are contributing to the solution of the Palestine problem.

The United States now reached a compromise with the Soviet Union. In the period between the departure of the British administration—for which the British still refused to announce a date—and the evacuation of their military forces, to take place by August 1, 1948, a committee of the United Nations, composed of representatives of five of the smaller nations, would take over governmental authority.

The final proposal took shape at last, and boundaries were laid down. The British were called upon to open a port by February 1 to enable the nascent Jewish state to bring in its repatriates.

In growing excitement first the Political Committee, then the Assembly, voted. On November 29 the partition plan was passed by a two-thirds majority. Nowhere in the plan was there any hint of how its implementation was envisaged against the violence of the Arabs and the sabotage of the British Government.

Yet when the magic words Jewish state were pronounced by the assembled nations, the mass of Jews shut their minds to the surrender of half of the already reduced territory of their Homeland; shut their ears to the loud rumblings of the mortal peril which they, and the little infant state, were now to face; did not realize the price in blood and tears they were about to pay.

The news from the United Nations was reported on the radio late at night. I was almost asleep when I heard the noise of singing and jubilation bursting in from the street. Then came a knocking at the window. One of the neighbors called excitedly "Come out. We have a state. We have a state." I did not go out. I felt utterly out of tune with the jubilation. There was nothing to sing about. I knew we had a new war on our hands.

Part Three

A NEW WAR

22

The Arabs Attack

Sporadic Arab violence broke out the day after the United Nations decision was announced. The Jewish Commercial Center in Jerusalem, just outside the Old City walls, was razed. Jews were killed in Haifa and in the border area between Jaffa and Tel Aviv. In all three cities Arab snipers from high vantage points opened a campaign of incessant harassment of the Jewish areas. Jewish transport on the main roads was attacked from ambush. The part played by the Palestine Arabs was small, the bulk of the fighting element having arrived from Syria, where a training center for volunteers had been established.

From day to day the attacks ranged farther afield, the main objective being Jewish transport between Jerusalem and Tel Aviv and on the Negev roads. Casualties mounted.

So much had been made of the military potential of the Haganah and its capacity to deal with any attack that most people took it for granted that such an attack would be suppressed with ease. For years we had been told that they were prepared for action against the Arabs should the need arise. The Haganah spokesmen had maintained that there could never be a repetition of 1936 with its lethal *havlaga*. Since the summer we had heard that the Haganah was preparing for the possibility of Arab attack. We knew of large sums of money for the purchase of arms assigned to them by the Jewish Agency, the fruits of special appeals throughout the world. Yet during these first days of Arab attack they took no action.

The British Government had already begun a campaign at Lake Success and in Washington to demonstrate that Arab opposition was fierce enough to make impossible the establishment of a Jewish state. The Jews instead of acting, talked of "moderation." The

Agency was even praised for its restraint by Creech-Jones, itself surely a matter for suspicion.[1]

For some weeks a thorough reorganization of the Irgun had been in progress. Its structure, its skills, and the nature of its striking power had been developed over the years to wage the special kind of war dictated by the character and dispositions of the British regime. The technical specialization whose efforts had evoked the admiration of the world and even of the enemy was the fruit of concentrated training and the development of a distinctive attitude of mind. Conspiracy and camouflage were its central ingredients. Now the character of the enemy had changed. The clash with the Arabs would predictably be largely in the open, whatever the disparity in numbers and whatever the degree of interference by the British forces.

Only a few of our members had had experience in open warfare, and these now formed the nucleus of a planning unit, presided over by Giddy, to carry through a program of retraining. We set up camps among the citrus groves near Ramat Gan, where hundreds of our veterans and a steady flow of new volunteers trained.

The full meetings of the High Command were now more frequent, although the character of our consultation followed its earlier pattern, with Begin as the moderator.

The British Government announced that its administration would come to an end on May 15 and the army would be evacuated by August 1. We were thus, as we warned the people, to be subjected to five months of battering by the Arabs and those who were helping them, while the British frustrated counteraction on our part and maintained a blockade on the coast to prevent the entry of Jewish arms or manpower. This would be followed—on May 15—by an Arab invasion.

The widespread underestimation of the grave dangers that hung over us—and especially of the British role behind the Arab aggression—forced on us an intensive campaign of enlightenment. Our propaganda sections worked day and night.

Early in December, I prepared an analysis of the situation and sent hundreds of copies to England—to the editors of newspapers throughout the country, from the major London dailies to the remote provincial weeklies, and to the municipal authorities throughout the land. I warned them of the part their government proposed playing in helping the Arabs fight us, and of the Irgun's intention to take the necessary counteraction.

We issued appeals to the Arabs for peace between our two peoples, warning them that the only beneficiary of civil war would be the British. Although many Arabs agreed with us, their voices were silenced. We learned of the liquidation of many Arab nonconformists. Peaceful Arab villages were converted gradually into bases for offensive action.

For ten days the Arab partisans held the field, suffering substantial casualties when encountering Jewish defense but undisturbed by any counterattack.

On the eleventh day the local Arab headquarters at Tireh near Haifa, Yazur near Tel Aviv, Shaafat near Jerusalem, and Yehudiyeh on the Tel Aviv-Lydda, were all attacked by Irgun units, blown up, and scores of casualties inflicted. In Haifa and Jaffa the Irgun attacked concentrations of Arab partisans. The traditional foregathering place of Arab terrorists at the Damascus gate in Jerusalem was bombed. At Haifa and Jaffa, at Tireh and Yehudiyeh, pitched battles took place.

These attacks had a salutary effect on Jewish morale. The descent on Tireh village had a piquant aftermath typical of the clashing motifs in the official Jewish leadership. At Haganah headquarters it was assumed, for some unexplained reason, that this attack had been delivered by their own Haifa contingent, and the official Haganah bulletin that evening reported it as such. Mr. Ben-Gurion in Jerusalem promptly seized the opportunity to praise its effectiveness. When, however, the Haifa Haganah command hastily gave their headquarters the true facts, *Davar,* the chief mouthpiece of the Jewish Agency next morning reported the same attack as a "senseless provocation."

Then at last the Haganah itself was given leave to take action, but their choice of targets proved singularly unfortunate. They blew up houses in Haifa and in several Arab villages which they described as "nests of Arab rioters." In Khasses village in Galilee, of the ten people killed in the explosion, five were children. At Selwan village outside Jerusalem, a woman and two children were injured. Near Rehovot the only casualties were a cow and a calf.

Accidents and bad luck, even inefficiency in execution, are understandable, even inevitable. What was disturbing throughout those weeks was the strangely unreal political aspects of all Haganah activity. They persisted in describing these reprisals as "punitive operations"—an empty phrase which emphasized their failure to recognize the fact that they were waging a war of life and death. But the Jewish Agency's official policy was still "moderation and non-provocation."

In mid-December the Irgun and the Jewish Agency began initial talks on the need for joining forces. We had long called for the formation of a provisional Jewish government under which all the fighting forces could unite, but this had apparently never been discussed by the Jewish Agency. Now at last they invited us to negotiate with them.

When Begin, Avraham, and I arrived at our first meeting place—the house of Tel Aviv Mizrahi leader David Zvi Pinkas—we found one member of the dominant Mapai Party, David Remez, and with him two nonconformists of the Agency Executive, Rabbi Yehuda Leib Fishman and Yitshak Gruenbaum, with another Mizrahi leader, Moshe Shapiro. Although we were soon convinced of the sincerity of their intentions, through them we measured the extent of unreality which dominated the Agency thinking. They were still persuaded that the British Government would implement the United Nations decision to open a port on February 1. Indeed, when Begin had concluded a detailed analysis of the grave consequences of the British blockade which for five long months would prevent the entry into Palestine of men and arms, Remez said, "We do not know yet on whose side the British will be," while Shapiro perfunctorily dismissed his observations with a wave of the hand: "But we shall have a port on the first of February!"

Although we tried to convince them otherwise, they were sure that within six weeks the port would be opened, allowing arms and men to arrive. Little progress was made on the major issues, but we reached an understanding on some of the practical problems of the defensive positions in Tel Aviv, already being manned by both Irgun and Haganah units, and agreed to meet again. Our negotiations were to prove protracted and difficult.

The Arab attack had been in progress for six weeks when in mid-January, Ben-Gurion, certainly the most militant of the Jewish Agency leaders, began impressing upon his followers the fact that we were at war and that a spirit of offensive was consequently crucial. Ten days before the first of February he cautiously conceded that the British would not open a port.[2]

In mid-December, the British evacuated their police from the

Jewish urban area stretching from Tel Aviv to Petah Tikva. Their troop dispositions were unaffected, but our underground precautions were substantially relaxed and there was a greater freedom of communication.

But we were far from being jubilant, knowing as we did that the gulf between our needs and our resources was large and forbidding. It was not enough to decide to convert the five thousand strong Irgun into an effective army; we had also to arm our men. The surprising intelligence that the Haganah was also painfully lacking in arms only deepened our sense of inadequacy.[3] The small quantities in our stores had to be distributed with great care in the light of emergency priorities.

We appealed to all our branches abroad to send arms and money. We began to organize, under Reuven (David Groszbard) of the High Command, our own manufacture of Sten guns and hand grenades. The willing co-operation of a manufacturer of zip-fasteners, Moshe Rubin, made possible, after several false starts, a steadily increasing supply of such weapons. Small quantities of rifles and ammunition reached us from Europe. We still had too few arms for our needs; still less for the great need that stared out at us from the calendar. For we knew that on the fifteenth of May a full-scale Arab invasion would be launched.

The immediate pressures and dangers did not deflect us from pondering larger objectives. With the rejection of partition by the Arabs we saw the obliteration of the frontiers laid down at Lake Success. The war could not be contained within the lines drawn on the map. In repelling the impending invasion we should not rest until the whole of Palestine, at least down to the Jordan, was in our hands; but the Jewish Agency had no such visions and had pledged themselves to the partition boundaries.

For the Jewish Agency, the stamp of the United Nations gave to the frontiers of the proposed state a kind of sanctity. Again and again, they repeated that they were defending the partition frontiers. Their obsession was understandable. Since they had neither fashioned nor foreseen the events that opened the road to international intervention, the decision of United Nations was in the nature of an unexpected gift.

We were certain that military exigencies would break this ridiculous spell and tried to hasten the process. We wanted to carry the war to the enemy, to break out from the partition frontiers and to push those frontiers eastward. We envisaged the evolution of tactical co-operation between us and the Haganah. We had four fronts specifically in mind: Jerusalem; Jaffa, which stabbed into Tel Aviv from the sea; the central "triangle" in the heart of the country between Shechem (Nablus), Jenin, and Tulkarm; and the Ramleh-Lydda Plain.

All these objectives might not be within reach, but we had to turn the Irgun into an instrument capable of seizing, or creating, the opportunity.

There was a second crucial question. The Jewish Agency might still be persuaded to renounce or postpone the declaration of the Jewish state. Even now two factions were in conflict within the Agency. Under the pressure of physical setbacks or foreign influence, the defeatist element might well gain the upper hand. From London, Weizmann, out of office but still commanding a substantial following in the Agency, counseled "moderation" in Palestine. To the survivors of the concentration camps in Europe, now overtaken by a third winter since their liberation, he urged "patience." There was little comfort even from the so-called militants. The United States Secretary of State, inspired by Bevin's "charges" that there were Communists among the "illegal immigrants," pressed the Jewish Agency to suspend organization of Aliyah B from Eastern Europe, and the Jewish Agency complied.[4] If the Agency could collapse so easily at such a request, how would they stand up to four more months of physical and diplomatic battering?

We resolved to give immediate and unequivocal support to a provisional government established by the Jewish Agency on or before May 15. We would place ourselves at its disposal, and under its orders disband throughout whatever territory it claimed. If, however, the Jewish Agency failed to set up a Government by May 15, the Irgun would establish a provisional government by itself or in concert with others.

The flames of Arab attacks licked at an ever-widening perimeter. Communications on all the country's main arteries were disrupted and maintained only by the organization of convoys, protected, as in 1936, by the British and again, as in 1936, denied the effective protection of counterattack. Sniping in the towns continued. Many hundreds of Jews from the Hatikvah Quarter contiguous to Jaffa had to be given shelter in Tel Aviv. The Arabs began making probing sallies into Jewish villages.

Then came the first massed attack on an outlying settlement by some five hundred Syrians on Kfar Szold at the Syrian border. It was followed by an onslaught on the Ramat Rahel Kibbutz outside Jerusalem. The offensive against the Jewish rural perimeter went on for five months, but from the first there was a resolute defense, inspired by the new and bolder policy of the Haganah: that all settlements must be defended to the last.

The scale of Haganah counteractions mounted very slowly, however. There were a few effective sallies into Arab village bases and a series of demonstrative, if minor reprisal attacks—shooting at an Arab bus near Haifa, blowing up a garage at Ramleh. Still, in the wake of the Irgun's successive engagements of the enemy at his own bases, the tactics of the Haganah were assuming the same counteroffensive pattern.

The Agency's subservience to the British remained unchanged, although the latter were openly exerting themselves to arm the Arabs and to disarm the Jews. A number of police armories in Arab centers were "taken over" by the Arabs. Again and again British police patrols met Haganah units and demanded the surrender of their arms. Haganah soldiers, acting on standing orders, meekly complied.

The Irgun tried to apply its still limited resources to the most effective possible use, penetrating and destroying Arab bases; once, to that end, even landing a small unit in Jaffa from the sea. The Lehi which, like the Jewish Agency, had given way to a strange optimism, resumed activity and used similar tactics.

As 1948 approached there was disheartening news of a slackening of support for the Irgun from abroad. This had its own logic. As the Jewish Agency was using the Haganah to fight in defense of the new state, there was no need for the Irgun's continued separate existence.

This mood was soon to pass. At that moment it caused us great concern and did considerable damage. It was particularly manifest in South Africa, from where so much of our earlier overseas support had come. When two or three gloomy reports arrived from Raphael Kotlowitz, the head of the Irgun branch there, indicating that the Revisionist Party leaders there were following the popular trend, accepting Jewish Agency assurances that the Irgun was now superfluous and refusing to co-operate in raising funds, we decided to send a member of the High Command to South Africa.

Unfortunately for me, I was the only candidate for the mission. Every other member of the High Command might have to wait for weeks for a South African visa, and would expose himself to the scrutiny of the British who now performed South Africa's consular business in Palestine. I was away from Palestine for almost three weeks. After initial difficulties my mission was successful. Kotlowitz and his group were enabled to launch an "unofficial" drive for funds. In the months that followed South African aid was indeed invaluable.

During my absence, the Irgun broke off formal negotiations with the Jewish Agency. Three of our officers were kidnaped by the Haganah in Haifa. Later one, Yedidia Segal, was found dead in an Arab village, in circumstances that suggested he had been shot while in the custody of the Haganah.

The tautened pitch of the war impressed itself on me within minutes of my return to Palestine. The driver of the taxi service from Lydda airport hurled his car toward Tel Aviv at frightening speed, a good twenty kilometers an hour faster than on my outward journey three weeks earlier.

The Arab assault had spread. Jewish transport throughout the country was now in many places moving along improvised routes. Traffic from Tel Aviv to Jerusalem made a wide detour to the west of Ramleh, rejoining the main road at Bab el Wad. The only road through the narrow valley in the Judean Hills was under constant attack. Supplies to Jerusalem were maintained only through the cool courage of the truck and bus drivers and their Haganah escorts, but at a mounting cost in casualties. There had been mass attacks against outlying Jewish settlements. The group of settlements centered on Kfar Etzion near Hebron was almost entirely cut off. In mid-January an effort to reinforce the beleaguered inhabitants had failed tragically. Thirty-five members of the Haganah had been ambushed as they picked their way through the hills near Hebron. Fighting to their last round of ammunition, they had been killed to a man. The British provided protection to convoys bringing supplies to the Etzion bloc and to beleaguered Yehiam in Galilee—provided they did not carry arms or ammunition. Both villages continued valiant defense. In the Old City of Jerusalem a force of Haganah and Irgun soldiers, under unified command, were defending the Jewish

Quarter and its 2000 inhabitants. The Quarter was cut off. Haganah efforts to break through from the New City had failed.

There were still few Haganah counterattacks. The Irgun was grievously restricted for lack of ammunition and unable to mount its own attacks.

An attempt by an Irgun unit to confiscate arms from a British military camp near Haifa had failed. The funds we raised in our underground tradition from known sympathizers were pitifully small in relation to the infinitely greater needs of the war. In early February we were faced with the prospect of suspending our own manufacture of arms.

After much debate we decided to make a direct appeal to the people and launch a public campaign for Irgun funds. This meant drawing a large part of the organization out of the underground and removing the cloak of conspiracy from many hundreds of our members. Although the British police had retired from the Tel Aviv zone, they were still no farther away than Jaffa.

The alternative at that moment however was to suspend our only dependable source of arms: our own production. Through our radio and our wall literature we announced the "Iron Fund." In Mograbi Square in Tel Aviv every afternoon over a loudspeaker an Irgun spokesman addressed the crowds. We mobilized every available man and woman, armed them with official receipt forms bearing our emblem, and sent them out on a house-to-house collecting drive. The results exceeded our most optimistic expectations.

Few heeded the Jewish Agency's frantic exhortations to them not to help us. Several days after the opening of our campaign, the Irgun unit in charge of the Mograbi Square meetings discovered on arriving at the square that they had been preceded by a group of Haganah members who occupied their speaking platform. A crowd gathered. Our men proclaimed that they would speak from a building on the other side of the square. The crowd objected and told the Haganah men to move away. The latter refused. The Irgun men repeated their appeal to the crowd to join them on the other side of the square, but the people still refused loudly. The commander of the Haganah unit gave an order and a shower of hand grenades was flung into the crowd. Many were wounded. When an armed Irgun patrol, attracted by the tumult, raced into the square the Haganah unit at last moved. Some were caught and searched and a quantity of hand grenades confiscated from them.

We appealed to our members not to be tempted into retaliatory attacks. These appeals were effective. The provocations of the Jewish Agency never developed into civil war.

How deliberate the provocation was now emerged from an unexpected source. The British High Commissioner angrily revealed that it was in response to an Agency proposal that the British police had been withdrawn in December from the Tel Aviv area. The Agency had promised in return that they would establish a public force of their own to liquidate the Irgun and the Lehi. This promise they had obviously not kept. They had made it in the belief that within a month or so (specifically when the British opened a port on February 1) the Arab "disturbances" would be over.

There was no mistaking the range and thrust of British strategy that winter. All departments—military, economic, administrative, propaganda, and diplomatic—were in full operation in London, New York, Europe, and Palestine itself. There were some unforeseen aberrations in the general pattern of behavior. When in early February a group of British soldiers or policemen blew up the building of the *Palestine Post* in Jerusalem, there was no reason to suppose that this act of terror had been ordered by the High Commissioner or the G.O.C. No one believed either that official orders were given for the pre-dawn attack in Ben Yehuda Street in Jerusalem where fifty men, women, and children, still sleeping in their beds, were killed and a hundred more were injured. The official explanation was that these operations were carried out by groups of deserters.

The tactics of official assaults were more devious. Haganah groups guarding Jewish positions in Jerusalem, in Haifa, on the main road near Tel Aviv, again in Haifa, again in Jerusalem, were disarmed by British army units and left, or delivered, to the mercy of armed Arab crowds. In one memorable incident four boys on watch in the Meah Shearim quarter in Jerusalem were rounded up by a British patrol, disarmed and driven in a British truck to the Damascus Gate, the base for Arab irregulars. There, they were forced to alight from the truck and in a few minutes they were done to death by the Arab crowd.

Another operation in the same spirit was successfully carried out at the Hayotsek Factory near Tel Aviv on the Jerusalem road. The factory having been partially destroyed in an Arab attack, a Haganah unit was sent in to help the workers restore the damage and to set up a guard on the premises. A British unit in two trucks arrived and its officer asked for permission to enter the factory. Permission was granted. The Haganah soldiers and the workers were at once lined up and disarmed, the premises being searched for more arms. The British unit then drove off. As they disappeared round the first bend in the road, a mass of Arabs armed with axes and iron bars, obviously waiting in the ditch across the road, came rushing in to the attack and eight Haganah men were killed.

These were extreme applications of the policy of disarming Jews.[5] Occasionally whole districts were searched, but usually the actions were directed at small or isolated Haganah groups.

A similar operation was the frequent removal by the British of road blocks set up by the Haganah to impede the progress of potential Arab attack. When the Jewish Agency protested, the British authorities intoned the traditional formula that they were responsible for maintaining law and order and announced that road blocks required a government permit!

Jewish areas surrounded and cut off by Arab offensive action were denied reinforcements or military supplies. All approaches to the Old City of Jerusalem, where the pitifully small joint force of Haganah and Irgun soldiers desperately held off Arab onslaught, were sealed off by the British patrols stationed at its periphery. To the Etzion bloc in the Hebron hills beating off increasingly powerful mass assaults, and to embattled Yehiam in Galilee, the British did indeed allow convoys of supplies to go through—but under strict check to ensure that they included neither men nor arms.

The cumulative circumscription of Jewish defense was a very real problem, but the major thrust of the British physical offensive was far grander in scope. A naval blockade prevented arms and men from reaching us, while the British allowed a steady stream of Arab soldiers to cross the frontier from the Arab states. By the end of February, according to British official estimate, five thousand Arabs had crossed into Palestine in this way.

Finally, the British Government continued to send arms and military equipment to the Arab countries. They did not conceal this. On the contrary: Mr. Bevin made plain his resolve, in statements in Parliament, that the shipments would continue, as he explained it, in fulfillment of treaty obligations to the Arab states. The Arab states, he concluded, had a right to expect Britain to honor her undertakings.

The British diplomatic and propaganda offensive was equally energetic and skillful. It was not a difficult matter to make nonsense of the United Nations timetable for setting up the two states. The government was in British hands. If there was a danger that the implementation committee appointed by the United Nations might at least lessen the impact of administrative chaos which the British were arranging for May 15, it was simple enough to prevent the committee from entering Palestine at all. This in fact they did, announcing their refusal to allow the committee to come before May 1.

As for the dispatch of an international militia (which would have to include a Soviet unit) to defend and maintain the United Nations decision, the British did not even have to exert themselves to prevent that eventuality. Such an idea was in fact only wishful thinking on the part of the Jewish Agency.

The only remaining possibility of United Nations action was a decision to authorize and arm a Jewish militia to guard the partition frontier. This was indeed proposed at Lake Success by the implementation committee but died a natural death.

As counterpoint to this many-pronged policy, the British urged on the world that partition was impossible, that the decisions of November 29 were a grievous blunder perpetrated by well-meaning amateurs, and that some other solution to the problem must be sought.

Britain's official resolve to "get out come what may" was now tempered by unofficial observations that if pressed hard enough she would consider resuming the heavy burden of government, but on her own terms.

23

Battle of the Roads

If our fate had depended on action by the United States we should
have been either subjugated anew by the British or overwhelmed by
superior Arab force. The subsequent friendship of the United States
for the State of Israel has obscured this simple truth. It may be that
at first the American Government believed that the Jews would be
able to withstand any conceivable attack; that they underrated Britain's resolve to frustrate the partition plan; that the problem of its
defense simply did not occur to them.

This myopia, if it ever existed, could only have been a temporary
affliction. When events showed that we were in desperate need, at
least of arms, and that there was a danger of the United Nations
resolution being nullified by force, it became clear that the United
States Government was not going to lift a finger to help us. Whether
Mr. Truman even tried to assert himself, as he had done successfully
in November, against the traditional policies and the pressure of his
State Department, is difficult to say. Reading between the lines of
his memoirs,[1] it seems likely that he did; but if so he was overborne
by the State Department Establishment.

In January an American embargo on all arms to the Middle East
was added to the British blockade. Since the Arabs were assured by
the British of all the supplies they wanted, the only practical significance of the embargo was its manifestation of American indifference to the fate of the Jews.

Zionist appeals against the embargo were vigorous and sustained.
Public criticism by Americans was outspoken and bitter. The Government was charged with hypocrisy and collaboration with Britain.
Neither protests nor attacks had any effect on the new policy. The
embargo was never lifted; indeed it was rigidly enforced. A consign-

ment of explosives destined for the Haganah in January, a consignment of arms and ammunition acquired for the Irgun in April, were impounded by the American authorities and the organizers arrested.

In the shadow of the embargo, the words and the diplomatic maneuvers employed by the United States spokesman at Lake Success made little difference. Yet it was soon evident that even there American policy seemed to follow the British line.

When, in early February, Britain's formal reply to the recommendations of the Implementation Committee made it utterly plain that the committee would not be allowed to operate, Washington did not even enter a formal protest. By the end of February, United States participation in the discussion at Lake Success was confined, in effect, to cataloguing reasons why it was constitutionally impossible for the Security Council to enforce partition.

Sabotaged by Britain, torpedoed by the United States while the other member states looked on, the partition of Palestine as a United Nations project was all but dead. Then the United States itself boldly delivered the final blow. On March 20 Mr. Warren Austin officially announced American abandonment of the partition plan. In its place he proposed a system of international trusteeship. He had no detailed plan ready. The wish that fathered the new theory became apparent a week later when Mr. Truman, in a speech defending the trusteeship proposal, said in a burst of impetuous petulance:

"Of course I don't want the British to leave. They were going to leave on August 1 and then suddenly decided to leave on May 15. I don't know why."

Now, at this admission, there came an answering British voice. Not an official one, but that of the respected Washington correspondent of the London *Times,* who wrote what was being whispered confidentially by British agents everywhere: the British would be prepared, out of a sense of international responsibility, to remain in Palestine, on condition, as so often repeated by Mr. Bevin in 1947, that there should be an "agreed policy"—the British grand design with U.S. approval.

The collapse of United States support for Jewish independence stemmed from the traditional policy of the State Department that the Arabs must be appeased because of the oil resources in their territories allegedly vital to American defense and to the profits of the American oil companies. In his memoirs Mr. Truman suggests that some of the men in the State Department "were also inclined to be anti-Semitic."[2]

Yet American policy would not have faltered if at the same time there had not been a swift deterioration of relations with the Soviet Union. The breach, whose growing shadow had inspired Bevin's belief in the United States inevitable acquiescence in the British solution for Palestine, widened ominously that winter. Mutual fear and suspicion produced tension similar to that of the summer of 1939.

Ever since the Soviet Union in the summer of 1947 had set her face against the Marshall Plan, the outline of two solid hostile blocs had become increasingly clear.

That winter any Western statesman with a claim to realism occupied himself with the practical problems of a possible war with the Soviet Union. The five countries of Western Europe negotiated a comprehensive treaty of economic and military co-operation. Liaison between London and Washington grew closer and warmer. The pressure of the British representatives in Washington on their American colleagues to reverse their Palestine policy assumed a new significance. To jettison partition and abandon the Jews was now presented as a necessity for Western defense. In an address at the end of January, James V. Forrestal, Truman's Secretary of Defense, bluntly told a Senate committee that "partition endangered American oil resources." The picture of an America attacked by Russia at any moment and hamstrung for lack of oil because of a sentimental whim began to frighten many American policy-makers.

The climax came at the end of February. In a swift coup, the Communist Prime Minister of Czechoslovakia forced a change of government on President Benes which effectively transferred full powers to the Communists. In a telegram to his government a week later the American military governor in Germany reported "a subtle change in the Soviet attitude which I cannot define but which gives me the feeling that (war) may come with dramatic suddenness."

Thirteen days after the Communist coup in Czechoslovakia, Jan Masaryk jumped—or was pushed—through a window to his death. In the Western countries, particularly in the United States, the impulse to forceful Western unity attained a passionate climax.[3] On March 18 Mr. Truman, in a trenchant speech attacking Russia's drive for expansion in Europe, announced the resumption of selective service for the American armed forces. Two days later came the announcement of the abandonment by the United States of the United Nations partition plan for Palestine.

A month went by before the United States even presented a new plan to the United Nations. State Department experts no doubt expected a collapse of Jewish will or the exhaustion of a starved Jewish defense. Some of the leaders of the Jewish Agency showed signs of bowing to American pressure. The power of Jewish determination now pervading the people as a whole proved stronger than the strange alliance of forces ranged against us. Whether the Jewish Agency would have withstood an actual decision of the United Nations to reverse the partition decision it is impossible to say. In actuality, no such decision came before May 14, when the Jewish state was declared.

In Palestine, the undeclared war continued as throughout March the battle of the roads raged. By the end of the month nearly all the main arteries of Jewish communications had been cut. The Negev was severed from the rest of the country. Jerusalem was cut off from the coast and from the settlements in the Judean Hills. Only the road from Tel Aviv to Haifa was held open. The Haganah's store of armored vehicles had been gravely depleted. Casualties, in men and officers, were very heavy.

Arab attacks on Jewish transport in the Negev had continued without any counteraction by the Haganah. When, after two months, the Haganah did launch retaliatory attacks, the British intervened and offered in appeasement to provide escorts for Jewish transport. They made it a condition that the convoys should be completely unarmed.

The Haganah rejected this offer. Their armored cars, they said, must accompany the convoys. They agreed only that while the convoy was passing through the Arab villages on its way, the green berets would not protrude through the peepholes in the armored cars.

The arrangement lasted a month. In mid-March, the British liaison officer baldly announced that no further British escorts would be provided. When the Haganah tried to resume its independent escorts, it was discovered that the road had suddenly been torn up at numerous points. The road was abandoned.

Communications were now transferred to the roundabout coastal road, used by both British and Arabs and left intact. The Arabs had now learned how to use electrically operated mines against specific targets and did so frequently and to great effect. Attacks by Haganah units to prevent the mine laying or to engage the Arabs laying mines were barred by British patrols. The Haganah orders were not to get involved in shooting with the British and so they withdrew. After running the Arab gauntlet for ten days, with a heavy toll of vehicles and men, the Haganah gave up this road too.

On that same March 26, a convoy got through to Jerusalem, the first in ten days. It included the major part of the armored cars operating on this road. The convoy was sent on to the Etzion bloc—which for more than two months had received neither supplies nor reinforcements. The Arabs, taken by surprise, did not attack it on its way south from Jerusalem.

On the convoy's return journey, they set up road blocks along its route. The convoy succeeded in breaking through some of them, but was finally stopped at Nebi Daniel. The men abandoned the vehicles and entrenched themselves in a building in the village. Here for two days they fought back an attack sustained by successive waves of Arab soldiers. Left with a few rounds of ammunition to each man, they sent a radio appeal to Jerusalem for help.

A British unit now intervened. The officer undertook to escort the besieged Jews to Jerusalem on condition that the armored cars were handed over. The Haganah commander, with a number of his men wounded, accepted the British offer. The British officer did not even pretend to take the armored cars but simply handed them over to the Arabs.

That catastrophic month in 1948 stiffened the resolve of the Jewish people to fight to the last. It was in the battles for the roads as the winter turned to spring that the Haganah found its soul. Those battles convinced them that we were engaged in a life or death struggle; that sheer survival required victory and that only a supreme effort of will could bring us that victory.

Traveling today through the hills of Judea, up from Bab el Wad to Jerusalem, one can see by the roadside, at frequent intervals, the burnt-out husks of the little armored vehicles destroyed in the bloody battles fought by the Haganah and the Palmach, as the Arabs, holding the heights on both sides, poured fire into that valley of death. They are a modest monument to an epic.

Begin, Avraham, and I renewed negotiations with the Jewish Agency representatives. We urged the immediate proclamation of a government. We offered our loyalty to one dedicated to the establishment and defense of the Jewish state. To no avail. We therefore continued the discussion, clause by clause, of an operational agreement with the Haganah.

There was no difficulty in reaching agreement in the area of operations where we were both fighting. The difficulties arose out of the historic differences of our attitudes toward the British. We insisted on recognition of the "presence" of the British in the struggle, refusing to countenance or accept hostile British action without resistance or retaliation. We would not allow our men to be disarmed by the British; nor would we forego any opportunity that offered of seizing British arms. The Haganah had by now officially abandoned its policy of timidly surrendering arms to the British whenever called upon to do so, but they would not consider retaliatory action against British forces.

The negotiations were beclouded by our knowledge that a group of Mapai led by Ben-Gurion and some of the Haganah leaders were opposed to the negotiations; and by our memory of the December deal with the British High Commissioner when he was "promised" the liquidation of the Irgun and the Lehi.

Finally, on March 8, the last clause was hammered into shape; and we all signed the agreement, which was brief and uncomplicated:

In the static defense sectors, Irgun posts would be under Haganah command, effected through Irgun officers.

Irgun plans for attack on the Arab sector would be subject to prior approval of the Haganah. This would apply also to plans for reprisals against the British.

The Irgun would also carry out operations assigned to it by the Haganah Command.

The Irgun however would always resist attempts at disarming them by the British irrespective of Haganah policy.

Plans for seizing arms from the British would be worked out jointly and carried out by mutual agreement.

The Irgun would not be interfered with in its objects of raising funds, though not by confiscation, and the Jewish Agency would make it known that we were *not* receiving funds from Agency sources.

This agreement was to come into effect only after we had worked out all the details and after its ratification by the Zionist General Council. We drank an optimistic toast. We did not know that the diehards in the Jewish Agency were strong enough to delay the agreement for seven whole weeks.

24

A Desperate Mission

The day after we signed our agreement with the Jewish Agency, I began to prepare for a trip to Europe and the United States. I was to mobilize help and reinforcements in arms and men; I was to determine why help had not already reached us; and I was to take whatever action I could to speed up the process. I arrived in Paris on March 27.

Two days earlier, Dr. Ariel, in the name of the Irgun, had handed to the French Foreign Ministry a memorandum proposing a secret agreement between us. It outlined the common interest on which such an agreement would be based "between France and a Hebrew Palestine as the Irgun envisages it." The Irgun, for its part, could offer only future good will in return for the practical help we proposed France should accord us.

We had two specific immediate requirements. We asked France to provide "the necessary facilities for the organization of a base for training and, for the time being, for concentrating one brigade in its metropolitan or colonial territory." We also requested the provision of "the armament and the supplies necessary for the modern equipment for two infantry brigades. One of these," continued the memorandum, "is in Palestine. The other will be concentrated in French territory and should reach Palestine about 15 May."

This memorandum was the culmination of a diplomatic campaign Ariel had been waging in a number of departments of the French Government for the past two years. His unfortunate suspension at the end of 1946 from his post in the Irgun had not discouraged him. In the meantime he had been invited to work for the Hebrew Committee of National Liberation, which was well served by Ariel's excellent political connections. He had maintained good personal relations with Irgun officers. Lankin and Eli kept in touch with him and on my own visits to Paris I always spent a few hours with him.

With the help of Madame Vayda, Ariel obtained permission for more than 20,000 "displaced persons" to enter France. During the tensions surrounding the *Exodus 1947* at Port de Bouc in the summer of 1947, he had learned from Marc Pages, Head of the Aliens Department in the Ministry of the Interior and his assistant François Rousseau, that the Jewish Agency seemed ready to succumb to British pressure; and Ariel, accompanied by Eri Jabotinsky, persuaded Shaul Meirov, the Haganah officer responsible for operations in Europe, against such a surrender.

Toward the end of 1947 Lankin had restored Ariel's status as the Irgun's diplomatic representative. Ariel tried to persuade his friends in the administration of the profound importance to France that the Jews repel the Arab onslaught, and of the Irgun's vital need for immediate help. On March 23, Jacques Boissier, *chargé de mission* in the office of the Foreign Minister, asked Ariel to set down the proposal in writing for the Minister.

On March 27, the day I arrived in Paris, Boissier wrote Ariel that he had communicated the memorandum to the Minister who "would no doubt study it and discuss it with his colleagues."

Ten weeks later the French Government gave us the arms, which were landed on the *Altalena*.

The *Altalena* was an American landing ship tank, bought from the Second World War surpluses by the Hebrew Committee. The ship had originally been intended for an Aliyah B operation, but because of the intensification of the Arab attack, the Hebrew Committee had agreed to the Irgun request to hold it for the purpose of bringing to Palestine a contingent of fighters from Europe, with as large a consignment of arms and ammunition and supplies as the ship could carry. It was in recognition of this design that the boat had been given its name, *Altalena* being the pseudonym used by Jabotinsky in his early writings.

Manned by American Jewish volunteers, the ship had arrived in European waters, the crew being ready to continue the voyage eastward to make their contribution to the defense of the Jewish state. But we could not give the order to sail before the second week of May, the eve of British departure from Palestine, and we had no arms for them. Lankin persuaded them to "fill in" by sailing the

Altalena as a cargo ship on the short run between Marseilles and the North African ports.

When, on the eve of my departure from Paris for New York, Lankin and I had a final discussion of our situation, we could not see the link that was being forged between our approach to the French Government and the ship which that week had berthed at Port de Bouc. The prospect was one of almost unrelieved gloom.

Two months had passed since Begin's appeal for help to all our units and friends abroad. So far the only response was from South Africa—and that after I had gone there. The fateful fifteenth of May and the Arab invasion were only seven weeks away.

Our great lack was money. The ship was at our disposal. Many thousands of men were available. We had only to arrange the formalities for their crossing various frontiers and their transport. However, in France, a supplies committee headed by Colonel Jakson[1] had achieved astonishing results. Large stocks of various supplies, from steel helmets to boots, had been donated by enthusiastic Jews. There were hopes of obtaining quantities of arms—rifles and ammunition—from various irregular sources.

But this was a small fraction of what we needed. Most frustrating was the situation in the United States. We had not received one single dollar from America. The propaganda machine of the Hebrew Committee was now operating in Europe, and their expenditures were no doubt greater than ever before; but of all our "family," it was least conscious of the change that had taken place in the nature of the Irgun's fight or the mortal dangers which we all would face by the middle of May.

The next day I flew to New York, where I spent three and a half unpleasant weeks. I was the first member of the High Command to visit the United States and had to make several difficult decisions without reference to headquarters.

First I was faced with the problem of the Revisionist Party. Though it had an energetic and able executive director in Dr. Benzion Netanyahu, it was still a nearly moribund branch of the world movement, failing to attract more than a handful of American-born members and sympathizers. In the preceding years one of its primary activities had been to work against the Hebrew Committee of National Liberation. Its initial hostility to the Hebrew-Jew thesis had been broadened into an all-embracing antagonism. Whether for this reason or otherwise it had not distinguished itself by any special support for the Irgun during the underground struggle.

Dr. Israel Lifschitz, the South African Betari who had carried out several missions for the Irgun in Europe, had recently been sent to the United States to investigate the possibilities of direct fund-raising for the Irgun. Lifschitz's instructions were to seek co-operation wherever he could find it. He told me that the Revisionist Party in America was now very keen to launch a campaign for funds for the Irgun. They believed that they could reach many sources which the Hebrew Committee was unable to tap. They made one condition. The proceeds of their collections would be shared fifty-fifty between the Irgun and the Revisionist Party of America.

I rejected this condition emphatically. Lifschitz informed the Revisionists of my veto. Several unpleasant meetings with the local leaders followed. Their anxiety to make some contribution to the struggle seemed to be strictly conditioned by the benefits that would accrue to their local organization. My arguments failed to move them.

Even more unpleasant was my encounter with the Hebrew Committee. I presented Samuel Merlin, the acting Chairman of the Committee,[2] with an urgent demand from the High Command for the transfer to the Irgun of a substantial sum of money. Merlin is a man for whose qualities my admiration has never wavered, but the emergency was harsh and I put our demand in forthright terms. There was little need to explain the situation. Merlin understood it as well as we did. No doubt he wished to help; but the machinery built could not be retooled overnight. Merlin pleaded poverty—heavy expenses and reduced income. The American League for a Free Palestine—their mass organization—was launching a new campaign which would take time. They had transferred moneys to Europe to finance the League in France, and to maintain the *Altalena,* which was a heavy burden. There was no money to be found for the battle in Palestine itself.

He was critical of our establishing an authority in the United States independent of the Hebrew Committee, told me that Lifschitz was said to be working with the Revisionists, and demanded that he be withdrawn or subjected to the authority of the Hebrew Committee.

Turned down by our representatives in the richest Jewish community in the world, I applied the decision we had reached in Tel Aviv.

With Merlin's *non possumus* in my ears, I sought out Rabbi Abba Hillel Silver.

Rabbi Silver, then at the height of his public career, was the head of the Zionist Emergency Committee which conducted the Zionist political effort in the United States. He was the most forceful of the so-called "activist" leaders in the movement. He was forthright and dignified in his public posture. These qualities, combined with an unusual oratorical excellence, suggested a colorful and determined leader. There is little doubt that his diplomatic interventions at the White House in the autumn of 1947 had strengthened the hand of President Truman in overcoming the resistance of the State Department to the idea of a Jewish state.

Silver was sympathetic to the Irgun. Notwithstanding his routine denunciations of "terrorism" to which on suitable occasions he felt he had to give expression, he did little to hide his true feelings and opinions. In a meeting with Begin in the underground, he had once promised to help if circumstances permitted. He had been vigorous in opposing the efforts of our enemies in the American Zionist Organization to achieve far-reaching resolutions against us. His hostility to the Hebrew Committee was as fierce and unrelenting as that of all the other official Zionist leaders. He would never admit that the success of Zionist propaganda in America had been made possible by the brilliant work of the committee. Like the other Zionist leaders, Silver vigorously opposed the Hebrew-Jew thesis and was repelled by some of the committee's publicity methods.

At this time he represented the thoughts and feelings, and was backed by the resources, of most of the organized Zionists in the United States. In Tel Aviv we had decided that if the Hebrew Committee would not send us direct help commensurate with our need and their own propaganda, we must at least try to secure that help from other sources in America. We would call on Silver to translate his sympathy and that of a large segment of American Zionists for the Irgun into material help in the struggle in which we were engaged.

My effort failed. Yet I feel that the truth will not have been fully served if I do not reveal the second part of the decision we took in Tel Aviv which shaped my attitude to Silver. If it became clear that the substantial and immediate aid we required was obtainable only through Silver, and if the promise of such aid was made conditional on our public repudiation of the Hebrew Committee as our representatives in the United States, I was to accept the condition.

I met Silver a few days after my conversation with Merlin and found him a good listener. I said all I had to say without a single interruption. He kept all his comments to the end. I spoke at length, but the thesis was simple.

The continued separate existence of the Irgun was essential for two reasons. First, we could not be certain that a majority of Silver's colleagues in the Jewish Agency in Palestine (at this time under severe pressure by the American State Department) might not decide to "postpone" setting up a government and declaring a state. The second reason was our strategic purpose of canceling the frontiers of partition. Whenever and wherever the offensive was possible, the Irgun would carry it as far as possible this side of the Jordan. When the long-delayed direct talks with the Haganah took place we proposed to reach an understanding with them on these lines.

On the proclamation of the state, we would disband and place our forces at the disposal of the government. As for Jerusalem, if the Jewish Government submitted to its internationalization, the Irgun in Jerusalem would continue to exist as a separate body with the avowed aim of bringing the city within the area of Jewish sovereignty.

We could not fulfill these purposes without substantial help. We expected Dr. Silver to push through the Zionist Emergency Committee the immediate grant of a half million dollars for the Irgun. I assured him that the very publication of such a decision, with its implication of co-operation between the official Zionists and the widely beloved Irgun, would evoke an explosion of enthusiasm, with a corresponding financial response far exceeding the sum granted to us.

Silver astonished me by the warmth of his reply. He was, he said, most impressed with our conception of the "division of roles" between the Irgun and the Haganah. He believed that the zeal and efficiency of the Irgun made its execution most feasible and he favored it wholeheartedly. Moreover, he believed that an Irgun striking force would have a greater psychological effect on the enemy than the Haganah. This would be the case especially if a Jewish offensive was in progress. He certainly believed that the Irgun were entitled to the help of all Jews irrespective of affiliation.

Nevertheless he could not accede to my appeal. He would have had no reservations in putting our case to the Emergency Committee, he said, but he had no hope of persuading a majority of the committee to allocate money to the Irgun. He was certain to be outvoted. The result, therefore, of his even raising the proposal in the committee would only be a loss of influence.

I asked him:

"Dr. Silver, if you agree with our thesis, isn't it obvious that acceding to our request may make a substantial difference in the very size and conformation of the state, may eliminate the monstrous and dangerous features of partition not only in the east but in the north as well? If the Lebanese join in the attack on us, we might well, in counterattack, reach the Litany River and break the back of our water problem. At the crucial, pivotal moments in history, great results may be achieved with relatively small effort. Do you not think, therefore, that at this moment in history perhaps the most important thing you could be doing is to find a way of helping the Irgun achieve this result? If you made this a major issue at the Emergency Committee, you would overcome the opposition. In view of what is involved, it is surely worth trying, it is surely worth risking being in a minority."

Silver did not change his mind, nor did I find a more receptive attitude in his chief colleague, Emanuel Neumann, whom I visited between my two talks with Silver.

To this day, I believe that I did not misjudge the strength of Silver's position at that moment. Though opposed and often sabotaged by his opponents—who were backed by Ben-Gurion and the Mapai—he was still, in April 1948, indispensable to the Zionist image in the United States, as an advocate of the Jewish cause. For a brief two or three years it had seemed that a new great leader had appeared in the Jewish national movement. That afternoon in New York, however, I made my own evaluation. Silver for all his qualities, was something short of great. His later career confirmed my estimate.

In spite of Silver's lack of co-operation, the financial tide turned while I was in New York. One hundred thousand dollars arrived from the Argentine, collected by Dr. Mirelman, the veteran Revisionist, and one hundred thousand from China, the result of the visit of Mordechai Olmert. Another fifty thousand dollars was scraped together by various friends.

Isaac Kaplan of Johannesburg arrived in New York with good

news from Central Africa. In Kenya he had helped organize the escape from the internment camp there of four Irgun and two Lehi members. The escaped men were headed by Yaacov Meridor, Begin's predecessor. It was his sixth escape. The camouflage arrangements in the camp, including the construction of padded figures to represent the escapees in bed, had been so successful that for a whole fortnight the British did not even know about the escape. Our South African branch had played a crucial part in organizing the escape from the moment the six emerged from the tunnel they had dug at Gilgil. The men were met near the camp by Bernard Woolf, a South African pilot. He had prepared relays of motorcars to bring the escapees to the Belgian Congo. Passports with forged visas, all prepared in the camp, had brought them safely past the Kenya, Uganda, and Belgian Congo frontier authorities. In the Congo they were met by Isaac Kaplan, who arranged their flight to Brussels and thence to Paris. They were now in Paris.

Isaac was on his way to Canada. Woolf was already there, negotiating for the purchase of planes. The plan, Isaac told me, had the backing of H.Q. in Palestine and might even have originated there. Isaac had been told by Meridor to ask me to introduce him to the Hebrew Committee for financial help. I was dismayed at this development. Our capacity to carry out our essential and crucial plans was gravely jeopardized through lack of means. How could we afford to buy planes? I made my attitude clear to Isaac. However, since Woolf was already in Canada, I put Isaac in touch with the Hebrew Committee.

I failed to follow up my opposition to the scheme. I did not exert myself on my return to Paris to get it dropped. Though it probably would not have helped, I should at least have tried. The Canadian planes were to prove a source of prolonged and expensive anxiety.

25

The Refugees

In April 1948, the scene in Palestine was transformed. The Arab monopoly of offensive was broken. Jewish counteroffensive achieved results of historic significance.

The plight of Jerusalem, cut off from the rest of the country, was of much concern. The Haganah Command decided to make a supreme effort to reopen the road into the city and decided to capture the villages serving the Arabs as forward bases along the route. Operation Nahshon was born, in which for the first time the Haganah carried out a two-pronged offensive operation, with a substantial force of 1500 men.

The scale of this operation was made possible by the arrival at the last moment of two consignments of arms from Czechoslovakia —one by a plane that landed on an abandoned airfield, the other by boat, the *Nora,* which evaded the British blockade. The Haganah was enriched by 4500 rifles and 200 machine guns.[1]

The offensive was only partly successful. It was launched at the two ends of the road in Arab-held territory. At the western end, in the plain of Ayalon—where once the moon had stood still for Joshua —the villages beyond Latrun were captured without resistance. At the Jerusalem end the road was largely cleared from Bab el Wad, the entrance to the defile through the hills for fifteen miles, to Jerusalem.

The most important victory was that at Kastel, a village set in the hills five miles from Jerusalem. The village was captured on April 2, but was lost again under heavy counterattack by a superior Arab force. The battle swayed back and forth for five days before the village was finally captured by the Haganah on April 9.

The central stretch of three miles from Latrun to Bab el Wad was not attacked at all, because a British force was stationed at Latrun. With the two sections of the operation completed, three large convoys got through to Jerusalem in quick succession, bringing substantial supplies to the hard-pressed population. On the third convoy the Arabs mounted a fierce attack at Bab el Wad, where a running battle continued all day. The casualties were so heavy that now no further convoy was attempted. The siege of Jerusalem began, and was to last eight weeks.

In the midst of these battles, on the eve of the Haganah's final attack on Kastel, three miles away a combined force of Irgun and Lehi attacked and captured an Arab village on the outskirts of Jerusalem. From this village the Jewish western suburbs of the city had been subjected to constant sniping. Through it ran a north-south line of Arab communication to the front in the hills, where the great battles for control of the road were raging. With the prevailing shortage of arms, its capture was a major undertaking. Hence the combination of forces between Irgun and Lehi, eighty Irgun and forty Lehi soldiers taking part in the attack.

Though the over-all operational agreement between the Irgun and the Haganah had not yet been ratified by the Jewish Agency, there was contact between the commands in Jerusalem. When Colonel Shaltiel, the district commander of the Haganah, learned of the plan to capture the village, he asked Raanan, the Irgun district commander, to co-ordinate the timing of the attack with the renewed Haganah offensive at Kastel. He also expressed satisfaction in a note with the plan which, he said, was a stage "in our over-all plan." He stressed the importance of holding the village after its capture.

"If you are unable to do so," the note continued, "I warn you against blowing up the village which will result in its abandonment by the inhabitants and its ruins being occupied by foreign forces. Such a situation will increase instead of lessening our difficulties in the general struggle. A second capture of the place will involve heavy sacrifices of our people."

Shaltiel concluded this message with this significant information:

"A further reason I wish to put to you is that if foreign forces are attracted to the place this will interfere with our plan to lay down an airfield there."

This operation became one of the strategic turning points in the war and, for good or ill, its political consequences are with us to this day. The name of the village was Dir Yassin.

Two hundred Arabs, including many women and children, were killed in the battle which ensued. The Arab soldiers as elsewhere failed to evacuate their women and children. The Arab snipers fired from houses which were used by the families concerned. The attackers had taken this into account. They made provision for a warning to be broadcast to the villagers through a mobile loudspeaker to remove their women and children from the fighting area.

The plan of operations was overtaken by events. No sooner had the attackers taken up their positions than they were detected by Arab outposts. Far from taking the initiative they were met by an initial hail of fire from the village. Their one armored car, carrying the loudspeaker, was stuck several hundred yards from the village.

Zero hour for the attack had been 4:30 A.M. and it was to have been concluded by daybreak, in under two hours. But the Arab resistance proved so fierce that the battle went on for nearly eight hours. Almost every house in the village was defended, and progress was painfully slow. By ten o'clock, forty of the attacking force, one in every three, had been hit, including Devorah Lederberg, an Irgun First Aider; four of their number were dead and one dying. By now the whole village was in their hands, except the house of the mukhtar (headman), from which sustained firing was maintained for two more hours. It was only when a platoon of the Palmach, bearing a two-inch mortar, arrived voluntarily in the village to "help out" that this last strong point was subdued. About 120 women and children from the village were taken out to safety.

I learned the salient facts about the battle at Dir Yassin during my stay in Jerusalem the following summer as commander of the Irgun, from Devorah Lederberg—who acted as my secretary—and from others who took part in the planning or in the fighting. Irgun soldiers wounded there testified to the same story in a Jerusalem court three years later when they sued the government successfully for inclusion among the beneficiaries of the law providing for the maimed in the War of Independence.

The version I heard on the radio in New York in the early morning of April 11 was completely different. It told of a massacre inflicted upon an innocent and peaceful Arab village by wild terrorists who slaughtered its inhabitants without reason or warning.

For the British and Arab propagandists at Lake Success, the

death of women and children at Dir Yassin was good ammunition to weaken at least momentarily the moral strength of the Jewish case.

Until the truth could penetrate we were doomed to suffer unpleasantness. The Jewish Agency leaders made one of their great propaganda efforts. They added their voices to the British and Arab propaganda. The account of the Dir Yassin battle which has served to calumniate Israel to this day, was provided by the Jewish Agency.

Shaltiel issued a statement no less untrue than the enemy attack. He claimed that he had not even been given advance information of the attack on the village. In fact, immediately after the battle he had been in touch with Raanan as to who should garrison the village —the Irgun, or the Haganah, and the latter had actually taken over. In his statement, Colonel Shaltiel declared that the Irgun and Lehi soldiers had "run away from the village."

To crown the episode, Ben-Gurion sent a telegram to one of the enemy Arab leaders, King Abdullah of Transjordan, expressing his horror and regret at the incident.

The aftermath of the propaganda on the Dir Yassin battle had decisive and ironic consequences on the outcome of the war. The Arab population throughout Palestine took the propaganda at its face value. It struck terror in their hearts, reduced their will to resist, and added impetus to their flight from the country.

Leaders of the Jewish Agency must accept responsibility for the fact that the Arabs used the Dir Yassin incident to demonstrate that the Jews drove the Arabs from their homeland and were therefore responsible for the Arab refugee problem. The Arabs have used the *Jewish Agency's own denunciation of Dir Yassin,* with embellishments and additions of their own, as a microcosm of the origins of the entire refugee problem. The fantastic image of the peaceful Arab and the murderous Jew is taken straight from the Agency texts.

The causes of the Arab flight from the area of the Jewish state were various. The flight had begun long before April. Indeed, in January, thousands of Arabs had fled from Haifa and Jaffa. By March many of the villages in the Sharon plain were empty. The flight was part of the programme of the Arab Higher Committee, the leadership of the Palestine Arabs, headed by the exiled Mufti. The committee called on all civilians to leave their homes so as to lighten the task of the soldiers, telling the people that they would be able to return later and recover not only their own homes but all the possessions of the Jews. After Dir Yassin, the propaganda of the Arabs was intended to stiffen Arab resistance in the Jerusalem hills; but after so much earlier pressure to evacuate, the Arab villagers took it as a cue to leave.

The tragedy of the Arab refugees is all the more poignant in that there is nothing to suggest that, even at the height of the fighting, more than a minority of the Arabs of Palestine felt themselves really deeply involved in the conflict. The events of 1948 have not shaken my belief that, freed of the interference of the British and the pressures of the neighboring Arab states, the Palestinian Arabs would have acquiesced to peaceful relations with us in the Jewish state. The facts of 1948 strengthen this belief.

At the end of March 1948 a report submitted to the Palestine Committee of the Arab League by the command of the Arab forces operating in Palestine established the total number of Arab soldiers as 7700. Of these 5200 had come from the neighboring states. Of Palestinians there were 2500—"volunteers," the report takes care to emphasize—"who serve as regular soldiers for a wage." The report claims that this figure *could* be brought up to 5000 or 6000 if arms and equipment were available. On even our own conservative estimates of the size of the Arab population of western Palestine, there were, at the outbreak of the armed conflict, well over 100,000 Arab men aged eighteen to thirty-six in the country.

The report of the Iraqi Parliamentary Committee appointed in 1949 to investigate the causes of the Arab defeat claims that the poor participation of the Palestine Arabs themselves in "the struggle for their freedom" was due to the internal quarrels of their leaders.[2] This can only be a small part of the truth. In the face of the great and violent events of those months it is impossible to believe that the Arab youth in Palestine would have accepted the role of fleeing civilians or bystanders if they had really believed that this was essentially a "struggle for their freedom."

In a Jordan newspaper on the fifth anniversary of the battle at Dir Yassin, one of the refugees from the village wrote without heat:

> The Jews never intended to harm the population of the village, but were forced to do so after they encountered fire from the population, which killed the Irgun commander. The Arab exodus from other villages was not caused by the actual battle but by the exaggerated description spread by Arab leaders to incite them to fight the Jews.[3]

In the third week of April Tiberias fell to the Haganah almost without a struggle: it was swiftly succeeded by Haifa where the British surprisingly announced their evacuation of the city. A quick Jewish offensive (by the Haganah with Irgun support) brought surrender by the Arabs. In this town, where relations between Jews and Arabs had always been correct and often cordial, the Jews, learning during the surrender negotiations that the Arabs meant to evacuate, appealed to them to stay. Obeying the orders of their leaders, they refused, all but three thousand of Haifa's 50,000 Arabs abandoning their houses and their businesses. Yet there was no panic flight; the evacuees had their luggage checked for arms by the Haganah and by British soldiers at the exits from the town.

Many of the Arabs traveled no farther than Acre. There, on a clear day, they could gaze at their home city across the waters of the bay. There they waited for the day four weeks later when, they hoped, in the wake of the victorious armies of the Arab states, they would re-enter Haifa as its exclusive masters. Four weeks later, however, Acre, with hardly a semblance of struggle, was captured by the Haganah. The evacuees moved north again, but now they were called refugees.

Three days after the fall of Haifa, the Irgun, in one of its greatest operations, changed the face of the struggle in Palestine, this time with conscious purpose, breaking across the frontiers of the partition plan and eliminating Jaffa as an Arab base, actual and potential, to ensure the town's inclusion in the Jewish state.

The attack on Jaffa could have been mounted much earlier. From the early days of the Arab attacks Tel Aviv had been subjected to a daily barrage of sniping which took a steady toll in dead and maimed. The whole of the center of the city was a target. Bullets whistled across Allenby Road and other main streets from a dozen directions. The border zone had been largely evacuated of its Jewish inhabitants, who took refuge in northern Tel Aviv and in Ramat Gan.

In the Irgun High Command we had early concluded that the immediate harassments from Jaffa, annoying and serious as they were, were but a prelude to the employment of the city as a major base of attack on the Jewish state after May 15. We calculated that Jaffa, stabbing topographically at the heart of Tel Aviv, could be developed into a dire threat to our defense. Forces could be landed there from the sea by the Egyptians, and from here a massive attack could be launched against Tel Aviv. The city could supply the base for a northern pincer of a dangerous encircling movement in co-ordination with a landward thrust from the south.

As early as January the capture of Jaffa was included in our list of strategic objectives. The sniping from Jaffa continued and was later reinforced by mortar shelling. Every week we learned of the reinforcements of Arab strength in the city by volunteers from the neighboring Arab states.

The strategic significance of Jaffa, and the potential danger it represented, was not so clear to the Jewish Agency. The Haganah, according to the official accounts, refrained from attacking Jaffa because they did not want to clash with the British and because they believed that when, on May 15, the British withdrew, the city would be "surrounded on all sides" and would fall like "ripe fruit." The official account states that they decided to capture all the "surrounding villages" but not to make a direct attack on Jaffa.[4] The sea, on Jaffa's fourth side, did not enter their calculations.

The three days of the Irgun attack on Jaffa revealed the several actors in the Palestine drama in characteristic attitudes.

Jaffa was well defended. The Irgun's objective was to cut off the elongated Manshieh Quarter, which thrust into Tel Aviv from the main body of Jaffa. Its frontal attack was supported by a fierce shelling of the whole city.

The Irgun at first made no progress against the fortified Arab positions at Manshieh, either on the first or second day, although there was panic in the city among the civilians. As casualties mounted, Begin proposed suspending the attack and digging in. The junior officers and men pressed for a renewed effort, and Begin consented. Giddy, in command, evolved a new plan of attack, based on incessant demolitions of the enemy buildings and strong points by a group of intrepid sappers. Slowly, for fifteen hours, the enemy was pressed back inch by inch across the four or five hundred yards that separated our men from the sea. Early on the morning of the fourth day the Irgun force dominated the Manshieh Quarter and was ready to move into the heart of Jaffa.

The ferocity of the defense was not due simply to Arab determination but to British co-operation. Suddenly at Jaffa the reason for British evacuation of Haifa became clear: the bridgehead by which, if Bevin's plan succeeded, they would reverse the process of evacuation, was not to be at Haifa but at Jaffa. They made no pretense of "neutrality" but went into action behind the Arabs, with tanks and artillery, as soon as the Irgun attack started. It was their direct intervention in the battle that upset the Irgun's original plan and nearly resulted in its defeat.

Even when the Irgun had broken through, the British still hoped to turn the tables and launched a counterattack. Tanks, guns, and mortars took toll of Irgun life. In an official announcement, the British stated that in consequence of the Irgun attack on Jaffa, they had sent in reinforcements from Cyprus and Malta.

Whatever their tactical purpose it was at once frustrated. Through the Haganah, with whom our agreement had now come into force, the British demanded that the Irgun hand over to them the Manshieh Police Station, the strategic center of the area. This was refused, and to ensure against that contingency the building was destroyed without delay. The Irgun did however agree to the second demand: not to advance, although we emphasized that what we had we would hold.

Ten days later, after a cease-fire agreement with the Haganah, the British left Jaffa for good.

The British Army involuntarily made a substantial contribution to the fall of Jaffa. A large part of the arms and ammunition used by the Irgun was British. Without them the attack could not have been made. Three weeks earlier the Irgun had carried out two major raids. One was directed at a British military camp near Pardess Hannah in the Sharon Valley, when a fierce battle developed and the camp was captured. A counterattack by reinforcements from outside was repelled. A second counterattack was launched, this time supported by armor, and was also repelled. The Irgun lost one killed, the British eight. At the end of the battle, during which the armory had been systematically emptied of its contents, the Irgun had acquired a large quantity of rifles, Bren guns, sub-machine guns and ammunition, as well as a few armor-piercing shells and an armored car.

The second raid, against an ammunition train, was equally successful. Twenty tons of ammunition, including a large quantity of mortar shells, were captured. It was these shells, fired lavishly into Jaffa a week later, that probably decided the fate of the city.[5]

After the first day of the battle for Jaffa, when it was clear that the first Irgun attack had failed, there was a suspiciously uniform reaction in the Hebrew Establishment newspapers. They could hardly hide their satisfaction that the Arabs had succeeded in throwing back the Irgun attacks.

Leading articles were peppered with words like "irresponsible" and "sabotage" and denounced the Irgun for daring to launch such an attack, arguing that the dissident Irgunists were inefficient and reckless.

Three days later, when the Irgun had broken through to the sea, the same newspapers published articles which learnedly discussed the strategic importance of the capture of Manshieh, and proclaimed that "the Jews could not permit Jaffa to be used as a base of operations against Tel Aviv."

The newspapers of course took their inspiration from the Haganah leadership, who, after that first heartbreaking day, had issued a vicious statement, describing the Irgun attack as abortive and accusing the Irgun of "exhibitionism."

The very next day the Haganah leaders changed their attitude completely. They now remembered that two weeks had passed since the ratification by the Zionist General Council of the agreement signed six weeks earlier between the Irgun and the Jewish Agency.

Ben-Gurion, the chief architect of delay, had apparently hoped to reach May 15, when the Jewish government was to be set up, without having to submit to the indignity of co-operating with the Irgun.

The independent Irgun attack on Jaffa presumably forced the issue. On the second day of the battle two Haganah leaders, Galili and Yadin, met Begin and Avraham, and the agreement became operative.

Thereupon the attack on Jaffa became strategically wise, tactically legitimate, and politically sane. Now indeed the Haganah decided to proceed with the plan for the capture of the Arab villages adjacent to Jaffa and all but one fell without a fight.

On May 13 the leaders of the Arab remnant in Jaffa officially surrendered the nearly deserted town to the Haganah.[6]

26

The Jewish State

The great debate at the United Nations continued throughout that April, but its sterility was absolute. The United States Government's retreat from partition did not enhance its image with the American people, nor with the representatives at Lake Success. When Warren Austin finally revealed the details of the trusteeship plan which was to supersede the partition scheme, it was received with marked coldness, and when he announced America's readiness to impose the new plan by force (in co-operation with other nations) the reactions were heated and sharp. The trusteeship project, formally submitted on April 21, was referred to a subcommittee but came to nothing.

Meantime the Americans and British concentrated their efforts on the more plausible proposal of a "cease-fire," their conception of which included a suspension not only of hostilities but also of all political action in fulfillment of the partition decision. Palestine, they proposed, would have an umpire (Britain, for example!) or an umpiring force (consisting preferably of Americans and British) who would initiate renewed efforts "for a peaceful solution of the dispute between Arabs and Jews."

Britain and America knew perfectly well that the debate in the United Nations was pointless without Jewish acceptance of the "postponement" of their independence. The State Department continued to press the Jewish Agency. The British Government rightly believed that as long as America pressed for a cease-fire she would refuse to lift the arms embargo. All this time the British continued to pour arms into the Arab states, to ignore the Arab "volunteers" pouring across the frontiers into Palestine, and to maintain the blockade at sea against the Jews.

In London, the myth of British neutrality was firmly entrenched.

In the four days I spent there on my way back from New York at the beginning of May I did sense a hint of bewilderment at the deployment of troops to Jaffa from Cyprus and Malta. It was difficult to square this blatantly executed reversal of evacuation with the previously projected picture of a neutral Britain, delicately lifting her skirts from the mud and blood of the conflict. As always in foreign affairs, Bevin had a loyal press. In varying degree, but with few and uninfluential exceptions, in the editorial columns and dispatches from Palestine, the British newspapers fostered the belief that Britain had no interest in Palestine now except to withdraw in peace.

If there were doubts and qualms over the government's obvious anti-Jewish policy they were no doubt easily suppressed. For beyond the immediate political antagonisms there was the old sense of Jewish inferiority deep-seated in the gentile consciousness, as well as in that of the ghetto-minded Jew. Its now crucial manifestation was the inability to recognize the Jew's right to defend himself or to fight back. His highest striving should be for pity. If he retaliated, he was a criminal. If he attacked, it was an outrage. If, even when outnumbered, he won a battle, it was murder. Neutrality could therefore in his case be stretched and distorted beyond recognition without seriously troubling the national conscience or disturbing the national equanimity.

There was triumph in Bevin's speeches and replies in the House of Commons during those dying days of the Mandate. The understanding between him and the Arabs in preparation for the invasion was apparently complete. Bevin's hopes were centered on Abdullah of Transjordan. Abdullah was little more than a puppet ruler, maintained and guarded by the British, his Arab Legion—the strongest and most efficient of the Arab forces—trained and led by British officers, his frontiers guaranteed by Britain, his arms supplied by Britain. The installation of Abdullah as the ruler of all Palestine must have seemed to Bevin to be the ideal second-best solution.

From Lake Success the news was also grim. No reinforcements could reach the Jews in the two remaining weeks before they would be attacked by five Arab armies at once.

In London there was much activity to bring help to the Irgun (as well as to the Haganah). The Jewish Legion, led by Major Samuel Weiser and Lieutenant De Lange, distributed large posters throughout the city calling for volunteers. During my few days in London on returning from New York in early May, I learnt from Bella and Yonah of plans to acquire arms and ammunition and I have a vague recollection of some kind of marine vessel for sale. In the atmosphere I sensed a sudden awareness of a common danger and a common destiny among the Jewish community.

Back in Paris on May 4, I met Yaacov Meridor for the first time. As he had been second-in-command of the Irgun at the time of his capture by the British, Lankin had given way to him as the head of the Irgun abroad. Meridor and his five comrades had escaped from prison in Kenya, and now we heard that both Aryeh Ben Eliezer and Yitzhak Izernitsky, who had also escaped from British internment in Africa, had, after a year in French Somaliland, been granted the right to asylum in Metropolitan France. When it was suggested that, traveling by way of the Suez Canal the two men would be subject to British surveillance and possible recapture, the French Government decided that the "refugees" would be transported under their direct protection. The day after my return to Paris, Ben Eliezer and Izernitsky arrived at Toulon aboard the French warship *Dixmude*.

I had not seen Ben Eliezer since the day twelve years earlier when he had driven me and Haskel to Jerusalem from Tel Aviv at breakneck speed. He had been active in America in the Bergson group and returned to Palestine at the end of 1943. It was he who proposed the transfer of leadership from Meridor to Begin. He cooperated with Begin in planning the opening moves of the revolt and served on the High Command for three months before his capture by the British.

There was little time for celebrating or reminiscing. We set up a provisional European Command of the Irgun, consisting of Meridor, Ben Eliezer, Lankin, Eli, and me. Eitan, organizing training courses, was seldom in Paris. Yoel, the head of our Intelligence, had also been in Europe for several months. He had sent a number of small consignments of arms to Palestine, disguised as immigrants' luggage, and had been jailed twice. Now free again, he was, like Eitan, forever on the move.

The headquarters of the Irgun was now established in the spacious offices of the Hebrew Committee on the Avenue de Messine and hummed with activity. The European Command met every day at noon in an apartment on the other side of the city. There we received reports regarding the organization of manpower—over which

Eli presided—and on the various negotiations taking place for the purchase of arms. We were kept informed on the progress of friendly talks being held by Jeremiah Helpern with a group of Spanish anarchists who had offered arms in our cause. From the south of France we were apprised of the prospect of being given an underground armory which had been cached by former members of the French Maquis. We received reports from Canada of our protracted efforts to acquire planes there.

Our spirits were low. A bare week separated us from the fateful fifteenth of May and we still had only a quantity of small arms, which we now stored together with the substantial quantities of personal equipment and other supplies gathered under the direction of Colonel Jakson. The heavy quantities of arms which we needed still eluded us. Persistent reports also reached us that the Jewish Agency would succumb to the pressure of the American State Department, over the protests of Ben-Gurion, and decide to "postpone" the declaration of the state. I informed Meridor and Ben Eliezer of the decision taken in Tel Aviv that if the Agency failed to set up a government by May 15, the Irgun would do so.

That very weekend in Palestine, the Irgun High Command found it necessary to publish a concisely worded statement of promise and warning:

> . . . If next Sabbath the message goes out: "The Hebrew State is hereby established" the whole people, the youth will rally and fight shoulder to shoulder for our country and people.
>
> If on that day a declaration of shameful surrender is published, if the leadership succumbs to the tactics of the enemy and Hebrew independence is destroyed before it comes to life—we shall rebel. There will be no surrender except by the "Vichy" leaders. The Hebrew Government will certainly be established . . .

We received reports that the British Government intended to persist in its blockade against Jewish immigrants after May 15. We therefore issued a blunt warning that any persistence in such a blockade after May 15 would be regarded as an act of war against the Jewish people. Unless this intention was immediately repudiated the Irgun would operate outside the borders of Palestine in order to retaliate and every British ship, merchant or navy, would be regarded as a legitimate target. A statement would be issued to warn shippers and passengers against the use of British vessels. We thus revived the tactic we had planned in 1947. At that moment we did not know whether the Portsmouth operation I had frozen eight months earlier was still feasible, but we could sink a vessel in Shanghai and possibly Hong Kong.

To make sure that the British took our warning seriously, we sought a particularly effective way of delivering it. Reuben Hecht was asked to convey the warning to Sam E. Woods, the American consul general in Munich. Hecht was one of the colorful figures in the Hebrew renaissance movement. Born into a wealthy, assimilationist Jewish family which controlled gigantic business enterprises in Switzerland, Hecht had been active in Aliyah B operations for the Irgun before the war and had indeed contrived to work in Yugoslavia until the Nazi invasion in 1941.[1] On returning to Switzerland, he had helped American airmen interned there. A close friendship grew up between him and Woods, then American consul general at Zurich, who had, in December 1940, when serving in Germany, brought to Secretary of State Cordell Hull the first warning of Hitler's plan to invade Soviet Russia.[2] Subsequently Woods, with Hecht's frequent assistance, had sent considerable information to Washington on conditions in Nazi-held territory and had recommended Hecht for the American Medal of Freedom. We were thus certain that the warning transmitted by Woods would be treated with the appropriate seriousness and dispatch by the State Department and that the British Foreign Office would be left in no doubt as to its authenticity.

Hecht met Woods at the Hotel Crillon in Paris. He read him the draft of our warning and asked him to pass this information along to Washington without delay. Three days later Woods informed Hecht that the British had assured the United States Government that they had no intention of prolonging the blockade beyond May 15.[3]

For six weeks Ariel was obliged to be patient as he watched the calendar creeping inexorably toward May 15. Throughout the month of April, he was assured by his contact, Boissier, that his proposal was moving along the proper channels, and was under consideration by Bidault. During the week I was in Paris, Ariel called on Pierre Boursicot, Director-General of the Sûreté-National. On the afternoon of Friday, May 7, he visited the Permanent Chief of the Foreign Office, Jean Chauvet, and was told that the Irgun proposal was to be discussed formally in the Cabinet. After further talks with Chauvet and Pages, Ariel reported confidently that agreement was in sight. But no definite commitment was made by the French Government at this moment. We had failed: there would be no Irgun ship to enter Palestine by May 15. We decided that Meridor and I must leave at once for Palestine and report on the situation. There was no quick way to reach Palestine, all the regular airlines having suspended operations, so we decided to charter a plane. Meir, a Palestinian-born former bomber pilot in the Free French Air Force, negotiated a British plane, despite the fact that the British Government had forbidden all civilian flights to Palestine. The company made the reasonable condition that immediately after landing in Palestine the plane would take off for Cyprus, but it would come back three days later to pick us up for the return journey to Europe. We took with us a small contingent of men, among them Eitan, who wished to persuade the High Command to allow him to resume duty in Palestine, Hillel Kook and Alexander Rafaeli, his colleague on the Hebrew Committee, as well as Dr. Yunitchman and several other Revisionist emissaries in Europe.

The decision to proclaim the Jewish state was made on May 12 in the newly established Jewish National Executive in Palestine. The motion was carried by a very narrow majority of six to four. Ben-Gurion led the six, after Shertok, fresh from America, had presented an account of the pressure to which he had been subjected in Washington by George C. Marshall, the U. S. Secretary of State, and the Under Secretary of State, Robert A. Lovett. The Americans had impressed upon him the fact that no American aid could be expected if the Jews did not "postpone" the proclamation and freeze all action, military and political, in what was euphemistically called a "cease-fire." They felt that the conflict in Palestine might lead to a world war and to bolster their arguments they expressed a pessimistic opinion of Jewish military chances against the regular Arab armies scheduled to invade Palestine the following week.[4]

Ben-Gurion was now as determined as before he had been hesitant. A week earlier he had sent an emissary to Begin—Eliezer Liebenstein (now Livneh)—to express his appreciation of the continuing Irgun pressure for the establishment of the state. It was proving helpful, he said, in overcoming the opposition.

We ourselves knew nothing of the proclamation when we set out from Paris at noon on Friday, May 14. I cannot remember at what point on our journey we heard the news that the state of Israel had been proclaimed that afternoon.

We arrived in Tel Aviv the next day. We were perhaps the first air passengers to land in the new Jewish state. When we disembarked from the plane, the field seemed empty, but within a few minutes, people began to emerge from behind various huts and vehicles and we were soon surrounded by a mixed company of immigration and customs officials and a few Haganah Intelligence officers. It appeared then that an Egyptian plane had aimed bombs at them a little earlier. The bombs had fallen in the sea. They had mistaken us for Egyptians coming back for another try, and had rushed for shelter, as they had no antiaircraft gun.

The joy of Meridor's surprise homecoming after four years' enforced absence was soon overshadowed by the grim tones of our conference with Begin and Avraham. Instead of a ship filled with men and arms we brought eloquent explanations for our failure. Even a few hundred rifles and a few thousand rounds of ammunition could have a decisive effect on the battle in which our Irgun force, under the operational agreement with the Haganah, was at that moment engaged: an attack on Ramleh.

A courier from Giddy arrived to ask for ammunition, but there was none available. The Haganah, Begin told us, was equally short of arms. He was confident that with proper equipment our men could liberate the whole of western Palestine.

We decided we must find a way to bring the *Altalena* to Palestine. At midnight, at the Irgun headquarters in the Freud Hospital, we held a meeting with three representatives of the Haganah: its commander, Israel Galili, Levi Shkolnik,[5] and David Cohen. The Irgun was represented by Begin, Avraham, Meridor and myself. We told them of the *Altalena* and proposed that they should supplement our funds so that we could buy an adequate quantity of arms to equip our men when they went into the army which we expected would soon be created. We estimated our need at $250,000.

With our thousand men and our arms on board, the Haganah could add 1000 of their own men from their reserves in Europe together with arms. On the completion of its mission in Palestine, we would make a gift of the ship to the Provisional Government of Israel.

We also told them of our negotiations for planes in Canada and offered to hand them over to the government as soon as they reached us.

That evening, for the first time in the four years of Irgun operations, Begin had spoken over our radio, abandoning his anonymity. It was a poignant moment for him and his listeners. Begin was unequivocal about the intentions of the Irgun.

> The Irgun Zvai Leumi is leaving the underground within the boundaries of the Hebrew independent state. We went down into the underground, we arose in the underground under the rule of oppression. Now . . . we have Hebrew rule in part of our Homeland. In this part there is no need for a Hebrew underground. In the State of Israel we shall be soldiers and builders. We shall respect its Government, for it is our Government.

That evening we learned from Begin that the agreement with the Haganah was in effective operation. Relations on the operational level were cordial. Moreover, the Haganah commanders had made it plain that as far as they could influence events the partition frontiers would not be an obstacle to Jewish advance and had no objection in principle to Irgun operations beyond those frontiers. This operational agreement was of course temporary and would come to an end when the national army was established. That would take a couple of weeks. We believed then that with adequate equipment, the Irgun could in those weeks have broken the back of the Arab forces on the central front, and the combined Jewish forces could have pressed on to the Jordan.

During an Egyptian air raid, Begin took us on a tour of Jaffa, now divided into two defense zones—one guarded by the Haganah, one by the Irgun. I recall the sense of achievement I felt—political and military—when I saw Irgun boys and Haganah boys armed with Sten guns keeping guard on the city. Jaffa was a bright interval in the clouds. Another happy phenomenon was the enthusiasm with which Begin and indeed any obvious Irgunist was received by the people. The Irgun, indeed, was at the height of its popularity and fame in that month of May.

President Truman accorded *de facto* recognition to the state of Israel eleven minutes after its proclamation. He surprised everyone by his swift action, including his own representatives at the United Nations. Soviet recognition of the state came three days later.

There was no relaxation in British policy.

Bevin launched a vigorous diplomatic campaign to prevent other nations from recognizing the Jewish state. Holland, France, and the Scandinavian states were all subjected to British pressure.

At Lake Success in the first days following the birth of Israel, Sir Alexander Cadogan pursued four arguments in Britain's name:

a) The Jewish state had no legal basis—because the United Nations timetable preceding its establishment had not been carried out (by the British themselves, though he failed to add this fact).

b) Since the Jewish state did not legally exist, it could not claim to have been invaded.

c) The attack by the Arab states was not a threat to peace.

d) British aid to the Arab states—in arms, in money, and, for Transjordan, in officers—would continue unless the Security Council of the United Nations decided otherwise. (Britain, he neglected to say, had the right of veto in the Security Council and could block any decision by its members.)

The Anglo-Arab alliance against Israel was complete and open. The Arabs, for their part, were not ashamed of it. On May 19, Azzam Pasha, the Secretary of the Arab League, expressing confidence in the outcome of the struggle, told a correspondent of the London *Times:*

> Dangerous and unfounded rumours are beginning to circulate that the Arab Legion is being restrained by the British. I can state categorically that no restrictions whatever have been made or even suggested by the British.

The United States, having recognized the state of Israel, had its clashes with the British point of view as pronounced by Cadogan; yet the one American measure by which Bevin's policy could be countered and defeated, lifting the arms embargo, was never adopted.

Six days after the Arab invasion, the Security Council appointed Count Folke Bernadotte, head of the Swedish Red Cross, as mediator to bring peace to Palestine. He arrived in Palestine at the end of May. By then the Security Council had adopted a British proposal for a truce to last four weeks, during which a solution to the conflict would be sought. While the Israeli Provisional Government agreed promptly to this proposal, among the Arab states there was a protracted discussion on its merits.

Meanwhile, our offer to the Haganah regarding the *Altalena* had been transmitted to Ben-Gurion. On May 17, Galili gave Avraham Ben-Gurion's reply, which was negative. There was no countersuggestion and no explanation.

I flew back to Paris the next day, accompanied by my wife, who came in order to join the team of agents seeking weapons for the Irgun all over Europe. She had in my absence gone through a course of training in a woman's unit and given auxiliary service during the capture of the Arab village of Yehudiyeh (now Yahud) near Lydda. Alexander Rafaeli of the Hebrew Committee, who had been a member of the Irgun in Raziel's time, asked to be allowed to re-enlist in the ranks. He was requested to return to Paris and there place himself at our disposal.

27

The Altalena

The activity at Irgun headquarters in Paris had intensified during my absence. Volunteers, offers of help, commercial proposals for the sale of arms came from all sides. Two agents had traveled to several countries to arrange transportation through France of members selected to sail on the *Altalena* for service in Palestine.

Two days before my return Ariel had at last had a conclusive reply from the French Government. He had met for the first time Jean Morin, Director of the Foreign Minister's Cabinet, who informed him that the government had decided to accede to our request for arms. This decision was a turning point in the relations between France and Israel. It came at a time when the French attitude to the new state was still equivocal. The decision was confirmed in formal terms by Bidault when he received Ariel that May 19. It was a long and bold step toward close relations between Paris and Jerusalem.

It had taken almost two months for the government to make up its mind. Now the execution of the plan had to be arranged through the necessary but numerous channels. Day followed day and no final date for the delivery of arms was set. At the Foreign Office, Ariel was now in constant touch with Morin, who worked hard to speed the process. Ten days went by before Ariel saw General Revers, the Chief of Staff of the Army. On the last day of May, Ariel reported that the army had received the necessary instructions for the actual delivery of the arms. He had already seen General Coudraux, the officer responsible for the operation, and had been assured that we would receive the arms on June 5.

On Sunday afternoon, May 30, we had a business meeting about the arrangements for the *Altalena*. Ariel was there, in a buoyant mood; Monroe Fein, the captain of the *Altalena,* a U. S. Navy veteran of the War in the Pacific, came from Marseilles; Abraham Stavsky came with Fein. For years Stavsky had been occupied with Aliyah B projects. He had negotiated the purchase of the *Altalena* for the Hebrew Committee, and he appeared and acted as its owner. He was its business manager. Fein raised two practical problems on which he asked for decisions. The first was the point of landing. The *Altalena* was a product of American wartime shipbuilding ingenuity —an LST built for the speedy landing of tanks. The ideal beach for this type of landing boat is one that is steep, so that the boat can be brought square up to the land. None of us had the necessary scientific knowledge to give Fein an intelligent answer. In any case this was not merely a physical problem. Without co-operation from the Haganah our choice of sites would be limited. At that stage, envisaging the need for bringing many of our own members to help in the unloading, we suggested the beach opposite Frishman Street in Tel Aviv.

Fein's second problem dealt with signals for visual communication when the ship came in sight of land. The proposal I had brought with me from Tel Aviv did not satisfy him and he made an alternative one. We sent Aryeh Ben Eliezer to Palestine to clear up these questions, as well as to bring us an up-to-date report on the situation there. Niko (Nathan Germant), one of Meridor's companions in the great escape from Kenya, accompanied him. We asked for one of them to return without delay, although it was doubtful whether this could be arranged. There was still no regular air service to Palestine, though a South African Jewish group of businessmen who had set up the Pan African Air Company were now keeping the route open. Still, the *Altalena* had its radio, and there was one on shore at the other end, while in a villa some distance from Paris a radio transmitter was being erected for us by our "Scientific Committee"—a group of physicists who had volunteered for service and whom Lankin had organized as a unit. We felt that this three-way communication would be adequate to overcome any problem that might arise from a failure by Ben Eliezer or Germant to return before the ship sailed.

The next day, from his own tiny headquarters in the one-room flat of the Homeski family on the Champs Elysées, Eli telephoned to every corner of Europe our instructions for the timing of the transports of people. They were to arrive by June 6 at one of the two camps prepared for them near Marseilles. Lankin, appointed by the

High Command as commander of the evolving military unit on the *Altalena,* took up his duties in Marseilles, while I remained in Paris.

The reports from the fronts were not heartening. The Arabs had not yet won any resounding successes, but they had certainly had the better of the fighting. In the north the Syrians had made progress along the Jordan. In the center the Irgun frontal attack on Ramleh had bogged down. Haganah assistance on the flank had not improved the situation. A new Haganah attack on Latrun had failed, with heavy casualties. In the Negev two Egyptian columns had made considerable progress. On the coastal road they had forced the evacuation of only one Jewish village: Yad Mordekhai. Repulsed both at Negbah and at Nirim, they had changed their tactics, bypassed the villages on their route, and were now pressing on toward Tel Aviv. At the end of May they had reached a point north of Ashdod, twenty miles from the city. In the central Negev they were progressing toward control of the dominating roads. Egyptian and Arab Legion forces had reached Ramat Rahel, the kibbutz on the southern outskirts of Jerusalem—for the Etzion bloc in the Hebron Hills had, after its epic defense, fallen to the enemy in mid-May. Only after heavy battles, during which the village was wiped out, had the Arabs been repulsed at Ramat Rahel. In the north of Jerusalem the battle with the Transjordanians fluctuated; but in the Old City, on the penultimate day of May, the remnant of the Jewish force had surrendered.

It was a gloomy picture. Most depressing was the overwhelming superiority of enemy material. Their planes carried out daily air raids. Their artillery and armor were everywhere in evidence. We were convinced of ultimate victory. But the price was growing day by day. In April a comparatively small quantity of arms had won Jaffa. In May an adequate supply of arms could bring our forces to the Jordan. Two or three months later even five times their weight might not be enough.

Then the French Government informed us that the delivery of arms for the *Altalena* was postponed for three days. Meanwhile hundreds of young men and women had arrived in the camp and had to be fed. The owners of the land on which one of the camps was set up threatened legal proceedings. Tension at Port de Bouc (and at Avenue de Messine) was heightened when the French police discovered a mysterious consignment of rifles in the Marseilles railway station.

Though the Ministry of the Interior had made arrangements with the police, the Customs, and with all other possible authorities to ensure the unmolested dispatch and movement of our arms to the ship, this odd consignment from Paris was by some error in the invoice delivered to the baggage room at Marseilles. When our agents arrived to claim it, the police arrested them. There followed a complicated diplomatic operation to achieve the unpublicized release of our unlucky representatives.

By June 2, both the Provisional Government of Israel and the Arab states announced their acceptance of the truce decided on by the Security Council. Although the conditions of the truce were designed to maintain the status quo between the two fighting sides, it was in fact a grotesque weighting of the scales against the Jews. The truce did not prevent the landing of arms from Britain in Iraq or Transjordan or even Egypt, whose ports were decently remote from the fighting zones. The only effective check on the import of arms was from the sea to our forces in Palestine.

The truce complicated our calculations about the *Altalena,* which would now be open to attack by the Egyptians, or by the British, as a breach of the truce. We discussed our problem with Monroe Fein, who had handled the same type of vessel against the Japanese. He was confident of his ability to evade, even to repel attack.

We decided: that in the light of the gravity of the arms situation, we must take the risk that might ensue from a formal breach of the truce; that the ship should therefore sail, taking whatever action its commander thought necessary to evade or resist enemy action; that the commander should do whatever possible to evade United Nations truce surveillance. To this end, unloading of the arms on the Palestine coast should be carried out at night, and the ship stand off during daylight.

Tuesday, June 8, was finally fixed for the delivery of the arms by the French Government. On that day I traveled down to Marseilles and to Port de Bouc. At the camps some nine hundred young men and women were waiting impatiently for the signal to leave. I found Rammy, summoned from Geneva to take charge of the larger camp, exhausted but very cheerful, having succeeded in maintaining order, cleanliness, and discipline and in holding the owners of the land at bay.

Late in the evening, accompanied by Dr. Ariel and Madame Vayda, I paid my first and only visit to the *Altalena.* Fein took me round the ship, explained its proposed organization, and showed me the substantial arms and supplies from diverse sources that had already come aboard, including half a dozen caterpillar tractors.

I went on to the pier, got into the car we had come by, and fell asleep in sheer fatigue. I was awakened by voices and movement. A convoy had arrived, led by a major who got out of his car and walked up to where Ariel was standing with Madame Vayda and the divisional commissioner for the Surveillance de la Territoire of the Sûreté. He saluted and said, "I am Major X, head of this convoy of arms directed to you. I am at your disposal." There were 27 trucks, with 5000 Lee-Enfield rifles, 5 million rounds of ammunition, and 250 Bren machine guns. It was now about 2 A.M. on Wednesday, June 9. The steel-helmeted soldiers began unloading the trucks and a team of stevedores loaded the contents on to the ship. We decided that the ship would sail on Thursday.

I flew back to Paris. That day it was announced that both sides in Palestine had agreed on terms and a cease-fire would begin on Friday morning. The situation in Palestine had meantime changed for the worse. The Egyptian column halted near Ashdod, had indeed been bombed by Jewish planes and had remained halted, but across the breadth of the Negev the Arabs now controlled a line of strong points and strategic crossroads. The Negev was cut off. News from all the fronts had two common ingredients: dauntless Jewish fighters and a striking Jewish inferiority in fire power.

On arriving in Paris I found a telephoned message from Marseilles. The stevedores working on the *Altalena* had gone on strike, having been ordered out by their trade union. Ariel intervened with the union, while the French soldiers set to work, helped by men from the Irgun camps. A precious day was thus lost.

At midday on Friday, June 11, the loading was completed, and the *Altalena* sailed for Palestine at 8:30 that evening. Early the next morning a telegram arrived from Begin asking me not to send the ship and to await instructions. I was shocked and dismayed. On Tuesday, the day I had gone to Marseilles, I had received a telegram from Tel Aviv asking whether the ship had sailed. The next day Germant had arrived with the signaling information and with instructions for beaching at Frishman Street. They must therefore have known we were sailing. What had happened in the interval?

Actually, Begin had assumed that he would be informed in advance of the date fixed for sailing. He, too, was watching the negotiations for a truce and its likely effect on the affairs of the *Altalena*. His estimate of the probable effects of a breach of the truce was different from ours. We in Paris believed that the Israel Government would give its blessing to an accomplished fact. He was not prepared to commit a breach of the truce without the prior consent of the government.

I drafted a message to be sent on our radio to the ship, but found that our transmitter did not work. I cabled Tel Aviv that the ship had sailed and that I had no contact with her. I advised them to try to communicate with her direct. I then raced to the Yugoslav embassy. While the ship had enough supplies for four weeks, the prospect of a thousand people sailing aimlessly around the Mediterranean for a month in the midsummer heat was not a pleasant one to contemplate. A friendly port might give her discreet shelter for at least part of the time. The only government I believed might agree to this was the Yugoslav. Yugoslavia had broken with the Soviet Union and had indeed opposed partition, but was not unequivocally hostile to us. This I had gathered from Brilej, whom I had met in Geneva and who was now an assistant to the Minister of Foreign Affairs.

I do not know what Brilej's own reaction would have been, but when I applied for a visa, I was told that the application must be sent to Belgrade. I asked that this be cabled and referred to Brilej. This may have been a mistake. Certainly in the ten days I remained in Paris I heard nothing.

The days passed in unrelieved anxiety, deepened by the knowledge that from the moment it sailed, the *Altalena* had been reported, though not prominently, in the British press. I was also kept occupied by the dozen airmen sent from Canada and the United States to man the planes which had been bought on our behalf, although the planes themselves had not arrived. On Thursday, June 17, Aryeh Ben Eliezer returned from Palestine. He told me what had happened there since the receipt of my telegram of the previous Saturday. Begin had sent a telegram to Lankin on the ship, instructing him to keep the *Altalena* away from the Palestine shore until further notice because of the truce. As we learned later, the order was received on board, and Fein and Lankin made the necessary arrangements, Lankin instituting rationing of food, drink, and cigarettes.

Immediately after sending the instructions, the Irgun High Command applied itself to securing the government's permission to land the ship. They communicated with Galili and gave him a full account of the ship's contents, its sailing from France without permission, and of the order now given to the ship to keep away. At a meeting on Tuesday, June 15, Shkolnik and Galili informed the Irgun leaders that the government had decided to ask the ship to be brought in with all possible speed. Begin had sent a new order to the *Altalena:* "Full steam ahead." "There are now no internal problems," Ben Eliezer told me. "Galili has promised that the Haganah will send trucks to help us unload the ship as quickly as possible so as to reduce to a minimum its exposure to possible UN intervention." They were due to discuss other details later as to where to beach the ship and how to distribute the arms.

I told the good news to Ariel, who had been brooding in his own way over the developments of the preceding week. He was overjoyed. The anxiety which had hung over the office those several days was quickly transformed into a disproportionate lightheartedness.

There was no further need for a large Irgun organization in Europe. With the dispatch of the *Altalena,* we had fulfilled our responsibilities, while the planes, when they arrived, would be forwarded to Palestine. Now the Irgun in Europe could be reduced to skeleton proportions. We would not disband entirely. We never forgot Jerusalem, where the Israel Government refused to claim sovereignty, where the Old City had fallen and the New was in danger. There the Irgun would have to continue its independent existence to struggle for the inclusion of the whole city in the Jewish state. Until then a remnant of the Irgun abroad had to be kept in being.

Of all our officers, only Aryeh and Ariel remained in Paris, with Yehoshua Halperin to look after finances. There were about twenty-five of us ready to leave for Palestine. I decided to charter a plane, a French one. With us on this occasion were Major Samuel Weiser, from London, Konrad Berkovici, one of the band of writers in America who had for years given dedicated service to our cause through the Hebrew Committee, Samuel L. Katz, and Gusta Feingold, a young woman with a baby, whose husband and brother, both former officers in the British army, had sailed on the *Altalena.*

As we waited on Tuesday, June 22, for taxis to take us to the airport, Ariel arrived. He called Eli and me aside and showed us a slip of paper, with a telephoned message from the French Foreign Office. A telegram had arrived concerning the *Altalena.* The ship had been fired on off Kfar Vitkin—a communal village north of Natanya peopled exclusively by the Mapai, always enemies of the Irgun.

28

Blood and Tears

We reached Haifa the next afternoon and at the airport we rushed to buy the newspaper. There we read that twenty members of the Irgun had been killed, among them Abraham Stavsky, and that the *Altalena* was now burning off the shore of Tel Aviv.

It is not difficult to reconstruct the story of the *Altalena*. Begin has published his account and so has Eliahu Lankin.[1] At my request, Monroe Fein wrote his own report immediately after the event, and this was supplemented by Jerry Salaman, the crew member who had been charged with the defense of the ship.[2] All these accounts confirm and supplement each other.

It had been agreed between the Irgun and the Haganah early in June that on the official proclamation of the national army the Irgun would be incorporated into it unit by unit under its own junior officers. The Irgun High Command would continue to function as a military staff recognized by the new army command until the transfer of our forces was complete. By the middle of June, a number of Irgun units were serving in the army. One of them had participated in the heroic defense of Negbah, another had captured the Arab village of Yibneh north of Ashdod.

Once the government agreed to our bringing in the *Altalena*, Galili (now Assistant Minister of Security) and his colleagues determined Kfar Vitkin as the best place for the ship to land, Galili explaining that it would be easier there to evade United Nations surveillance. Hence Begin ordered the *Altalena* to head for Kfar Vitkin. Eliahu Lankin was delighted by these instructions. He told Fein that since Kfar Vitkin—an exclusively Mapai and anti-Irgun village—was the government's choice, it meant that the latter was cooperating with the Irgun in the operation. "All our troubles," he told Fein, "are over." Fein, however, was wary of air attacks and trained men as antiaircraft gunners. By the time the ship arrived off the Palestine coast, he had mounted twenty-two guns and thirty Browning machine guns as antiaircraft defense.

On shore the next phase of the discussions began on the distribution of the arms.

The very raising of the question came as a surprise to the Irgun. The arms were a collective achievement of the Irgun crowning years of effort and sacrifice. They should have arrived much sooner in order to equip Irgun units taking their place in the national army and the independent Irgun unit in Jerusalem. Galili told Begin that while the government agreed that 20 per cent of the arms should be allotted to our contingent in Jerusalem, the rest must be handed over unconditionally to the provisional government itself. Begin has published what he said to Galili: "Had the boat come several weeks ago, as we had planned, the Irgun would have had all the arms. Wouldn't you agree that our boys should come into the army at least fully armed and equipped? You yourself demanded that in view of the gravity of the situation all arms and equipment in the possession of the Irgun should be issued to the Irgun boys who were going into the army. What has changed? These particular arms were merely late in arriving. Our boys are already in the Army or will be within a matter of days. It would only mean that they will be mobilized with the full equipment which we in any case would have given them. What is wrong with that? Why can't you agree?"

Galili remained adamant, and announced that since no agreement had been reached on the distribution of the arms, the government would not help with unloading the ship.[3] This was a severe blow. It would not be easy for the Irgun to mobilize the men and equipment to unload the arms. All available Irgun manpower not yet actually in the army was alerted, as well as all possible sources of transport. Avraham optimistically decided to try the army once more. He telephoned David Cohen, the liaison officer at the Ministry of Security who had been present with Galili and Eshkol at our midnight meeting a month earlier, and who was now serving as the liaison officer with the Irgun staff, and appealed to him for help in unloading. Cohen promised to convey this request and suggested that Avraham should telephone again later.

The next day Cohen told Avraham that the army would send trucks to Kfar Vitkin. It was now Friday, June 18. On the evening of June 19, the *Altalena* was sighted off the coast. She was a little too far south, so that it was some hours before her crew spotted the signal lights on shore. At 3:30 A.M. the following morning the ship reached the beach at Kfar Vitkin. "It was impossible to bring the LST all the way up to the shore," wrote Fein. "The bow of the ship . . . was approximately forty meters from the end of a small pier which extended 100 meters from the shore . . . The shore parties had constructed a number of rafts made out of empty oil-drums and we attempted to lash these together with hopes of forming a bridge. However the surf was too high to handle them safely and this attempt was abandoned. We also attempted to land a group of passengers on the LCVP (small boat) but the coxswain, after attempting to run up on the beach several times, decided not to risk the boat and the people and returned with them to the ship. By this time daylight was approaching, and we gave up the attempt to land anything that night and put out to sea once more with the intention of returning as soon as darkness had fallen in the evening."

What had happened on shore?

There was an atmosphere compounded of action and celebration at Kfar Vitkin. At last all the months of striving and hard work were successfully concluded, and not too late to turn the scales in the battles soon to be renewed. For Begin, it was a great and historic occasion. He understood the significance, after years of underground struggle, of this dramatic and open manifestation of Irgun achievement. Landing the *Altalena* seemed a fitting last act for the Irgun Zvai Leumi.

David Cohen, the liaison officer, came that Sunday afternoon to Irgun headquarters at the Freud Hospital building. There he found his opposite number, Amitzur (a member of the Irgun High Command) who informed him that the ship had been ordered out to sea and would be back after dark for unloading. Cohen repeated the promise of army assistance in unloading the arms from the ship, adding that he himself would mobilize additional help in the neighborhood. The promised trucks never reached Kfar Vitkin, nor did Cohen, Galili, nor anybody who had taken part in the negotiations with the Irgun.

On the contrary: no sooner had Galili received information that the boat was within reach than he gave certain orders. The task of carrying them out fell to the army commander in the area, Dan Even, who headed the Alexandroni Brigade. In later years Even wrote a foreword to a book about this brigade which told in detail the briefing he was given that Sunday. According to his account (which has never been denied) Galili said to him: "The I.Z.L. has brought a boat filled with arms and ammunition to the shore at Kfar Vitkin. We knew the arms were due to arrive and reached an agreement whereby we and they were to unload the arms together. The I.Z.L. has broken the agreement. They did not inform us of the date of the boat's arrival nor where it was going to anchor."[4]

On the strength of this briefing, delivered in the presence of the Chief of Operations, Yigal Yadin, Brigadier Even proceeded to prepare the attack on the *Altalena* and the Irgun.

At nine o'clock on Sunday evening of June 20, the *Altalena* returned to shore. Begin went aboard and was given a tumultuous welcome. Two hours later, with the help of the LCVP, the whole Irgun contingent was landed. Nearly a thousand happy men and women were taken by truck to a rest camp at Natanya. A few remained with the crew to help unload, together with a large contingent of Irgun members. During the night a group of Palmach soldiers came to lend their assistance, asking Lankin to show them around the *Altalena*. He took them out in a motorboat to the ship, they expressed amazement at the size of the arms shipment, then left and were not seen again. Unloading proved very slow work, which would have taken a week, working nights, to complete. It was decided not to suspend work during daylight hours and the unloading went on till Monday midday or later.

Avraham had returned to Tel Aviv. There, accompanied by Amitzur, he requested the mayor to arrange for the dispatch of lighters from the port to speed up the work of unloading. On his way to Tel Aviv, Avraham saw troops going toward Kfar Vitkin, and wondered why.

During the night two strange ships had taken up positions near the *Altalena*. They were identified as corvettes of the Israel Navy. On the beach, Begin and Meridor noticed soldiers taking up positions around them in a wide circle. Soon, an officer arrived with a note for Begin, signed by the local army commander. It was very terse. The ship and the arms must be surrendered within ten minutes; otherwise the army would apply all the force at its disposal. Begin sent a reply that "this was no matter that could be settled in ten minutes." The army commander did not carry out his threat. Yaacov Meridor was permitted to leave the area to see the heads of the local councils of Kfar Vitkin and Natanya, who promised to intervene with the government. Begin sent word to the ship to stop unloading. Meridor returned and proposed that Begin should board the ship and make his way to Tel Aviv. After much discussion, Begin agreed.

"In this way," writes Begin, "we could extricate ourselves from these siege conditions and I would be able to communicate directly with the Government and put an end to what I still hoped was a perilous misunderstanding somewhere. I was doubtful about leaving the boys, surrounded as they were. But Meridor insisted that I go."

The men on the beach were called together, and Begin explained what he was about to do. At that moment, the army launched its attack from all sides and with a variety of weapons, including rifles, machine guns, and mortars. The Irgun members were unarmed. Begin shouted to the men to scatter, while he and Lankin and a number of others raced to the motorboat waiting at the shore and took off for the *Altalena*. Abraham Stavsky was in this group, as was Merlin of the Hebrew Committee, who had come from Tel Aviv. Monroe Fein, startled by the burst of shooting, "suspected some sort of a sneak Arab attack and my thought was to protect the ship by going to sea." He wrote:

> I then learned that there was a party of people coming from the beach in our LCVP which had been tied up at the pier at the time. I gave them instructions to stand off until I was clear of the beach and then I would take them aboard. As we started our engines and began to move off the beach, we saw the boat leaving the pier with approximately thirty people on board. As the ship swung around and headed seaward, our starboard side was facing the two corvettes which remained in the same position as they had all during the day and the previous night.
>
> Suddenly, and without any warning whatsoever, both corvettes opened fire on the "Altalena" with heavy machine-guns. We were completely unprepared for such an attack and could not begin to return fire. *I noticed the gunfire was aimed towards the LCVP as well* and swung the ship around to a position between the boat and the corvettes. *As soon as we had completed this maneouvre the firing from the corvettes stopped* and we began to receive a signal from them. As we were taking the men in the boat aboard, one of the corvettes again began firing but this time the shots were placed across the bow and were obviously intended as warning shots to make us comply with their order, which was to proceed immediately to Tel Aviv. We signaled back that we would comply with these orders. As soon as the LCVP was stowed aboard, we turned south and set a course for Tel

Aviv. One of the corvettes had taken up her position to the west of us and the other astern of us. As we continued, the latter gradually dropped out of sight.[5]

As the *Altalena* sailed southward to Tel Aviv she naturally hugged the coast, as Fein felt she would be safest there from attack by the corvette. Suddenly the corvette sent an order to change course and head for the open sea. The ominous significance of the order was patent.

"As we had no intention of complying with this order," wrote Fein, "we adopted various ruses to stall them off . . ."

It was after midnight on June 21 when the *Altalena* reached Tel Aviv. Running in at full speed, she was grounded opposite Frishman Street, and was greeted by a flurry of fire from the shore. Soon after, the two corvettes took up positions nearby. When dawn came, those on board saw that the shore area was surrounded by soldiers.

The last act of the tragedy may be simply described. After its arrival off Tel Aviv, no proposal or demand was made by the provisional government to the leaders of the Irgun or the captain of the ship. The white flag hoisted that day was disregarded, a formal "surrender" ignored.

In Tel Aviv, Avraham, on hearing what was happening at Kfar Vitkin, went to see Yitshak Gruenbaum, a member of the provisional government in whose name agreement to the *Altalena*'s coming had been given. Gruenbaum was startled to learn that there had been any prior discussions with the Irgun leaders concerning the *Altalena*. The members of the government, he insisted, had not been told of its expected advent. Ben-Gurion had informed his colleagues that the Irgun had sprung a surprise on the government by bringing in a ship with arms which they now refused to hand over to the army. This was a revolt, declared Ben-Gurion, which had to be crushed.

Gruenbaum promised to see Ben-Gurion immediately, and he and Avraham worked out an interim proposal for a compromise. The arms should be landed and stored while a reasonable arrangement was worked out for their distribution. Avraham explained that the Irgun would regard it as a great injustice if the Irgun soldiers were not given priority for these arms, although the final word would rest with the government. Twenty per cent of the arms, however, must be sent to the Irgun men in Jerusalem, where the government did not claim sovereignty.

Avraham never heard from Gruenbaum again. When they parted the *Altalena* was already on its way to Tel Aviv, carrying a prize for Ben-Gurion worth more than a few thousand rifles and a few million rounds of .303 bullets and the rest. Begin was aboard, having been maneuvered into a position where he might be treated as a rebel, the Irgun organization itself crushed.

On board the ship, Begin concentrated on getting the arms off.

"A group of armed men was sent ashore in the LCVP to take up positions round the beach," writes Fein, "in order that discharging of cargo could begin."

When a second group approached the shore they were fired on from the beach on all sides. The boat succeeded in landing this party but it could not return to the ship because it was subjected to heavy fire each time it approached. "The fact that the crew of the boat was waving a white flag," writes Fein, "did not seem to diminish the firing."

His account continues:

> On the ship, the order was given to the men in the defence unit to fire on such of the army troops as they could definitely see were firing on the ship. When the order to open fire was given the after battery mistakenly fired one burst at one of the corvettes, but this gun was immediately silenced, as the corvettes had shown no inclination to join in the fight. The ship continued to receive heavy firing from the shore for a period of about one and a half hours. Some of the heavy machine-guns ashore were using armour-piercing ammunition which passed right through steel bulkheads of the ship. This fact began to cause numerous casualties. We had no doctor on board and some of our casualties were very seriously wounded. We contacted, through Etzel[6] headquarters ashore, the army commander and requested a cease-fire in order to allow us to remove the wounded men from the ship. We arranged that we would use our own LCVP for this purpose. Cease-fire was agreed to almost at once and all firing on both the shore and ship had stopped within a few minutes. *From this point on there was not a single round of ammunition fired from the ship for the remainder of the afternoon.*[7]
>
> Immediately after the cease-fire order we attempted to contact the LCVP which had remained on the beach to the north of the ship. However, we discovered that we were unable to reach them as apparently their radio set had gone dead. Jack Baron, the Chief Officer volunteered to swim to the boat to tell the crew of the arrangement that had been made. As soon as he was in the water, he was fired

upon many times from the shore. He succeeded in reaching the shore, only to be captured by army men. He was not allowed to walk up to the boat. When we saw there was no possibility of communicating with our own boat, we immediately made this fact known to the Palmach commander and asked that a government boat be sent from the harbour to take off the wounded. This was immediately promised us. We then settled down to wait for the appearance of this boat, meanwhile caring for the wounded as best we could.

During this time one of them died. One hour and a half later, and after repeated requests there was still no sign of any boat. We had also tried to signal to the two corvettes to make the same request, but they gave no indication that they even saw our signal. At this time, we were suddenly taken under fire by a large gun which was located on the coast to the north of the city. This gun fired three shots all of which passed over the ship and exploded in the water beyond. We immediately got on the radio and asked whether or not the cease-fire order still was in effect and if so, what was the reason for the renewed gun-fire. A reply was made that the cease-fire order was still in effect and that the gun would be silenced immediately. Following this there was a period of about fifteen minutes in which no more gunshots were made.

During this time I conferred with the Commander-in-Chief of the Irgun and told him that if the gunfire should hit the ship, the ship, the cargo and possibly a good many lives would be lost and that he should at all costs maintain the cease-fire order until there could be further negotiations. This he agreed to do, but as he himself came up to talk on the radio to the headquarters ashore, the heavy gun resumed firing.

As soon as the gun started a second time, I struck the flag as a sign of surrender. We again inquired of the Palmach commander whether the cease-fire order was in effect and the reply came that the cease-fire order was in effect but that he had been "unable to contact all fronts." Within a few seconds after this message was received, there was a direct hit on the ship which started a large fire in the cargo hold. The ship's crew made immediate and valiant efforts to put out this fire, but because of the nature of the cargo it proved beyond our capacity and I ordered all men aboard to prepare to abandon the ship.

The first thought all of us had was to remove the wounded men. There was no panic. Everyone behaved in an extremely calm and heroic manner. As the men began jumping off the ship and swimming towards the shore, those of us still on board saw that they were being shot at continuously from rifles and machine-guns on the

e attack on Goldsmith House, the British Officers Club; Jerusalem, March 1, 1947.

e Irgun "barrel bomb" designed to lob over the high fences around British army
d police buildings.

Irgun attacks a British police tender in the heart of Tel Aviv, 1947.

Looking down Ben Yehuda Street BY COURTESY OF REX HOUSE, LONDON

The water tower at Yed Mordechai after Arab attack.

An Egyptian Air Force plane being salvaged on the Herzlia Beach.

This Way to Freedom!

Lash for lash the Irgun strikes back — and the Hebrew is no longer the British whipping boy in Palestine.

The Hebrew fights today. He stands battling for a spot on earth to call a home.

The Hebrew fighter is fed up with promises and sympathy. He is through asking . . . the eloquence of his weapons tells the world that he intends to live.

Of all the underdogs in the world today the Hebrew is the toughest to liquidate, the most certain to win — thanks to the fighting Resistance.

Resistance in Palestine is not an empty gesture of desperation; it is a sober operation calculated to WIN. Americans — you — can tip the scale to Hebrew victory.

PALESTINE FREEDOM DRIVE

A sample of propaganda from the Hebrew Committee of National Liberation; 1947.

A letter from the French Government to the IZL representative (Ariel); 1948.

MINISTÈRE
DES
AFFAIRES ÉTRANGÈRES

LIBERTÉ·ÉGALITÉ·FRATERNITÉ
RÉPUBLIQUE FRANÇAISE

CABINET DU MINISTRE
LE DIRECTEUR-ADJOINT DU CABINET

PARIS, LE 25 mai 1948

Monsieur,

Le Gouvernement Français me prie de vous demander de faire parvenir au Commandement de l'IRGOUN TSEVAI LEOUMI en Palestine, la communication suivante :

" Des informations reçues de JERUSALEM indiquent que les établissements français dont certains sont occupés par les troupes et d'autres soumis à des tirs d'artillerie, ont été pillés ou sont menacés de destruction complète.

" D'autre part, le Consulat Général de France est l'objet de tirs violents des deux parties ".

"Le Gouvernement Français peut difficilement tolérer que se poursuive plus longtemps cet anéantissement d'une oeuvre de civilisation plus que millénaire. Il demande au Commandant en Chef, dans les termes les plus énergiques, de donner à ses troupes les ordres nécessaires pour qu'il soit mis fin immédiatement à cette situation."

Il indique que l'heureux développement de nos rapports avec l'IRGOUN risquerait d'être compromis s'il n'était pas tenu compte de cet appel.

La même communication et pour les mêmes raisons a été faite auprès de l'Agence juive des Etats Arabes.

Veuillez agréer, Monsieur, l'expression de mes sentiments distingués.

Monsieur S. L. ARIEL,
39, avenue de l'Opéra,
PARIS
-:-:-:-:-

Jean MORIN

1

On guard
at Irgun headquarters
in Jerusalem; July 1948.

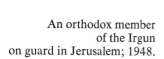

An orthodox member
of the Irgun
on guard in Jerusalem; 1948.

Relaxing on the *Altalena;* June 1948.

Monro Fein, captain of the *Altalena*.

Eliyahu Lankin, commander of the troops aboard the *Altalena*.

The *Altalena* in flames off Tel Aviv; 1948.

The New Gate of the Old City of Jerusalem penetrated by the Irgun in the last attack; July 17, 1948.

Begin visits the Jerusalem contingent of the IZL; August 1948.

End of the Irgun. Author and two staff members at the press conference.

beach. I rushed to the bridge and began waving a white flag and shouting to stop the fire on the men who were swimming for their lives. At the same time another man hoisted a large piece of white canvas on the halyard, but these efforts were of little avail, as the firing continued.

We continued our efforts to take off all of the wounded men and we received much assistance from those who rowed out from shore in a number of paddleboats, exposing themselves to the danger of the firing from the beach and the explosions on the ship which by that time had begun and continued in increasing frequency. Several men among us made a trip below decks throughout all parts of the ship which were still accessible and made certain that no man had been left on board. When this had been done and when the violence of the explosions warned us that it was highly dangerous to remain on the ship any longer, all men were ordered over the side and the ship left burning and exploding violently. By this time the harassing fire from the shore had ceased and the only danger to those of us still in the water was from the flying shrapnel of the ship itself.

Those of us who reached the shore were unmolested on the beach and most were taken immediately to Etzel headquarters where we received clothing and arrangements were made for shelter.

When the incredible news of this attack on their comrades reached them, members of one of the Irgun units now incorporated in the national army broke camp and made their way to Tel Aviv. They tried to get through the cordon surrounding the beach, but failed. The reporter of *Haaretz,* who saw their effort at two different street intersections near the beach, noted that in each case they did not use force nor open fire. Later, when the shelling of the boat started, the reporter noted, the Irgun called to the army soldiers to stop shelling and broke through their lines—but again refrained from shooting. Some of the army soldiers joined with the Irgun in shouting for shelling to stop. But no one seemed to know where the gun was and the shelling of the ship, and the shooting at those aboard who tried to save themselves by swimming, went on to the end. The ship was destroyed, along with the major part of the precious load of arms; sixteen members of the Irgun were killed and forty wounded. Two Haganah army soldiers were killed in the burst of retaliation and several wounded.

On my return, and for months afterward, I made as comprehensive a study as I could of the events surrounding the sinking of the *Altalena.* The facts (in spite of the strange distortions to which they

were subjected) are hardly disputable. I mulled them over, corre-
lated them with what I knew through my own direct experience, and
reached a bitter conclusion. From the moment it became clear that
Begin was on that ship, he became the target of the bullets and the
shells. There is no other rational explanation for the behavior of the
army.[8]

I write this fifteen years after the events, without heat. Very little
new information has come to light since that time. Yet I hesitated a
long time before reaching this conclusion. I would have preferred a
different explanation, to show that it was all a misunderstanding,
that something went wrong in the communications, that there was a
reason why none of the soldiers seemed aware of a white flag flutter-
ing on the ship and of white handkerchiefs waved frantically by men
swimming to shore.

There was a sprinkling of facts in the official version given by
Ben-Gurion and Galili when they released the story of those tragic
events. They maintained that suddenly one morning the Irgun
brought in a ship loaded with arms. That no one knew about it. They
reasoned that this shipment must be part of a conspiracy against the
government and, of course, it flouted the UN truce conditions. The
provisional government naturally could not tolerate either the threat
to itself or the breach of the truce regulations and demanded that
the boat and its contents should be handed over—so that they could
be placed under UN control. The Irgun refused to do so, obviously
meaning to arm its members for the purpose of holding the government to ransom. An Irgun contingent gathered on the beach at Kfar
Vitkin and opened mortar fire on the army, while the *Altalena* left
Kfar Vitkin, evaded two corvettes, and escaped toward Tel Aviv,
where she beached opposite Frishman Street. Here the Irgun was
again ordered to hand over the ship and its arms. It refused. There
was nothing left for the government to do but to destroy the ship,
which, said Ben-Gurion, was bringing ruin to Israel. "Blessed be the
gun that destroyed her," he proclaimed at the emergency meeting of
the Provisional National Council on June 23.

Not everyone was persuaded by this tale. Two cabinet ministers—
Rabbi Fishman and Mr. Moshe Shapiro—resigned. Several members
of the National Council asked unanswerable questions. Not all the
facts were known to them, but several could not be explained away.
First, Mr. Ben-Gurion's declared concern for the truce was sheer
nonsense. Second, the Irgun had brought the ship to, of all places,

Kfar Vitkin, a stronghold of anti-Irgun forces.[9] Third, the fighting men on board had been landed at Kfar Vitkin and sent away. Fourth, at Tel Aviv the ship had been fired on after raising a white flag. Finally, men who had abandoned the ship were fired on as they swam to shore.

Ben-Gurion had sufficient support among his party members and among the enemies of the Irgun to ignore the questions and protests of the more squeamish members of the National Council and of the Irgun sympathizers there. Public shock and bewilderment lasted long enough to enable him to emerge as the undoubted victor from the clash that had been so blatantly stage-managed.

The tragedy of the *Altalena* was the subject of considerable discussion within the Irgun. There was much criticism of Begin, particularly by some of those who had worked in Europe. He has been accused of naïveté because he believed that the government's agreement about the boat was sincere. But this naïveté we all shared. How otherwise would we have sent the ship at all? Everyone in Paris was overjoyed at the news brought by Ben Eliezer of the agreement with the government, taking it for granted that the ship and its cargo would be welcomed. Indeed, Begin was more cautious. He insisted on getting their specific approval, even ordering the ship to keep away from the coast until he had it.

On the shore at Kfar Vitkin, however, he failed in not recognizing at once there had been a betrayal. The ten-minute ultimatum on the beach was a great shock, but its implications should have been clear. Begin should have realized that he had been led into a trap. I believe that there was no alternative to "surrender," at Kfar Vitkin, followed later by a vigorous campaign of public enlightenment.

Begin's agreement to the proposal to board the boat and sail to Tel Aviv is also understandable, but by doing so he at once cut himself off from all possible channels of influence and communication and was exposed as formally resisting the army.

Unfortunately, when it became possible to tell the people the whole truth, it was done in such a manner as to nullify its effect. Once safely ashore, Begin went directly to the microphone. After the terrible events of the past two days, with the *Altalena* and its cargo destroyed, with sixteen of his young comrades dead and scores wounded, exhausted physically and nerves strained to breaking point, he was obsessed with one thought: the truth must be told for the people to realize the magnitude of the crime committed not only against the Irgun, but against the security of the people. He had a shattering story to tell, but did not realize that he was in no state to tell it. His performance was disastrous. The unprepared speech was too long. His voice broke and he wept. He sounded incoherent, out of control.

"There are times," wrote Begin in *The Revolt,* "when the choice is between blood and tears. Sometimes . . . it is essential that blood should take the place of tears. Sometimes, as the 'Altalena' taught us, it is essential that tears should take the place of blood."[10]

There is, however, another alternative; neither blood nor tears. Nearly fifteen years earlier, Jabotinsky had written about leadership in crisis. It was an article that none of us who followed Jabotinsky will ever forget. It was called "Kalt Un Fest" ("Cool and Firm").

Begin's excited speech helped to ensure Ben-Gurion's ascendancy. Many who saw Begin as a rising political star were disturbed by his emotion. They did not know that it was only the second time in his adult life that he had wept.

29

The Last Commander

The possibility of civil war was the first subject Begin and I discussed when I went to his home immediately after my arrival in Haifa, the day following the *Altalena* climax. The ship was still smoking off the beach. A Palmach unit had made a night raid on Metsudat Zeev, the headquarters of the Revisionist Party where the Jabotinsky Museum was housed. They had arrested a number of the people from the *Altalena* sheltering there for the night. Scores of Irgun members were arrested. On the road from Haifa our taxi had been stopped five times at road blocks and our papers examined.

The mood in the Irgun was explosive. Begin was haggard and tense, but he was against civil war. Within a fortnight at most the war with the Arabs would be resumed, he said. Our accounts with Ben-Gurion would be settled in the ballot box. We would set up a political party. Meanwhile, we must influence our people to join the army, ours now no less than Ben-Gurion's. We went together to a meeting of about 200 Irgun officers. Begin addressed them in this spirit. No voice was raised against his appeal.

We now planned the formation of a new political party. We started with a difficult financial problem. We had incurred heavy debts. The Irgun had been maintained for six months as a fighting force entirely at our own expense. We were claiming reimbursement from the provisional government for the period since our agreement with the Jewish Agency had come into effect, and negotiations were in progress. In the days following the *Altalena* incident Begin, Avraham and I met Shkolnik and David Remez, who was a member of the government. They did not deny liability. But the government never paid us a penny. Our new organization—Tenuat Haherut, the Freedom Movement—took over these liabilities, including a loan from the Bank Leumi, which Begin had obtained on his personal guarantee in order to ensure supplies during the battle for Jaffa. Tenuat Haherut also accepted part of the burden of financing the Irgun in Jerusalem. At meetings in Samuel Merlin's apartment, where he lay recovering from the leg wound he had received on the *Altalena,* we continually discussed our problems in Jerusalem.

At the end of June, the Irgun district commander there appealed to Begin to take over the active leadership. The commander, Mordekhai Raanan, occupied with the substantial problems of the organization and supply of the unit, suddenly found himself confronted with political problems. These were always the affair of the national headquarters. Now, strictly speaking, there were no national headquarters. Moreover communication was faulty, and with the resumption of fighting, urgent political decisions might have to be made.

Begin was prepared to accept the suggestion at once, but he was confronted with considerable opposition. Negotiations with the provisional government for the smooth entry of Irgun members into the army were still in progress, and there was much to be done to build the new political organization. Begin's presence in Tel Aviv seemed vital. On July 6, three days before the end of the truce, he proposed that I should go to Jerusalem. I accepted, and made hasty preparations to return to Jerusalem, to become the last commander of the Irgun.

On July 5, Count Folke Bernadotte, the UN mediator, had issued his proposals for peace. The Negev was to be included in the Arab state, as well as the whole of Jerusalem; Jaffa was to be excluded from the Jewish state, and Lydda and Haifa were to be free ports. He also proposed that the projected Arab state should be incorporated in Abdullah's Kingdom of Transjordan, placed, that is, under British control. In return, the Jews could keep western Galilee. He also suggested an economic union between Israel and this enlarged Kingdom of Transjordan—in effect, that the Jews, having had the revenues of their chief ports taken from them, should still subsidize the Arabs. Moreover, after two years, neither "state" would control its own immigration, which would be the concern of the Joint Economic Council, or, failing them, the UN itself.

The Bernadotte plan was published at the height of a new international crisis: the Berlin blockade. Again there was talk of war. Anglo-American collaboration was working smoothly, with a new level of harmony between London and Washington. Britain's unblushing welcome of Bernadotte's proposal was followed by a prompt announcement of the U. S. Government's approval. Nobody bothered to ask the Palestine Arabs for their opinion. Once the Arab states agreed to Bernadotte's plan, the whole Palestine issue could be reopened at the United Nations as though there had never been any earlier decision. Abdullah, the prime beneficiary of the scheme, actually traveled to Egypt and to Saudi Arabia to urge upon his old enemies peace with the Jews on Bernadotte's terms. They had no interest in handing Palestine to Abdullah. They turned him down, insisting on fighting to the end.

The provisional government rejected Bernadotte's plan, though they did continue to recognize the projected international status of Jerusalem. There had been rumors, while I was abroad, that a secret meeting between Jewish representatives, led by Mrs. Golda Meirson, and King Abdullah had ended in an agreement to allow the Old City of Jerusalem to remain in his hands. The rumor may or may not have been based on fact. That members of the provisional government long cherished the notion of a possible arrangement with Abdullah (whom, after all, they knew as a British puppet) was no secret.[1] Certainly Bernadotte's proposal revealed a new source of pressure against the Jewish position in Jerusalem.

The role of the Irgun, committed to the aim of restoring the city to Jewish sovereignty, seemed now to be invested with greater significance.

The Palmach had found an alternate route to Jerusalem, whereby the siege could be broken. It linked the two ends of the road by a rough punishing trail, which was promptly named the Burma Road. At one point, the terrain dropped 400 feet in a steep, sometimes impassable slope. When on July 8, the last day of the truce, my wife and I traveled to Jerusalem, the sand and stones at the steep descent were covered by a huge stretch of thick wire netting. All passengers dismounted, and the drivers edged the buses and trucks inch by inch down the slope while the wire squeaked and groaned under their weight. The rest of the road was pitted with potholes and bulging with rocks. Traffic proceeded along it at a snail's pace. The journey by bus from Tel Aviv took four or five hours. We were delayed by a breakdown near Bab el Wad. It was almost sunset when we arrived at Jerusalem.

Jerusalem had never been a bustling city. Now, as though in preparation for the resumption of the war, it seemed unusually hushed. People spoke in low voices, as if listening for some distant noise. The siege had been broken, and stocks of food replenished, but only with basic necessities. One commodity could not be replaced: water. The city was dependent on what it could draw from its own wells, and a strict ration was enforced of half a pail per person per day, for all purposes. Shortages of water and inadequate sewerage arrangements resulted in a pervasive smell which the midsummer sun baked into the stone buildings and into the very asphalt of the roads.

We took a stroll at twilight. There were few obvious signs of violent war. The buildings seemed virtually untouched. Yet we soon discovered that behind the stone façades considerable damage and destruction had been inflicted by Arab shells. There were few families that had not suffered some casualty—in battle or from the heavy shelling. Although all were certain of ultimate victory, they waited tensely for the ordeal that was to begin the next day.

The war resumed the next morning as the Arabs shelled a wide area of New Jerusalem. But by this time I was deeply immersed in the multiple problems of my new duties.

That Friday morning Raanan drove me to Katamon to see our base of operations. Konrad Berkovici and Major Samuel Weiser came with us. As we drove down Ussischkin Street there was a crash and a flash as of lightning that seemed to strike the car and lift it off the ground. It wobbled sharply, but Raanan brought it to a standstill. A shell had missed us by perhaps two yards and hit the pavement beyond. A young soldier was lying there, blood gushing from a wound in his throat. Two of his comrades lifted him into a vehicle but he died in a few minutes.

We spent that night at the Eden Hotel. Apart from my wife and myself, the only guests in the hotel were Berkovici, Weiser, and Shoshana Raziel, the widow of David Raziel. Amid the noise of the almost continuous shelling Berkovici relieved the tension by playing the piano.

We had previously agreed in Tel Aviv that my two main objectives in Jerusalem were to achieve the recapture of the Old City and to prevent a civil war. We succeeded in the second objective, ignoring all provocation, but we did not succeed in regaining historic Jerusalem.

The most direct threat of civil war was a bizarre by-product of the capture by the Irgun, two days before I came to Jerusalem, of five Britons alleged to be spying for the Arabs. The problem presented by these prisoners was placed before me as soon as I arrived.

There was a complicated background to their arrest. Jerusalem abounded with rumors of spies and traitors. The Arabs certainly had up-to-date information about strategic targets for their shelling, for they had demonstrated a very high degree of accurate selection. No sooner did the Haganah take over or move into a building than it was shelled. It was no accident that the Haganah and the Irgun Intelligence were attracted to the Jerusalem Electric Corporation. From its files of applications by new customers, no doubt, some of its employees possessed sufficient information to enable the enemy to pinpoint sensitive targets for attack.

The Haganah arrested a Jew—one of their own officers, and a senior official in the Jerusalem Electric Corporation—Meyer Tubiansky. The suspicions of the Irgun led them independently to capture five British officials of the corporation.

I studied the file of reports concerning the capture and interrogation of the five Britons. The men had been shadowed for some days before being arrested, when the Irgun had confiscated a radio transmitter with which, presumably, they had communicated with the Old City. The replies of one of the captives indicated glaring discrepancies. A second had in fact signed a confession. The remaining three continued to deny the charge of spying.

London was hard at work to secure their release. Britain had of course not recognized the state of Israel, so that British protests and demands were delivered to the provisional government through the Belgian consul. The reports which I had, suggested that the Jewish Agency leaders—now turned ministers—were in a panic. They assured the British that they had not arrested the men and would have them released. The Haganah had already court-martialed and shot Tubiansky, but replied in similar terms. At Lake Success Sir Alexander Cadogan brought what he termed the "kidnaping" to the attention of the Security Council and reported the assurances given by Bernard Joseph, head of the Jewish Civilian Administration in the city, that he was doing his utmost to have the captives released.

I rejected the idea of setting up a military court to try them. I decided to hold them until they could be brought to civil trial. The British Government continued to press for their release. Ben-Gurion urged Joseph to act; Joseph in turn urged the Haganah to do something. The Haganah Intelligence informed us that they were in possession of evidence against these men, who should therefore be handed over to them. We suggested that as we were in possession of the men they hand the evidence over to us.

A proposal of another kind came from Tel Aviv, via our radiophonic contact. Five of our men detained during the *Altalena* crisis—Yaakov Meridor, Lankin, Amitzur, Kook, and Hasson—were still prisoners; why not offer the provisional government an exchange? I turned down the idea. It would be an unequal exchange. Moreover I felt strongly that our men, far from seeking release, should insist on a trial. Ben-Gurion relayed a message through Joseph, threatening to take the prisoners from us by force.

I was not prepared to see a single Jew hurt over the five prisoners. I also did not want to enable Ben-Gurion to send them free. I replied, through our Intelligence chief, that we agreed to hand over the five prisoners in return for a prior public announcement that they would be taken into Israeli detention to stand trial. If it was refused, we would make public our proposal, and the prisoners would remain in our hands. Joseph, equally unwilling to risk bloodshed, accepted our condition. On Friday, July 16, we delivered the prisoners to the Haganah, and Joseph (or the Haganah) issued the agreed statement to the press. In due course, the Attorney General did not find enough evidence to try three of the five; of the two others, one was sentenced to seven years—a sentence quashed on appeal—the other was acquitted.

The membership of the Irgun in Jerusalem, as I found it, was roughly equal in numbers to the Haganah units in the city. There were about a thousand men and women serving, of whom some seven hundred were in the front-line units, quartered in evacuated Arab and British houses at Katamon in the south of the city. Our stores of food and supplies were maintained in the center of Jerusalem. In Talbieh we had turned a mansion into a hospital. We manned the defense posts on Mount Zion opposite the southern wall of the Old City with the Haganah, and also in the Pagi Quarter opposite Sheikh Jarrah in the north, where the Arabs held a segment of the city outside the walls.

In the military unit, the Gedud, were many men who had come from the coast—before and after the *Altalena* incident. For the most part it consisted of Jerusalem-born youths, with a common background with many of the rank-and-file members of the Haganah.

The fierce ordeal to which all those in the city had been subjected for seven months had developed a sense of comradeship and mutual respect among most of the people, and this the deliberate hate-mongering of some of the Mapai elements in the Haganah leadership could not undermine.

Nobody could ignore the considerable part the Irgun had played in securing and defending the city. When the British evacuated a day sooner than expected, it was the Irgun that prevented the Arabs from taking over the "Bevingrad" complex, almost adjacent to the Old City, which had served as the British headquarters. The Irgun had fought with great bravery alongside the Haganah in the Old City until its surrender. Though woefully lacking in heavy arms, the Irgun had under the operational agreement been assigned by Shaltiel to defend the Sheikh Jarrah Quarter, bearing alone the brunt of the first attack with armor by Abdullah's Arab Legion and then the obloquy of hostile politicians for the loss of the quarter.

It was an Irgun unit of sixty-five men, led by one of its brilliant young officers, Nimrod (Yehuda Lapidot), that had saved Ramat Rahel, the southern key to the city. The Egyptians had captured this kibbutz and driven out the resident defenders and a Haganah garrison. The Haganah had retaken it, only to be driven out again. An armored Haganah unit finally succeeded in holding the village. At a joint staff meeting of the three fighting organizations, it was agreed that a force of seven platoons (about two hundred men) would be sent in to replace the armored unit. Of these, three would be Haganah, two Irgun, and two Lehi.

Inexplicably the Irgun unit was the only one to arrive at Ramat Rahel. For thirteen hours, from 9 A.M. till 10 P.M. on May 25, Nimrod and his men held off a superior mixed force of Egyptians and irregulars commanding an armored car and a tank. Nimrod's heaviest weapon was a Lewis gun. When that night Nimrod and his men were relieved by a Haganah contingent, they had no ammunition left and half their number were wounded.

No one ever explained the failure of the Haganah to fulfill their part of the arrangement, or why they neglected to send reinforcements that whole day while a Palmach unit sat idly at Arnona, a mile from Ramat Rahel. It later became the subject of bitter recrimination between the Irgun and the Haganah.

Our forced marriage with the Haganah was uneasy and fraught with tension. According to the operational agreement, the Irgun officers were obliged to carry out the orders of Shaltiel, commander of the Jerusalem Haganah. This was not made easier by their suspicion of his animosity, nor by the low opinion of his military capacity which they shared with many of his colleagues and subordinates and even with a majority of the civilian population.

In my post as Irgun commander in Jerusalem I tried to combine overall responsibility with a minimum of detailed interference. There were suggestions from several quarters that I should make changes in personnel, but I left every officer in his place. Raanan continued to act as the district commander, without interference from me; nor did I interfere in the administration of the Gedud, though on two occasions I was asked to countermand decisions by the Gedud commander and once I persuaded him to change his mind. I took over direct control of all external relations and Intelligence as well as responsibility for the four-page daily newspaper which the Irgun had founded during the siege. I remained anonymous for several reasons. I had been appointed by the Irgun High Command which had officially—and in fact—ceased to function. Uncertain of Ben-Gurion's possible reactions against Begin and the others in Tel Aviv if a member of the national High Command were discovered directing the Irgun in Jerusalem, I judged anonymity to be the most discreet procedure, keeping my radiophone contacts with Tel Aviv down to a minimum.

Soon I learned that anonymity was also an aid to greater efficiency and to avoiding contacts not essential to my task. I made no change in our representation with the Haganah and with the civil authority (the Jerusalem Emergency Committee) headed by Dr. Bernard Joseph. I remained unknown to them. Raanan and our operations officer, Zeev (Menachem Shiff), continued their contact with Shaltiel and his officers. Dan (Kalman Bergman) and his assistant Aharon (Joseph Leiserowitz) dealt as before with Bernard Joseph and his subordinates in the civil authority of the city, betraying no hint by whom they were being briefed.

When it was difficult to gather together all the members of the command for discussion, I adopted Begin's underground method and filtered decisions to each of them individually. This was not difficult, as there were only five of them in all: Raanan, Dan, Nikko (Nathan Germant, the commander of the Gedud), Baruch (Eliahu Meridor, who was in charge of training) and Yitshak (Moshe Ariel), who served as the adjutant of the Gedud.

30

Ten Crucial Days

The next ten days of fighting throughout the country added considerably to the territory held by Israel, although we were not always victorious. In the northeast repeated attacks failed to dislodge the Syrians from the positions they had occupied west of the Jordan. In the center a fourth and then a fifth attack on Latrun failed. The direct road from Jerusalem to the coast was not restored. In the south, it was the Egyptians who took the offensive. They gained no ground, but no serious Jewish counteroffensive developed. The Negev remained cut off from the rest of the country.

Our victories, however, were impressive. Galilee, west and east, Upper and Lower, was all but cleared of the enemy, except for an enclave in the north-center held by an otherwise soundly beaten Fawzi Kaukji, and the troublesome northeast corner where the Syrians were entrenched.

On the central front both Lydda and Ramleh were captured, a large number of villages falling into Jewish hands. The corridor from Jerusalem to the coast was widened, adding space to the new alternative road. These victories began to shape Israel's attenuated outlines.

Transcending the victories was a buoyant new spirit of offensive, the verve and speed of action which infused the new Israel Army. Still underequipped, it had yet, with the aid primarily of Czechoslovakia, been considerably enriched in arms, including a small number of tanks, a small number of fighter planes and, finally, three bombers. These planes carried out raids on Cairo and Damascus, repaying in some small measure the substantial bombing to which the Egyptians had subjected our cities.

In those ten days it became clear that the Arabs' design had failed.

All their invading forces—the Transjordan Arab Legion with its British officers, the Syrians, and even the Egyptians—were still capable of hard fighting, and held large tracts of territory, but they were now on the defensive. The tide had begun to flow in our favor. The whole of western Palestine was within our grasp when the Jewish counter-offensive was halted by a new truce.

The decision to accept the truce had neither military origin nor justification. By that mid-July, in seven months of fighting, nearly one in every hundred of our population had been killed in the defense of our country.[1] The governments of the great Western nations which had refrained from any step to prevent or lessen the slaughter of our people by the Germans refrained also from helping us repel the attacks of the Arab states. While our one hope of national survival hung by a thread they withheld all aid from us. Now Britain once more was planning our final destruction. Their interest was now to prevent our turning the tables and to leave the aggressors as strong as possible for renewing their aggression if we rejected Bernadotte's plan.

London and Washington guided the Security Council to a quick decision for a new truce that, significantly, included the threat of sanctions against any unwilling party.

Why did Ben-Gurion and his government accept the truce? In a long speech in the Knesset nine months later (April 4, 1949), Ben-Gurion claimed that he had accepted the truce on "democratic" grounds. Had we occupied the whole of western Palestine in July 1948 we should, he declared, have been in a minority and the Arabs in a majority. We would have had to set up a Parliament, and the Arabs would simply have outvoted us. At which point, there would in fact *be* no Jewish state.

This was characteristic Ben-Gurion obfuscation, manufactured to extricate him from a difficult position in Knesset debate. If its implications were valid, Zionism was from the beginning undemocratic and immoral. Until 1948, the Arabs in the country were in a majority. Zionism claimed that the Arabs' residential rights were to be weighed against the rights of the Jewish people as a whole both inside and outside the country. Here lay the origin of the passion of aliyah, the insistence of all Zionists on immigration and more immigration. Here lay the root of the principle accepted by Britain in 1917, by the League of Nations in 1922, and, at that time, by the Emir Feisal and other Arab leaders. Why suddenly in mid-July 1948, when at last the Jews could come back freely, it was right to reverse this principle and make a temporary Arab majority the decisive factor, Ben-Gurion never troubled to explain.

In fact, even his statistics, as far as they were relevant to the argument, were hollow. That summer the Arab majority was on the verge of becoming a minority. There had never been more than 900,000 Arabs in western Palestine. By July 1948, when a quarter of a million Arabs had certainly fled western Palestine, large-scale Jewish immigration had already begun. By October, when the elections Ben-Gurion envisaged might have been held, the Jews were probably already in a small majority. In January 1949, when the first general election was held, the Jewish majority in the whole of western Palestine was unquestionable. All such estimates, moreover assume that the Arabs in the "triangle" west of the Jordan, would have refrained from flight and remained in the country.

Fifteen years later, Mr. Ben-Gurion demonstrated the cynicism of that Knesset explanation. In a newspaper interview in 1964 he declared that if he had had other generals—specifically General Moshe Dayan—in 1948 our frontiers might well have been different.[2] He implied that he had wanted to occupy all western Palestine but had been frustrated in his determination by the inefficiency of the soldiers. This attack provoked the soldiers, who throughout the years had maintained a loyal silence, to expose the realities of 1948. Three of them—General Yaacov Dori, the chief of staff, General Yigael Yadin, the chief of operations, and Brigadier Yigael Allon—made statements that constitute a formidable indictment of Ben-Gurion's leadership in 1948. Allon summed up their reactions in forthright language:

"Mr. Ben Gurion's words do not accord with the facts. They are a slur on the fighters in the war of independence who longed to liberate the entire country and were not permitted to do so. When the then Prime Minister and Minister of Defence ordered a halt to our advance we were at the height of our victories on all the decisive fronts, from the Litany River in the north to the heart of the Sinai desert. In a few days fighting we could have achieved the final destruction of the Arab invasion armies and the liberation of the whole country. The Army cannot be blamed for mistaken political decisions. The country has remained divided and the Old City of Jerusalem out of bounds not because of operations that failed but because of operations that were disallowed and omissions that were forced on the

Army by the political leadership headed by Ben Gurion. The country has remained partitioned and its borders distorted not because of incorrect strategic planning or inadequate military ability but purely and simply because of a political retreat in the crucial days. This was within the responsibility of Mr. Ben Gurion."

It was indeed. The blunder was historic. It was not only a question of liberating western Palestine. We threw away the opportunity of completing the military defeat of the Arab forces and thus denied ourselves the possibility of achieving a peace treaty with the Arabs.

In 1948 the people of the neighboring Arab nations were not passionately involved in the dispute with Israel foisted on them by their leaders. A peace treaty which provided for direct cultural and commercial contact with them could have helped crystallize, in time, the large element in these countries prepared for reasonable relations with the Jews. A peace treaty based on rational frontiers for Israel would have opened doors to the solution of the problem of those Palestine Arabs who ran away.

The half-achieved victory and the consequent unachieved peace were the natural parents of the tense and explosive near-belligerence that has never since ceased. They left the field open for the Arab politicians to pour forth an incessant and unanswered harangue of hate into the ears of the new generation of Arabs. They made inevitable their exploitation of the refugee problems as a focus for dreams of revenge and for the threats of forcible Arab conquest of Israel that still animate large sections of the population of the Arab states around us, after eighteen years of indoctrination.

31

The Failure to Win Back the Old City of Jerusalem

The story of the failure, in 1948, to restore the Old City of Jerusalem could be told in a few simple sentences. The Irgun, even with Lehi co-operation, did not have sufficient strength to recapture it alone. It could have been done with the help of the Haganah. To bring about any change in these essential circumstances required much more time than the eight days of military operations that began on July 9.

When I first arrived in Jerusalem, Raanan reported his negotiations with Shaltiel on the operations to be carried out as soon as the first truce was ended. Shaltiel had announced his determination to recapture the Old City, truce or no truce.

The people of Jerusalem blamed Shaltiel for the fall of the Old City in May. He failed, they said, to understand the immediate situation within the walls and treated the officers there without consideration. He seemed unconcerned with the fate of the city. It was said that he was much distressed by these charges, and would now make a supreme effort to rehabilitate himself by the triumphant capture of the Old City.

With this declaration of principle, Shaltiel announced to Raanan that the capture of the Old City could be effected only after essential operations on the other side of Jerusalem. It was vital to widen the corridor from Jerusalem to the coast. Strategically, he said, this was more important than control of the Old City. He had therefore decided to capture the Arab villages of Malha and Ein Karem and two Arab posts, Hirbet El Hamama and Mizmil, on the western outskirts of the city. Raanan and Zeev objected to this plan. They pointed to the unique significance of the Old City and the great moral effect its restoration would have on the Jewish forces; while the capture of the Arab villages west of Jerusalem could be effected at any time. Shaltiel was adamant. Under the agreement the Irgun had made with the Haganah, he had the last word. He comforted Raanan by giving him details of the timetable of operations. The Arab positions of Hirbet El Hamama and Mizmil would be attacked by the Lehi and a Haganah youth unit on July 9. Malha would be attacked on Sunday, July 11, by an Irgun force with Haganah support. This operation should be concluded by the twelfth. The attack on the Old City would be launched on Tuesday, July 13.

Raanan's report, designed to bring me up to date, was delivered at the first meeting I called of the Command.

It suggested an odd situation. Irgun platoons were occupying defense posts with Haganah men both at Mount Zion in the east and at "Pagi" in the north. A part of the remainder of the Irgun force would go to Malha. At the smaller targets in the west the main force would be provided by Lehi. In each case the Haganah would supply a "supporting" force. It seemed to me that the main strength of the Haganah was not to be employed at all until the actual attack on the Old City. Even there it could comprise at most half the total attacking force. One did not need to be an expert to see imbalance in this plan of timing and distribution of forces.

The supporting forces the Haganah was to supply in the attacks on the western positions of the Arabs were to be drawn from a Youth Battalion (the "Jonathan") consisting of sixteen- and seventeen-year-olds. This plan indicated a certain amateurishness, in striking contrast to the dash and intelligence with which the Israel Defense Army was preparing for the resumption of the battles in the rest of the country.

In spite of Shaltiel's alleged passion for personal atonement in the Old City, we had serious grounds for suspecting the provisional government of a less than zealous attitude to the restoration of Jerusalem. I asked the members of our Command the crucial question:

"Is the Irgun in Jerusalem capable of launching an attack on the Old City by itself (let us say, with Lehi) with a reasonable chance of success?" Germant said no; we had not enough strength. Raanan was equally definite: no. He gave as one reason the possibility of obstruction by the Haganah.

After sifting all the facts, I came to the conclusion that Raanan was probably right. If it had not been for the danger of obstruction by Shaltiel, and had we the time for planning, the Irgun could possibly have gone it alone; but we dared not try.

The bare narrative of the events that followed requires no analysis. The Lehi-"Jonathan" attack on Hirbet El Hamama was successful, but Mizmil was not captured until Saturday, July 10. The Ein Karem attack was postponed. On Sunday morning Shaltiel sent a message to Raanan announcing the postponement of the attack on Malha to Monday evening; then on Monday morning he told Raanan that this would be postponed to Tuesday evening. The attack on Malha was at last launched shortly before midnight on Tuesday, July 13. After a softening-up prelude by the Haganah mortars emplaced at Bayit Vegan, the four Irgun platoons and the two of the Haganah youngsters fought their way into the village. At dawn the village was in their hands, at a cost of one killed and one wounded.

Later that morning our Intelligence reported a concentration of the enemy south of the village. Shortly afterward the village was heavily shelled. An Irgun request to the Haganah to lay down mortar fire on the Arab positions met with the reply that the men manning the mortars had gone on leave. The Arab advance on the village was thus undisturbed. A fierce battle developed in the center of the village while the Irgun positions were heavily shelled without reply. The Irgun unit was pushed back slowly, suffering heavy casualties. They retreated to a row of houses on the fringe of the village, and succeeded in keeping the advancing Arabs at a distance of seventy yards. They held on till we could send reinforcements from the city. Then the tide turned. The Arabs moved back, turned, and ran. The Irgun had lost seventeen killed, and many wounded.

The battle for Malha thus lasted until Thursday, July 15. That day the Security Council at Lake Success passed its resolution demanding a truce in Palestine within three days and within twenty-four hours in Jerusalem. Zero hour for Jerusalem was fixed for Saturday morning, July 17, at 5:45 A.M.

On Tuesday evening, at the time our force was advancing on Malha I was at my "headquarters"—a room in Raanan's apartment which he had placed at our disposal. I was startled by the arrival of visitors from Tel Aviv: Giddy, with a veteran underground fighter, Haim Toyt (Shraga Ellis), and an Irgun ex-officer in the Jewish Brigade, Yerahmiel (Yehuda Segal). They looked pale and tense after their hazardous and dusty journey. "What about the Old City?" Giddy asked. "Why have we not attacked the Old City?"

It was painful to give him my answer. "If we were able to attack the Old City on our own," I said, "we should be doing so probably this evening, instead of attacking Malha. We are very suspicious of Shaltiel. But all the information our boys have given me tells the same story. Our strength is inadequate even in numbers. Maybe we could make up for numerical weakness by tactical ingenuity, but we cannot attack the Old City if the Haganah is prepared to prevent us. We can therefore only continue to press Shaltiel to carry out his promises to us."

Giddy was unwilling to resign himself to this sober conclusion. He had a strong feeling that somewhere, somehow there was an error in the facts or in my analysis. "I don't want to refuse any opportunity," I assured him. "Your ability may make the difference. You may see a way. You know the territory. Take twenty-four hours. Go over the ground. Get all the information you want. If you then tell me that an attack is feasible, that you can make a reasonable plan, we shall attack the Old City regardless of Shaltiel. I shall take the responsibility for breaking the agreement with the Haganah." Giddy agreed and went away with his companions. On Wednesday they toured the forward positions facing the Old City and examined the front, yard by yard. They pondered the relative positions of the Haganah and the Irgun units.

I count that Wednesday as one of my most trying days in the Irgun. I received reports of our initial success at Malha, of the inexplicable abandonment by the Haganah mortars, and of our dead and wounded. I waited for word of the impact of the reinforcements we had sent. Finally I waited impatiently for Giddy. He returned in the evening, grimy and disheveled. His report was negative. If we had had freedom of movement, untrammeled lines of supply, and were not threatened by interference or obstruction in the rear, he would have had no hesitation in planning an attack. But without Haganah acquiescence this was impossible.

Over the years more circumstantial evidence has accumulated to confirm that Shaltiel derived his inspiration, and perhaps his orders, directly and personally from Ben-Gurion. Ben-Gurion does not seem to have often consulted his colleagues in the provisional government and gave them little opportunity to decide on the deployment of the armies, even when the issues were purely political.

Ben-Gurion's handling of Brigadier Allon's plan to capture the Gaza "strip" is a case in point. At the end of 1948, Brigadier Allon had broken the last Egyptian pockets of resistance in the Negev. His rear secured, his flanks untroubled, he saw Gaza, lying on his homeward path, as a difficult but attainable objective. Yet, as his orders did not include the capture of Gaza, he hurried to Jerusalem to ask for permission to do so. Ben-Gurion was absent, resting at Tiberias. Allon made his request to the Foreign Secretary, Shertok, who acquiesced, but said it was not within his province to decide finally. Allon must see Ben-Gurion. Allon rushed to Tiberias, but Ben-Gurion refused permission. The United States Government had exerted pressure, he said. Gaza remained in Egyptian hands.

Where Shaltiel's procrastination had previously been measured in days, it had now to be measured in hours. He knew before we did that the provisional government had agreed to the truce, and that he had at most two days in which to attack the Old City. Yet there was no hint of impatience or haste in his behavior. We were embattled at Malha, our force preoccupied and weary, while Shaltiel's own forces were unemployed and rested, presumably waiting for action. Yet it was we who had to press him. Shaltiel seemed responsive to our pressure. Now, surely, the attack would be launched. Raanan and Zeev urged him to agree to the Irgun taking the Mount Zion sector, as the positions there were in any case manned mainly by the Irgun, whose officers had carried out detailed reconnaissance of the terrain. Shaltiel refused. The attack from Mount Zion, he maintained, would be executed by the Haganah. Meantime he let Thursday pass.

We did not propose to employ the Malha unit in the assault on the Old City. They would be required in a subsequent phase—as a second attacking wave, as reinforcement or replacement—depending on the course of the battle. We had the advantage of initial surprise. Except perhaps for Mount Zion, the Arabs could not know where the Jewish forces would breach the wall. The three Jewish forces would enter the Old City simultaneously. Once within the walls, they should be able to establish themselves without much opposition before advancing to effect a junction. We expected this second phase to bring hard fighting, followed by a mopping-up operation. The issue would be decided within twenty-four hours, the complete occupation of the Old City should not take more than three days.

On Friday Shaltiel fixed 4 P.M. as the hour to assemble forces, telling Raanan that preliminary shelling of the Old City would start an hour later. In reply to Raanan's anxious query, he repeated his undertaking that once Jewish forces gained an entry into the Old City they would remain there and he would disregard the truce.

At the Irgun base in Katamon one might have thought that a great victory had been won. A spirit of jubilation prevailed—of happy expectation, of personal fulfillment. After all, the Old City is Jerusalem to us. The dreams and prayers and hopes that find expression in the evocation of Jerusalem are centered not in some abstraction, but precisely in the Old City. The Irgun had traditionally given much to secure the Old City—ever since the Pelugot Hakotel in 1937, so many of whose members had died or been maimed in the defense of the Jewish Quarter; two months earlier Irgun men had fought heroically to save the Old City. All had since dreamt of the day when the battle to liberate it would be launched.

Indeed the units quarreled over the privilege of liberation. That morning the contingent from Malha, having handed the village over to a Haganah garrison, returned to base. Weary and weakened as they were, they objected strenuously when they heard that they were not to lead the assault on the Old City. Their commander, "Kabtzan" (Eliezer Sudit), all but mutinied. Four or five hours' rest, he said, would be enough for his men. But in the end he accepted the inevitable and agreed to Nimrod's platoon entering the Old City first.

Two men normally engaged in auxiliary duties requested to be attached to the attacking force, had already been turned down by the commanding officer. I had to disappoint them. One of them did smuggle himself into the attacking force: Joe Kohn, a volunteer from San Francisco, who had worked for the Irgun in Europe and had arrived on the *Altalena*. A veteran of the United States Army in the Second World War, he was killed that night at the post he had chosen for himself, manning our mortar in the Russian Compound.

At four o'clock our men piled on to the trucks ready to take them to the forward base: the Notre Dame building opposite the Old City. As I watched them from the pavement I saw a flash from the southeastern horizon. A moment later a shell landed in the road between me and the trucks. Then another landed a little further away. My reactions were slow. The others had flung themselves down. I stood still, looking for more flashes. A shell tore a hole in the pavement a few feet from me before I took cover. Though several hundred men were crowded into a small area and half a dozen shells fell in those few minutes, nobody was even scratched. The burst of fire subsided. With the men singing "On the Barricades," which had become the Jerusalem Irgun battle hymn in the months of open warfare, the trucks moved off toward the city. I did not go to the forward headquarters, which was in the Barclay's Bank Building opposite Notre Dame. I held to my resolution not to get in the way of the operations officers. I promised myself that I would visit Nimrod and his men inside the Old City the next day. Within the few hours left before the hour for the truce, Shaltiel twice postponed the operation. Of the sixteen hours left on Friday afternoon, another eight were lost. Zero hour was moved from four o'clock to eight o'clock, and at ten o'clock it was postponed to midnight. Only then began the shelling of Arab positions in the Old City.

At about nine o'clock the Arabs laid down a fierce barrage of shelling over the whole city. I could remember nothing so sustained even in the London duels between German bombers and British AA guns. From the weight of their attack the Arabs might well have been preparing their own assault on the New City. Their fire seemed to subside when the fierce Jewish shelling of the Old City began, a softening process which went on for three hours, although twice Raanan vainly asked Shaltiel to shorten the period.

At last the shelling of the New Gate area was stilled, and Nimrod was able to launch his attack. It was after three o'clock. Under Arab machine-gun fire, one of the veteran sappers of the Irgun, Yosef Danon, brought the load of explosives to the wall, set the fuse, and raced for cover. The explosion blew a large hole in the wall. The way into the Old City was open. Nimrod's platoon went in at once and encountered heavy fire as they took up their position in the lee of the wall before advancing.

Nimrod asked for orders. His first rendezvous inside the walls was with the small Lehi force which was to break in a little further north and now he wished to know where they were and how far the Haganah force from Mount Zion had come. But nobody had moved. The Lehi had suffered a disaster. The truck carrying their large conical explosive had been hit by an Arab shell on its way to their forward base and had been completely destroyed, along with a second truckload of ammunition. A second cone had been brought to their forward base, but the ground between them and the wall now came under such heavy fire that to venture through it was impossible.

The explosive applied by the Haganah to the wall opposite Mount Zion suffered a similar fate. At first an attempt was made to convey it through a narrow tunnel dug by Irgun sappers during the truce, but the cone proved too wide for this operation. Two Haganah men then carried the cone to the wall, under Arab fire. There it exploded, but merely inflicted scorching. No other explosives were available and no further attempt on the wall was made.

A short time remained before the hour fixed by the international authority for the truce. There was indubitably a Jewish force within the Old City. Now Shaltiel's promise was formally put to the test, and Raanan addressed a query to him. It would, he hoped, be in order for Nimrod's force to continue operations in the Old City after 5:45, when the truce came into effect. Nimrod could hold out until the Haganah and Lehi broke in.

Shaltiel's reply was explicit: "We shall treat you," he signaled, "as rebels. We shall attack you as we would the enemy. We shall cut you off from your supplies." Nimrod was ordered to withdraw. His little force had suffered no casualties. Two hundred and fifty yards to the rear in the Russian Compound, the same shell that killed Joe Kohn also killed Zwi Krinsky and inflicted multiple wounds on their officer "Chanky," (David Brisk) the Irgun's artillery officer. The authentic version of Shaltiel's attitude emerged from the report of Meshullam, the Irgun's liaison officer at Shaltiel's forward headquarters. He described how Shaltiel's staff languidly sat through the night, frequently examining their watches. No one complained, he said, that the hours were passing without action. Everyone seemed to be waiting for the hours to pass and the truce to come into effect, and when this came all were blatantly relieved. Within a dozen hours Shaltiel demonstrated that his passion for the truce was quite spurious. He gave orders that Saturday for the capture of Ein Karem, which was duly attacked and occupied by a mixed Lehi and Haganah force twenty hours after Shaltiel had forced the Irgun withdrawal from the Old City.

From a quite unexpected quarter years later, new light was shed on Shaltiel's actions, clearly establishing the source of Shaltiel's orders. This evidence comes from the memoirs of Dov (Bernard) Joseph, Shaltiel's civilian counterpart. He writes: "A memorandum I dictated at the time makes it evident that we should have had a legal right to continue the attack, which was going well for us, beyond the 5:45 deadline on Saturday morning. At 6 P.M. the evening before,

Colonel Shaltiel and I had met the Chairman of the Truce Commission and informed him that Shaltiel had been instructed by our government to order his troops to cease firing at 5:45 the next morning if we received information by midnight from the Truce Commission that the Arabs had also agreed. It was arranged between us that the Truce Commission would give this information directly to Shaltiel as soon as it was received . . .

"Only at about 2:30 on Saturday I learned that the Truce Commission had in fact received no official answer from the Arab side. According to my memorandum I then telephoned Shaltiel, who confirmed that he had not been notified by midnight that the Arabs had consented to the cease-fire. When I asked him why, then, our forces had stopped firing at 5:45 he replied that his instruction was that we were not to fire if the Arabs stopped firing, and in fact they had stopped firing. I expressed surprise at this and said my understanding from the explicit wording of Shertok's cable to me was that we would cease fire only if the Arabs had, at a fixed time, notified the commission that they would do likewise."

Dr. Joseph does not analyze Shaltiel's behavior. He merely describes his own further efforts to secure information until he learned that at no stage had the Arabs announced their acceptance of the cease-fire. He concludes: "Clearly if we had gone on fighting that morning the Security Council could not justifiably have held us to be at fault . . ."[1]

No one suspects Shaltiel of treachery. He had no reason, military or personal, for disobeying or distorting Shertok's instructions, still less for branding himself as a nincompoop—except that he must have had overriding instructions from an authority higher than Shertok. To Ben-Gurion's formal responsibility there accrues testimony not only that he gave Shaltiel specific orders designed to prevent the recapture of the Old City, but that he did so probably without consultation with his colleagues in the government.

Logically, in the circumstances known to us and even more in the light of Dr. Joseph's knowledge, an inquiry should surely have been held on this last phase as, indeed, on the earlier phases of the loss of the Old City. Subsequently in the Knesset, we proposed such an inquiry. Ben-Gurion, supported by his followers, including Dov Joseph and Brigadier Allon, successfully resisted it.

32

The Irgun Disbands

The fate of the Old City was sealed. The Arabs would certainly not hasten a renewal of the war. The provisional government had no intention of provoking its renewal in Jerusalem. That battle was lost to the Jews.

This reality ran counter to the United Nations decision to internationalize Jerusalem. Jewish control of the New City sharply frustrated the alternative proposal put forward in June by Count Bernadotte to hand the whole city over to the Arabs. Either of these alternatives would result in pressure to weaken the Jewish hold on the New City. It was therefore essential as quickly as possible to strengthen such a hold. We therefore began a campaign for the formal inclusion of Jerusalem in the Jewish state.

A week after the truce came into effect I traveled down to Tel Aviv. Begin was immersed in the many calls and duties entailed in inaugurating an ambitious new political party. He was intensely sensitive to the problem of Jerusalem, and I too was conscious of the party's material sacrifice, soon an impossible one, in the continued maintenance of the Irgun in Jerusalem.

We agreed that if the provisional government did not proclaim Jerusalem as part of the state of Israel, the Irgun must continue to hold on there as long as possible in order to emphasize our determination to resist any status for Jerusalem but Jewish sovereignty. We agreed to set up in Jerusalem a branch of the political party to rally support for its inclusion in the state.

Nine days later, in the name of the newly founded Jerusalem branch of Tenuat Haherut, we carried through a petition calling on the Israel Government to include the city in the state. More than thirty thousand signatures were collected in the two days of the campaign.

Some refused to sign. They obeyed the injunction of the organs of the provisional government in Jerusalem, headed by Dr. Joseph. Seventy-four-year-old Professor Joseph Klausner, the historian, had agreed to head our petition committee, but at the last moment was browbeaten into announcing his defection. Dr. Joseph told him that it was desirable to have the petition a few weeks later so that all groups could participate but that we had refused to postpone our campaign. I had the doubtful consolation of Klausner's apology when he heard the truth.

Colonel Shaltiel distinguished himself by issuing orders to all ranks not to sign the petition, although many soldiers laughingly or indignantly ignored the order. Some civilians requested the petition stewards to allow them to sign in the privacy of their homes. In the face of its success, Joseph proclaimed that the petition had failed, although six weeks later, he led a delegation to Tel Aviv to inform the provisional government—on unspecified authority—that its Jewish inhabitants demanded that Jerusalem be proclaimed an integral part of the Jewish state. Meanwhile the Arabs in Jerusalem hardly allowed a day to pass without some shooting. The Jewish forward positions, especially on Mount Zion, where Haganah and Irgun units served together, were repeatedly attacked. There were casualties on both sides. The cease-fire lines which cut through the heart of Jerusalem, the broad swathe of debris that marked No Man's Land became the boundary line that divided the city.

Yitshak Gruenbaum, now Minister of the Interior in the provisional government, opened negotiations with Begin in Tel Aviv for the dissolution of the Irgun in Jerusalem. I did not take part in the talks. Yitshak Avinoam, who had relieved Raanan as Jerusalem district commander, was sent with draft proposals. The talks dragged on for weeks, accompanied by the traditional reports that we were about to be liquidated by force. The first result of the negotiations was the release of the five *Altalena* prisoners, upon our insistence that they be either tried or released.

By mid-September the terms of an agreement had been negotiated. These satisfied at once the essential demands of the provisional government and the principle for which the Irgun had been kept in being.

The Irgun would disband and its members enter the Israel Defense Army.

The Irgun units would remain intact within the army, and their integrity would not be disturbed.

The Irgun units would not be sent out of Jerusalem.

The oath of loyalty taken by each soldier would bind him to serve in Jerusalem and not elsewhere.

These terms would be valid as long as there was actual Jewish rule in Jerusalem.

At this point Gruenbaum announced regretfully that while he had cautiously obtained official approval at each stage of the negotiations he was now finding difficulty in obtaining the final stamp of agreement. Mr. Gruenbaum's story had a familiar ring. Nine years earlier the Haganah leader Golomb after long negotiations had reached a tentative agreement for co-operation with the Irgun. He received an urgent telegram which, through inadvertent publication, became notorious: "If you have not signed, do not sign. If you have signed, repudiate your signature."

That 1939 telegram was signed by Mr. Ben-Gurion, as we now recalled. Gruenbaum, however, was quite confident that our new agreement, reasonable as it was, with its great advantage to the government of the end of "dissidence," would most certainly be ratified.

To prepare our men and women for the imminent dissolution of our organization, I called meetings in the mess room of each of the companies at Katamon. I informed them of the terms of the agreement we had reached, explaining the responsibility that would be theirs if foreign rule were to return to Jerusalem. Among the hundreds I addressed were men who had given to the struggle of the Irgun all the years and the sweetness of their youth. Each bore the consciousness of his own personal contribution to our freedom. All bore within them scars of suffering, of bitterness—and of mourning for the comrades at their side who had watered the soil of independence with their blood. The day was tinged by sadness.

The threat of foreign rule in Jerusalem was, in those days of August and early September, a real one. Pressure for the implementation of internationalization increased from day to day. Except for Transjordan, the Arab states led the campaign. They had a dual motive. Internationalization would deprive the Jews of the New City and equally deprive Abdullah of the Old City. The one objective was no less important than the other, Arab fraternity having resumed its normal tenor.

The Arab pressure harmonized with the desires of the Catholic Church and with the paragraph on Jerusalem in the original decision on partition of the United Nations, a decision the Arabs had previously willfully rejected and drowned in blood.

There had been many signs of the Israel Government's apparent resignation to a formal regime of internationalization. We knew that they were being tempted with a plausible alternative: "demilitarization," a semantic disguise for internationalization, for demilitarization could be ensured and controlled only by an international body —that is, by the United Nations; which meant, at least for the moment, by Count Bernadotte himself.

Throughout most of the nine restless weeks that followed the second cease-fire and until the last days of the summer, Count Bernadotte occupied the center of the political stage in Palestine. His self-confidence and his bold persistence in laying down ultimate solutions for the "Palestine problem" was supported by Ernest Bevin and the United States State Department.

In mid-September, Bernadotte submitted a last report to the United Nations in which he had modified one item in his plan. He no longer proposed that Jerusalem be handed over to the Arabs. As this idea was particularly dear to his heart, its abandonment must have been painful to him. He now proposed a United Nations regime for the city. In all other respects he kept to his first report: the Negev was to be handed over to Abdullah, as well as Ramleh and Lydda—except for the airport, to be under international control. Haifa was to be an international port. The 360,000 Arabs who had fled the country were to be brought back. Immigration was to be subject to Abdullah's agreement and, in the final analysis, United Nations control.

Bernadotte was openly angered and hurt when, as a result of this plan, he discovered that the Jews regarded him as a British agent. He denied the accusation vehemently. He insisted, both in public and to the Jewish and Arab representatives with whom he negotiated, that while he regarded himself as unfettered by the partition decision of November 1947, his only object was to bring peace to Palestine. His anger and his protestations did not modify the universal Jewish hostility. It was believed throughout Israel, and

bluntly expressed in speeches and newspaper articles, that Bernadotte was an instrument of British interests. That summer he was in
fact, after Bevin, the most hated man in Palestine.

The hostility to Bernadotte did not necessarily mean an equal
appreciation of his importance. I do not remember a single discussion in Irgun councils of the danger that Bernadotte might represent.
We felt that Bernadotte could be effective only in so far as he might
be capable of influencing members of the Israel Government. We
believed that, certainly in July 1948, the Jews could determine the
fate of the country as far as the Jordan in the east, the Litany River
in the north and, for that matter, the Red Sea and the Suez Canal
in the south.

Because we believed that our fate was in our own hands, the Irgun
did not regard Bernadotte as a real threat to our people. Evidently
others did. In the late afternoon of Friday, September 17, Count
Bernadotte was assassinated in Jewish-held Jerusalem. He was
traveling in a car with four of his subordinates. The car was blocked
by a jeep whose four occupants carried out the attack, killing Bernadotte and one of his assistants. The assailants were never caught
or identified.

Avinoam brought me the news of Bernadotte's assassination at
dusk. Our Intelligence Department soon assured us that no Irgun
men or arms were involved. At eight o'clock Aharon brought me
the news that a statement had been issued by a group called Hazit
Hamoledet (Fatherland Front) claiming responsibility for the action.
Later in the evening there was a report that Y., a non-combatant
member of Lehi had drunkenly boasted in the Yarden Cafe in King
George Avenue that Lehi members had carried out the attack.

There were a number of rumors concerning the identity and political affiliations of the men who killed Bernadotte, but most seemed to
indicate that the "Fatherland Front" was a splinter or dissident
group of Lehi. We found no evidence involving Lehi at all.

Lehi had, it is true, directed fierce propaganda against Bernadotte
and a few of its members had some weeks earlier demonstrated
against him, but no official decision to assassinate him was taken
in that organization. No one in Lehi had previously heard of the
"Fatherland Front," and it was never heard from again. Clearly, it
was a group created for the sole purpose of eliminating Bernadotte.

Yet the military governor of Jerusalem, Dr. Joseph (who had
been appointed in August) decided that the Lehi or a group within

it was responsible for the assassination and declared that action would be taken against them. In fact, as Joseph wrote in his memoirs, he had decided intuitively as soon as he learned of the death of Bernadotte, that "there was little doubt that one or other of the dissident groups was responsible for the outrage, and in all likelihood it was the Stern Gang." Colonel Moshe Dayan, who had replaced Shaltiel, agreed. They decided on "a large-scale military operation to round up the whole Stern Gang." Joseph rushed to Tel Aviv, where the provisional government gave instructions to send troops to Jerusalem for this purpose.

Under hastily promulgated emergency regulations, Lehi was declared an illegal organization. A curfew was imposed. Lehi members in Jerusalem and throughout Israel were rounded up. In the days that followed several hundreds were arrested, including the leader, Nathan Friedman-Yellin, who had gone into hiding.[1] Friedman-Yellin and his lieutenant, Mattityahu Shmulevitz, who three years earlier had been sentenced to death after electrifying a British military court with a stinging political speech, were later tried and convicted of belonging to a terrorist organization. Friedman-Yellin was sentenced to jail for eight years, Shmulevitz for five years. Friedman-Yellin was later elected to the Constituent Assembly on the slate put up by Lehi. My own first act as an elected member of the Assembly was to demand his release from jail. The government solved the problem by proclaiming a general amnesty.

When at midnight on the Friday Bernadotte was assassinated, I learned of the proposed wholesale arrest of Lehi members, my suspicions about the authenticity of the rumors of their responsibility deepened. United Nations officials and other observers subsequently charged the Israel Provisional Government with being overslow in taking steps to apprehend the assailants. The curfew, they said, was not imposed until twenty-one hours after Bernadotte died. These charges miss the point. The effort to find the men who killed Bernadotte was instituted and pursued by the police—unobtrusively, it is true, perhaps not too efficiently, and, in the end, unsuccessfully. The more spectacular steps taken by the government—the curfew, the sending of troops, the arrests—had nothing to do with the death of Bernadotte. They were designed to liquidate the Lehi. The government also had plans to eliminate the Irgun in the confusion and tension that followed the assassination.

Avinoam came to me early on Saturday morning, bringing with him a request from S., a member of Lehi and an old friend, that as many Lehi members as possible be given Irgun identity cards to shield them from the campaign of indiscriminate arrests of Lehi members already begun. I agreed at once. At least some of the Lehi fighters were thus spared the dual discomfort of Jewish incarceration in British Mandatory jails.

Ben-Gurion did not delay for long his action against the Irgun. No sooner was he certain of the elimination of the comparatively small Lehi contingent, than he turned on us, ignoring the draft agreement reached only a few days earlier between his colleagues and the Irgun. On Monday, September 20, an ultimatum was delivered to me. It was signed by Yigael Yadin, Chief of Staff of the Israel Defense Army, but the style was Ben-Gurion's. It said:

1. The I.Z.L. in Jerusalem must accept the Law of the State in regard to the army, enlistment and arms.
2. All members of the I.Z.L. liable for mobilisation must join the Haganah Army of Israel.
3. All the arms must be handed over to the Haganah Army.
4. Everybody joining the army must take the oath taken by every soldier.
5. The law applying to the I.Z.L. is the law applying to every other Jew.
6. If within twenty-four hours beginning today, Monday 20/9/48, 1200 hours you accept the terms: disband the I.Z.L. and its special battalions, hand over the arms and join the Haganah Army—none of you will suffer for the infringements you have hitherto committed against the law of Israel, and you will be treated like every other Jew.
7. If within the time stated you do not fulfill the demands of the Government, the Army will act with all the means at its disposal.

The reaction in Jerusalem to the news of the ultimatum was angry and bitter. One of the fiercest of our denigrators in the city, the correspondent of the London *Times,* was compelled to take note of it. He cabled his paper:

"The Israeli Provisional Government's ultimatum to I.Z.L. demanding the immediate disbandment of its armed forces was received with considerable resentment both by its members and by the majority of the population of the city."

We could have resisted. I calculated that it would be enough to hold out for three days in order to achieve a cease-fire and to restore the status of the negotiations with Gruenbaum. But Begin and I and the Irgun as a whole did not want civil war. We decided to accept the terms.

However, liquidating an organization has its obligations. I did not sleep that night. On Tuesday morning, two hours before the ultimatum expired, I announced the end of the Irgun at a press conference in the Eden Hotel. I told the journalists briefly what had happened, adding:

> Rejection of this ultimatum would involve considerable bloodshed. The strength of the Irgun Zvai Leumi in Jerusalem is sufficient to ensure that any attack would involve the attackers in heavy losses. We are not prepared to shed the blood of Haganah soldiers whose lives the Government of Israel is so lightly prepared to throw away. We are consequently informing the Haganah Army this morning of our acceptance of the ultimatum, and members of the Irgun Zvai Leumi will be told to join the Haganah Army.

> But this ultimatum comes *three weeks after* the Provisional Government had had the I.Z.L. reply to its previously stated demand of disbandment. Then too and for the same reason that we were not prepared to let the Government plunge us into Civil War—the I.Z.L. announced its readiness to yield to the demand. But then the demand was accompanied by proposals (verbal) made to the I.Z.L.

I described the proposal made by Mr. Gruenbaum, and went on:

> The Irgun Zvai Leumi representatives were told they could regard these proposals as official. On the other hand, non-acceptance would result in the Government's use of force. The I.Z.L. accepted the proposals in principle. On one pretext or another the matter dragged on for three weeks.

> Yesterday the Cabinet member who had been negotiating with us announced telephonically that the matter was now out of his hands. And the ultimatum was delivered by the Adjutant to the Minister of Security, Mr. Ben Gurion.

> We must add one comment on the central untruth in the document: the clause which offers an "amnesty" for all the infringements of the law of Israel. We have infringed no laws. This same Government, in earlier negotiations was told that we accept the military and administrative authority of the Military Governor and the Government recognised the Irgun Zvai Leumi in Jerusalem as a separate organisation. As such it negotiated with us, and as such we have operated. It is pitiful that a Government should issue untruths. What

is more, it is a historically impudent untruth, coming from men who collaborated with the British enemy while these boys they offer "amnesty" were giving their lives or suffering in prison and exile as a result of their denunciations. It is an impudent untruth directed at the soldiers of the I.Z.L. who fought to defend Jerusalem, the men of Ramat Rahel and of Malha and of the Old City.

33

"The End... And the Beginning"

After Bernadotte's death, the British and the Americans continued for a time to press the Bernadotte proposals at Lake Success. Without Bernadotte's energetic promotion, these proposals soon faded from public view. In any case during the fall and winter of 1948, the British and American governments were presented with new problems. The Israel Government moved against Kaukji in Galilee and against the Egyptians. Ben-Gurion refrained from liberating old Jerusalem and the Triangle, and it was true that there the threat to our security was not immediate. Abdullah was having too much trouble digesting this territory to be interested in renewing the fighting. In the Negev, however, the situation was intolerable. There the whole of Jewish settlement was held down by Egyptian occupation of vital outposts and by their control of communications. The only Israel contact with Negev villages was by air. In Galilee, Kaukji in the north was an ever-present threat.

In October and in December, the Israel army launched military operations which swept Kaukji out of Galilee and finally cleared the Egyptians from their northern outposts in southern Judea and from the Negev. In early March, the southern Negev down to Eilat was liberated. There was much agitation in London, echoed in Washington. The United States acted swiftly to intimidate Ben-Gurion into leaving the Egyptians in Gaza.

When in late December, Israel troops, in pursuit of the Egyptians, crossed into Egyptian territory, the British and Americans achieved a hasty resolution in the Security Council calling on them to withdraw. This they did at once.

It was at this point that the great and historic abandonment of British policy took place. Suddenly, on January 7, 1949, without warning, without provocation, without reason, five British fighter planes from the Suez Canal Zone crossed into Israel territory. All five were promptly shot down by planes of the infant Israel Air Force. This brief incident, with its drama for the world and for the British people, lit up sharply the unrealities of Britain's posture in the Middle East. A flood of violent protest surged forth from every corner of Britain against Bevin's policy toward the new state of Israel.[1] It proved the last straw. Quick action by the British Cabinet followed. At last the final failure of the long war on Zionism had to be admitted. On January 10, just before the elections to the Constituent Assembly of Israel (which became the first Knesset), His Majesty's Government accorded formal recognition to the State of Israel.

We had no time to savor the historic moment. I had to find an answer to many questions. I had supervised the orderly transfer of men and arms from the Irgun to the Haganah. I pressed on with the organization of the political party which was to campaign for the complete restoration of our national territory.

That was to be a new experience, on a new plane, in a different climate, against the background of an independent sovereign state, with its own evolving life and significance.

We came to the watershed in 1948. I had come to the end of the road on which, across the chasm of Jewish homelessness, I set out at Jabotinsky's call eighteen years before.

NOTES

1. Already in 1920 an Arab attack on the Jews of the Old City of Jerusalem had raged unchecked for three days while a Jewish self-defense unit, formed by Jabotinsky, was prevented by the British from entering within the walls. Jabotinsky was arrested and sentenced to fifteen years. A world-wide outcry resulted in the sentence's being quashed, but the pattern had been set. Another outbreak followed in 1921, and a more violent one in 1929.

2. Murals on South African history presented by him are still to be seen at South Africa House in London.

3. September 20, 1936.

4. Haganah (meaning *defense*) was the recognized military body of the Jewish community.

5. *Trial and Error*, London, 1950.

6. Ibid., pp. 478–86.

CHAPTER 2

1. The independent organization set up by the Revisionist Party after leaving the World Zionist Organization.

2. Palestine Royal Commission, Minutes of Evidence, pp. 287–90.

3. Ibid., p. 375.

4. A fascinating comparison of passages in Jabotinsky's memorandum on partition and Churchill's speech in the House of Commons appears in Oscar K. Rabinowitz's book, *Churchill and the Jews* (in ms.).

CHAPTER 3

1. *Trial and Error*, p. 488.

2. While this book was in preparation I was told by Avraham Selman, a fourth member of the group who escaped, that they had persuaded Bitker to start operating against the British, but through them as an independent group and not through the Irgun.

3. The World Executive.

4. Jabotinsky's impact on the Polish statesmen with whom he came into contact in that period is revealed in a remarkable article published in 1965 by Count Michael Lubienski, in 1937 the permanent head of the Polish Foreign Ministry, and later a university teacher:

   "During my work at the Ministry of Foreign Affairs, I had the opportunity of meeting many great and famous political leaders, like Hitler, Mussolini, Lenin and Churchill, prime ministers, ministers, ambassadors and parliamentarians. Knowing this, my pupils once asked me which Head of State had made the greatest impression on me. I had to think for a little while as I was not prepared for this question, but then I saw once more the shy, short and bent figure of the great Zionist leader [Jabotinsky], looking at me through his glasses with his clever and penetrating eyes." (Zeszyty Historyczna [Historical Notes] Instytut Literacki, Paris, 1965.)

5. He made this public himself to the Zionist Congress at Zurich in 1937.

CHAPTER 4

1. Literally "mobilization platoons."
2. New Moon, the first day of the Hebrew month.

CHAPTER 5

1. *Jewish Herald*, July 21, 1939.
2. These accusations are to be found in the South African *Jewish Chronicle* or *Zionist Record* of the first half of 1939, at that time my main source of information. Detailed denunciations also appeared in Palestine in *Davar* in anonymous articles and in Zionist newspapers in Europe, notably *Hajnt* of Warsaw.

CHAPTER 6

1. For organizing the famous expedition of the SS. *Sakariya* Eri Jabotinsky was sent to prison on its arrival in Palestine in mid-February 1940.
2. It appears in full in Isaac Zaar's *Rescue and Liberation*, New York, 1954.
3. *Davar*, August 5, 1940.

CHAPTER 7

1. His "Hayalim Almonim" (Anonymous Soldiers), originally the hymn of the united Irgun, afterward taken over by Lehi, has always been to me the most inspiring of its kind.
2. Friedman-Yellin (now Yalin-Mor) has published an eloquent account of Stern's plans in *Itgar* (January 25, 1962).

CHAPTER 8

1. Quoted from the minutes of the Jewish Agency by Yehuda Bauer in *Diplomacy and Underground* (Hebrew), Tel Aviv, 1963, p. 196.
2. Churchill's *War Memoirs*, Vol. IV, p. 849 (Cassell edition).
3. *Jewish Chronicle*, May 7, 1943.
4. *Collier's*, November 1, 1947.
5. Vol. II, pp. 1538–39.
6. Other people had also thought about the shipping problems. In the House of Commons on May 19, Professor A. V. Hill revealed that ships were returning empty from North Africa to Britain and America, and asked why they could not be used to transport refugees. To this Eden did not reply.
7. Hopkins' note, quoted in Robert Sherwood's *Roosevelt and Hopkins*, is also included in the U.S. official Papers on Foreign Relations 1943, Vol. 3, p. 38.
8. The London *Times*, October 9, 1944.

CHAPTER 9

1. Quoted by R. H. S. Crossman in *Palestine Mission* (p. 166).

2. On January 5, 1945, the *Jewish Chronicle* quoted Dr. Silver: "Dr. Wise was time and again criticized for unauthorized conduct and undisciplined actions. The worst and most recent instance was the fatal telegram he dispatched without my knowledge to the Secretary of State on the very Even when Senator Wagner and I were scheduled to see him to persuade the State Department and the President to withdraw their objections to the Palestine resolution . . . In this telegram he stated that while he would be happy if approval were given to the resolution he and many associates do not wish action to be taken contrary to the recommendations of the State Department and the President."

3. *Jewish Chronicle,* January 25, 1946.

4. *Palestine Mission,* London, 1946, p. 68.

CHAPTER 10

1. The full text is in Volume 2 of *Bamaarakha* (collected speeches of Ben-Gurion) page 289 *et seq.*

2. The Palmach were specially trained units enjoying internal autonomy in the Haganah. Their leaders claimed that denunciation to the British was not part of their program of action.

3. This account is the official Jewish Agency version. Brand's own account is in his book *Advocate for the Dead,* London, 1958.

4. Churchill's *War Memoirs,* Vol. VI, Chapter 12.

5. Letter by Marshal of the RAF Sir John Slessor in the London *Observer,* August 16, 1964.

6. Distances from Foggia: Warsaw, 750 miles; Auschwitz, 550; Budapest, 450.

7. Today they bear respectively the Hebrew names Yalin-Mor, Eldad, and Shamir.

CHAPTER 11

1. Based on figures, published throughout the period, which I have pieced together.

2. He had not remained unmoved by the heroism of the Jewish underground. R. H. S. Crossman, M.P., related years later that, in a conversation with Weizmann soon after the attack on the King David Hotel, "I suddenly saw that he was crying. As the tears streamed down his cheeks, he said to me: 'I can't help feeling proud of our boys. If only it had been a German headquarters, they would have got the V.C.!'" (*A Nation Reborn,* London, 1960.)

3. It is included however in Mr. Ben-Gurion's collected writings: *Bamaarakha,* Vol. 5, 1957.

4. A similar notion was perhaps present in the minds of British statesmen.

CHAPTER 12

1. Haim Landau, now a member of the Israel Knesset.

2. Ya'acov Tavin, now a businessman in Tel Aviv. Henceforth he will be referred to as Eli.

3. David Danon, now a Professor at the Weizmann Institute.

4. *Bamaarakha,* Vol. 5, p. 102.

5. A sour note was struck by the Jewish Agency. Its spokesman in London,

distressed by the understanding tone of a British newspaper report called a special press conference to express the "highest sympathy" with the "gallant officers" of the British Army and to announce that the "terrorists" deserved no sympathy at all. (*Evening Standard,* December 31, 1946.)

6. This was true even of liberal and supposedly knowledgeable people. Describing his own ignorance of the Palestine question up to 1946, Mr. R. Crossman, M.P., wrote in that year: "Palestine had for many years been one of those wearisome subjects which were always cropping up in the papers. The Englishman was uneasily aware that it might disturb his conscience if he thought too much about it, just as we had avoided knowing about India." (*Palestine Mission,* pp. 14–15.)

7. Women's International Zionist Organization.

CHAPTER 13

1. The account of his amazing escape and subsequent adventures is included in his book (Hebrew) *The Story of the Commander of the Altalena,* Tel Aviv, 1954.

2. American League for a Free Palestine Inc.: Statement of Receipts and Disbursements, Archives in Jabotinsky Institute, Tel Aviv.

3. Two years later in the War of Independence this trio were among the first pilots in the embryo Israel Air Force. Each of them was at some stage Chief of Operations. Weizmann came to be C-in-C of the Israel Air Force and is today (1967) Chief of Operations of the Israel Army. He is universally credited with the inspiration and drive that, in his nine years at the head of the Air Force, laid the groundwork for its brilliant achievement in the Six Day War.

4. Referring to Irgun "outrages" Barker wrote that the "Jews in the country are accomplices and bear a share of the guilt.

   "I am determined," he continued, "that they shall suffer punishment and be made aware of the contempt and loathing with which we regard this conduct . . .

   "I appreciate that these measures will inflict some hardship on the troops, yet I am certain that if my reasons are fully explained to them, they will understand their propriety and will be punishing the Jews in a way the race dislikes as much as any—by striking at their pockets and showing our contempt for them."

5. Rosenbaum's real name was Yehiel Drezner.

6. Ernest Bevin was never in jeopardy from the Irgun. Despite the personal "refinements" he introduced into Palestine policy, and though some believe, like Hugh Dalton, that another Foreign Minister would have pursued a policy at least less harsh, we did not regard his responsibility as personal. His colleagues, who acquiesced in all he did, were no better than he.

   He was, however, a target for Lehi attack. A member of the Lehi group in London that planned the attacks told me that they made plans on three separate occasions for Bevin's assassination, once as he was arriving at a meeting of Foreign Ministers, twice as he drove through the West End. In the first case as Bevin was leaving his car the lone attacker, at two or three yards' range, was reaching for his revolver when some accidental circumstance intervened. In the other two timing was wrong.

CHAPTER 14

1. Yaacov Amrami—today a publisher in Tel Aviv.

2. David Tahori—today a bank official in Tel Aviv.

CHAPTER 15

1. Frank Gruner, in the United States, submitted an appeal on his own account to the Privy Council. It was rejected on the grounds that he had no standing. The appeal later submitted by the mayor of Tel Aviv was actually decided by the Privy Council, in unperturbed formality, after Gruner's execution. It too was rejected.

2. Yehiel Drezner went to his death under the name the British knew him by: Dov Rosenbaum.

3. *Yediot Aharonoth:* September 28, 1962.

CHAPTER 16

1. There is little doubt that Arab oil resources were not in fact vital to any American war effort. The rulers of the Arab oil countries, Saudi Arabia and Iraq had no intention on any account of withholding oil from the United States and thus depriving themselves of fabulous sums of money. They made this utterly plain to the oil companies' representatives. It was the latter who, in return, promised not to mention this undertaking to the State Department and indeed did their best to persuade the State Department that the oil resources in the Arab states *were* in danger. This fascinating piece of skulduggery is described in Benjamin Shwadran's well-documented *Middle East Oil and the Great Powers,* New York, 1955.

2. Secret minutes of meeting on February 3, 1947, which have never been published. The newspaper reports at the time, in themselves substantially accurate, did not contain the crucial evidence of the Agency's complete *volte face* as revealed by this and the following passages, which I quote from the minutes. (Zionist Archives, Jerusalem, File No. 8141/8116. S25/7709.)

3. On February 13.

4. *Bamaarakha,* Vol. 5, pp. 174–75.

5. Dr. Brodetsky on February 3.

6. *Haaretz,* June 12, 1947.

CHAPTER 17

1. Housing estate.

CHAPTER 18

1. In the autumn of 1948 a new survey revealed that even we had slightly overestimated. The Arabs in 1947 had numbered 850,000 (and Jews 600,-000). The correction was by now, of course, only of historic interest.

CHAPTER 19

1. The remaining two, Michaeloff and Ziterbaum, who submitted pleas, were sentenced to life imprisonment.

CHAPTER 20

1. These details are based on the account of an American clergyman, John Gravel, who traveled on the boat as correspondent of the *Churchman.* It was substantially corroborated by other eyewitnesses.

2. Aryeh Gelblum in *Haaretz,* July 20, 1947.

3. *Haaretz,* July 30, 1947.

4. Ibid., July 31, 1947.

5. Some British opinion attributes to the hanging of the sergeants a high degree of causality for the British evacuation. This is an oversimplification, but it did have a climactic effect and tipped the scales at a crucial moment.

6. The account of the landing at Hamburg is based mainly on the reports of Marguerite Higgins in the New York *Herald Tribune;* and partly on conversations with *Exodus* passengers, one of whom (at the time a child of six) served in later years as my secretary. The description of the camp at Poppendorf is based on Robert Gary's report in the PTA News Service.

CHAPTER 21

1. The italics are in the printed version included in Ben-Gurion's collected speeches (*Bamaarakha,* Vol. 3, 1956, p. 244).

2. *Bamaarakha,* Vol. 5, p. 214.

3. Ibid., p. 220.

4. A lighthearted account of her exploits is contained in her book *The Lady Was a Terrorist* (New York, 1953).

5. *Bamaarakha,* Vol. 5, pp. 243–44.

6. Ibid., p. 233.

7. The Irgun proclamations of the period have been brought together and published by Menahem Begin in his *Bemahteret,* Vol. IV.

CHAPTER 22

1. Too late, as usual, they learned that their self-restraint had harmed Israel's cause. In the report submitted on May 12, 1948, to the Jewish Agency leadership, Mr. Moshe Shertok revealed as one of the causes of the American cooling-off toward the partition scheme "the military weakness of the Jews in the opening phase of the struggle." It is said, repeated Shertok, "that George Marshall remarked at a party that he was disappointed in the 'Haganah.' He had thought that if the Arabs were to start anything—the Haganah would liquidate them in short order. This did not happen." (Zeev Sharef, *Three Days,* London, 1953.)

2. *Behilahem Yisrael,* pp. 34–51 (speeches of January 15 and 21).

3. According to the official history of the War of Independence (*Toldot Milhemet HaKomemiut,* Maarakhot, Tel Aviv, 1959) there were at the outbreak of hostilities 10,000 rifles and 4435 automatic weapons of all kinds in the country, dispersed among many Jewish authorities and difficult to concentrate. The total mobilizable strength of the Haganah, according to the same source, was 40,000, of whom some 18,000 were called up in December 1947.

4. The facts became known only through the resignation from the Agency Executive on December 29 of Dr. Moshe Sneh. The Agency's decision was not implemented: the organizers of the current transport from Romania simply disregarded it.

5. Haganah members were still under standing orders not to resist disarming by the British. Irgun and Lehi members were never so disarmed. Standing orders in the Irgun were to disarm British soldiers wherever possible.

CHAPTER 23

1. Vol. II: *Years of Trial and Hope,* New York, 1956, p. 163.

2. Truman, Vol. II, p. 164.

3. Benes, a broken man, held on tenuously as President for three months. Three months after his resignation, he too was dead.

CHAPTER 24

1. Colonel Jakson's real name was (and is) Homeski. He was the father of Paul Homeski, the pilot in London to whom I have referred. His rank had come from his service in the British Intelligence during the war. He was also a French underground veteran.

2. Peter Bergson had gone to Europe after an internal dispute on policy.

CHAPTER 25

1. *Toldot Milhemet Hakomemiut,* Tel Aviv, 1959, p. 112.

2. The report was published in Hebrew translation in 1956 by Maarakhot (Publishing House of the Israel Defense Army) under the title *Meahorei Hapargod (Behind the Curtain).*

3. Yunes Ahmed Assad in *Al Urdun,* April 9, 1953.

4. *Toldot Milhemet Hakomemiut,* Tel Aviv, 1959, p. 143.

5. A full account of these raids and of the battle for Jaffa is in Begin's *The Revolt.* (Chapter 29, British edition.) A detailed study is in *Kibbush Yafo* by Haim Lazar, Tel Aviv, 1951.

6. Hence the legend, or the excuse for the legend, that Jaffa was captured by the Haganah.

CHAPTER 26

1. The German Staff chose the hotel at which Hecht was staying as its headquarters and had already begun moving in when Hecht made his escape.

2. Mentioned in Cordell Hull's *Memoirs,* Vol. 2, pp. 967–68.

3. I am indebted to Dr. Hecht, now of Haifa, for letting me see the correspondence between him and the late Mr. Woods.

4. This account is taken from *Three Days* (W. H. Allen, London, 1959, pp. 72–73), by Zeev Sharef, who was present at the meeting as Secretary of the "National Executive." Sharef was later Secretary to the Israeli Cabinet. Other accounts published at the time, by the American Zionist leader Emanuel Neumann, suggested a much fiercer American pressure.

5. Now Eshkol—the Prime Minister of Israel since 1963.

CHAPTER 28

1. Begin in *The Revolt,* Lankin in his (Hebrew) *Sippuro Shel Mefakked Altalena (The Story of the Commander of the Altalena),* Tel Aviv, 1954.

2. Preserved at the Jabotinsky Institute in Tel Aviv in manuscript.

3. *The Revolt,* p. 168.

4. *The Alexandroni Brigade in the War of Independence,* Tel Aviv, 1964.

At a press conference two days later Galili produced an entirely different version of the incident. He said:

"The crisis broke out because of the grave fact of a boat's arriving on the shores of the country during the truce without our prior knowledge, without our being asked, without our agreeing. About a month ago the Commander of the I.Z.L. signed a document in which it was stated that the members of the I.Z.L. would enlist in the army and take an oath of loyalty to the Government. The I.Z.L. members enlisting would in the transition period constitute separate regiments to be incorporated in various brigades on various fronts. The document also laid down that the I.Z.L. would cease separate operations for the acquisition of arms and their contacts in this field would be transferred to the army. The I.Z.L. and its Command were to cease operating and existing in the State of Israel . . .

Two or three days before the boat arrived we were surprised at the dead of night by news that the boat was approaching our shores. Our demand that the boat be handed over unconditionally to the Government and Army was rejected. They demanded that the arms be taken to the stores of the I.Z.L. and used primarily to arm the I.Z.L. regiments." (Report in *Davar,* June 23, 1948)

5. My italics.

6. Irgun Zvai Leumi.

7. Fein's italics.

8. Not every soldier joined the attacks. A number of army officers refused to obey the order to fire on the boat. They were later court-martialed—and acquitted.

   On the night of the *Altalena*'s arrival, the Tel Aviv area commander of the infant Israel Air Force received orders to fly over the *Altalena* and be prepared to bomb her from the air. This was an order he was not prepared to obey. The pilot, Boris Senior, flew over the *Altalena* and made strenuous efforts to signal down to her in the darkness. His signals were not seen on board. He was eager to send a personal reassuring message to Lankin who, he knew, was in command of the Irgun on board, for Lankin had been his own immediate officer in the Irgun.

9. Twelve years later, Dr. Dov Joseph, a faithful supporter of Ben-Gurion, found a solution in his memoirs, to this little difficulty by transferring the scene of action to Natanya. *The Faithful City,* New York and Tel Aviv, 1960, pp. 238–40.

10. P. 176 (British edition).

CHAPTER 29

1. After Abdullah's death authorized accounts were published of Golda Meirson's visit to him (made in disguise and at great personal risk) across the Jordan. There she certainly tried to persuade him to remain at peace with the Jews. The meeting is dealt with by Zeev Sharef in his *Three Days* (op. cit.). Neither his account nor any of the others mention any proposed deal over Jerusalem.

CHAPTER 30

1. The proportional equivalent of nearly two million Americans or half a million Britons. Throughout the six years of the Second World War 363,000 Britons and 322,000 Americans were killed.

2. *Haboker,* March 6, 1964.

CHAPTER 31

1. Dov Joseph, *Faithful City,* New York, 1960, pp. 254–55.

CHAPTER 32

1. He took shelter at the Haifa home of an Irgunist, my brother-in-law, Mi-

chael Kaplan, who was also arrested and held (without trial) in detention
in a kibbutz for several weeks.

CHAPTER 33

1. In his *My Mission in Israel* the first U.S. ambassador to Israel, James G.
McDonald, describes how on his way to Tel Aviv in August 1948 he called
on Bevin in London together with the U.S. ambassador there, Lewis Douglas. He was stunned both by Bevin's mendacity and by his vehemence
against the Jews. After the interview "Douglas remarked that Bevin was
perhaps 'slightly unsympathetic' to the Jews. I looked at him but remained
silent. His comment struck me as a tragic understatement, for Bevin, like
Hitler and Mussolini at my interview with them when I was League of Nations High Commissioner (for Refugees) in the 1930's, had impressed me
with a complete sense of ruthlessness."

APPENDIXES

CHRONOLOGY OF EVENTS

1915   Zionist moves to help Britain in Great War with a view to restitution of Palestine to Jews under British control. Weizmann opens diplomatic negotiations with British statesmen. Jabotinsky launches campaign for Jewish legion to fight in Palestine. Aaron Aaronson forms pro-British espionage group—NILI—behind the Turkish lines.

1917   NILI Organization crushed by Turks.
British Government issues Balfour Declaration promising to "facilitate establishment of Jewish National Home in Palestine."

1918   Jewish Regiments under Colonel J. H. Patterson take part in liberation of eastern Palestine (Transjordan).

1920   Arab attack on Jews in Jerusalem. Jabotinsky organizes defense (Haganah) and is sentenced to fifteen years' imprisonment by British military court. Sentence later quashed.

1922   League of Nations places Palestine in British control under a Mandate incorporating Balfour Declaration. First British (Churchill) White Paper, emphasizing Arab rights.
Eastern Palestine excluded from application of Zionist clauses of Mandate.

1929   Arab riots, mainly in Jerusalem and Hebron.

1930   Passfield White Paper imposes severe restrictions on Jewish immigration and land purchase.
Split in Haganah. Haganah "B" formed—later known as Irgun Zvai Leumi.

1933   Nazis come to power in Germany. Intense persecution of Jews begins. Anti-Semitic movements throughout Europe gain momentum.
Economic elimination of Jews in Eastern Europe accelerated.

1934   British drive against "illegal" immigrants into Palestine from the zone of disaster in Europe.

1936   Countrywide attacks organized by Arab leaders against Jews in Palestine with help of mercenaries from neighboring countries: the Arab "Revolt." Jabotinsky calls for evacuation of Eastern Europe by Jews and for urgent policy of pressure on Britain to open gates of Palestine.

1937   Irgun Zvai Leumi emerges as militant organization, defies "self-restraint" policy of Jewish Agency, carrying out reprisals for Arab attacks.
British Royal Commission recommends partition of Palestine, including partly autonomous Arab and Jewish zones. Plan later dropped.

1938   Nazi occupation of Austria.
       "Illegal" immigration into Palestine intensified.
       Shlomo Ben-Yosef hanged at Acre by British for attempted reprisal on
       Arabs.
       The Munich Agreement.

1939   Nazis occupy Czechoslovakia.
       British White Paper announces 75,000 immigrants in five years as the
       end of permitted Zionist development. Sporadic acts of anti-British vio-
       lence in Palestine.
       Germans invade Poland. World War II breaks out. All Zionist groups an-
       nounce solidarity with Britain against Germany. Irgun proclaims truce.

1940   Death of Jabotinsky.
       Split in Irgun. Stern Group (LEHI) rejects truce with Britain.

1941   David Raziel, Commander of Irgun, killed on mission for British in Iraq.

1942   Avraham Stern captured by British and killed in Tel Aviv.
       Nazis launch program for "Final Solution" of Jewish problem by ex-
       terminating all the Jews.

1943   British and Americans at Bermuda Conference make plain nothing will
       be done to save Jews of Europe. Practical proposals for saving specific
       groups of Jews rejected.
       Germans and Italians driven from North Africa.
       Allied invasion of Italy. Italian resistance collapses.

1944   Irgun under Menahem Begin launches revolt against British rule, calls
       for Jewish government. Fierce official Zionist reactions culminate in col-
       laboration between Haganah and British to crush Irgun.
       Jewish Brigade Group formed, takes part in Italian campaign.

1945   End of World War II. Bare remnant of European Jews found alive.
       Labor government elected in Britain (July).
       Foreign Minister Bevin manifests hostile policy to Zionism and indiffer-
       ence to fate of death camp survivors (November).
       Haganah joins with Irgun and Lehi in United Resistance Movement.
       Widespread campaign of violence against British.

1946   *June*   Jewish Agency leaders arrested.
       July   Irgun blows up British Government and Army H.Q.—
                   King David Hotel.
       August   British deport "illegal" immigrants, brought by Haganah
                   to Cyprus.
                   Jewish Agency Executive meeting in Paris decides to call
                   off armed resistance. Moshe Sneh resigns as head of
                   Haganah.
       October   Arrested Jewish Agency leaders released in return for
                   undertakings to co-operate in crushing Irgun and Lehi.
                   Irgun opens campaign abroad. British embassy in Rome
                   blown up.
       December Irgun flogs British officers in retaliation for flogging of
                   Irgun captives.

1947   *January*   Jewish Agency negotiates "unofficially" with British Gov-
                   ernment.
       February Bevin announces approach to United Nations on "how
                   to carry out Mandate."
       March 1   Irgun, by co-ordinated countrywide attacks on British,
                   provoke martial law.
       March 17 Martial law called off.

April		British hang four Irgun captives.
		UN appoints Special Committee to investigate Palestine situation.
May		Irgun blows up Acre Fortress.
July		"Illegal" immigrants on *Exodus 1947* turned back first to France, later to Germany.
		Three Irgun soldiers hanged.
		Irgun hangs two British sergeants.
August		UN Special Committee recommends end of British rule and partition of Palestine between Jews and Arabs.
September		British Government announces intention to give up Mandate.
November		UN Assembly adopts resolution for partition of Palestine.
		Jewish Agency agrees to partition as measure for peace.
		Britain announces refusal to co-operate in implementing UN resolution. Arab rioting begins.
December		U. S. Government imposes embargo on arms to Palestine.
		Bevin refuses to cancel arms shipments to Arab countries.
1948	*April*	Irgun captures Jaffa (outside of partition lines laid down by UN).
	May 14	State of Israel proclaimed, provisional government headed by Ben-Gurion set up.
		Arab states invade Palestine.
	June 11	Month's truce proposed by UN, accepted by both sides.
	June 20	Irgun arms ship *Altalena* blown up at Tel Aviv.
	July 9	Fighting resumed.
	July 17	Second truce.
	September 17	Bernadotte assassinated.
	September 21	End of Irgun Zvai Leumi.

GLOSSARY OF TERMS AND ORGANIZATIONS

ALIYAH (lit. going up)   Return of Jews to their homeland.

ALIYAH B (or Aliyah Bet)   "Illegal" immigration, i.e. repatriation of Jews to Palestine without British permission.

ALIYAH SHNIYA   The generation of Jewish immigrants from 1904–14 who dominated Zionist ideology and politics during the British Mandate period.

AMERICAN LEAGUE FOR A FREE PALESTINE   Organization of Americans founded to provide support for Hebrew Committee of National Liberation.

BETAR   Zionist youth organization founded by Vladimir Jabotinsky, dedicated to idea of Jewish state and service in its pursuit. The main source of Irgun membership.

ERETZ ISRAEL   Palestine.

HAGANAH, THE   Defense organization of the Jewish Agency and under its orders—had the great majority of young Jews in Palestine in its ranks.

HASHOMER HATZAIR   Left-wing Socialist Zionist Party.

HAVLAGA (literally self-restraint)   The policy of non-retaliation adopted by the Jewish Agency during the Arab attacks of 1936–38.

HEBREW COMMITTEE OF NATIONAL LIBERATION   Set up in America to preach Hebrew national independence, repatriation of Jews and support for the revolt against Britain.

HISTADRUT, THE   The Jewish Labor Federation in Palestine, which played a dominant part in the Zionist Establishment.

IRGUN ZVAI LEUMI ("the Irgun")   Literally National Military Organization, a breakaway group from the Haganah in the thirties, broke the policy of *havlaga* in 1937, launched the main revolt against British rule in 1944.

JEWISH AGENCY FOR PALESTINE ("the Jewish Agency")   The body recognized in the Mandate for Palestine as representative of the Jewish people to co-operate with Britain, as Mandatory Power, in establishing the Jewish National Home.

LOHAMEI HERUT ISRAEL (Lehi)   A splinter of the Irgun, formed in 1940 by Avraham Stern, who denounced the truce with Britain, proclaimed by the Irgun on the outbreak of the war against Germany.

MAPAI   Palestine Labor Party and dominant element in the Jewish Agency.

MIZRACHI   Party of Religious Zionists.

NEW ZIONIST ORGANIZATION   Formed by Revisionists on their secession from the Zionist Organization, 1935.

PALMACH   Shock troops formed by Haganah during World War II, active in "the season" against the Irgun (1944–45), then in co-operation with Irgun in the Resistance Movement (November 1945 to August 1946) and later against the Arabs in the War of Independence (1948).

REVISIONIST PARTY   Party in World Zionist Organization before 1935 and since 1946. See New Zionist Organization.

STERN GROUP   See Lohamei Herut Israel.

TENUAT HAMERI   The Resistance Movement—the combined force of the three underground movements (Haganah, Irgun, and Lehi) that fought together against the British from November 1945 until (August 1946) the Jewish Agency ordered the Haganah to end its armed resistance.

WORLD ZIONIST ORGANIZATION   See Jewish Agency.

PRINCIPAL CHARACTERS

ABRAHAMS, ABRAHAM Head of Political Department of the New Zionist Organization (Revisionists) in London during World War II.

ALTMAN, ARYEH Leader of the New Zionist Organization (Revisionists) in Palestine, 1936–48.

BEGIN, MENAHEM Commander-in-Chief of the dissident Irgun Zvai Leumi (1943–48) and leader of the revolt against Britain.

BEN-GURION, DAVID Chairman of the Jewish Agency (Zionist Organization) and leader of the dominant party, Mapai.

BERGSON, PETER (Hillel Kook) Irgun emissary in Europe 1937–40, later (in America) Chairman of the Hebrew Committee of National Liberation (1945).

BERNADOTTE, COUNT FOLKE United Nations mediator during the Arab-Israel War, assassinated in Jerusalem September 1948.

BEVIN, ERNEST British Foreign Minister in Labor government 1945–50.

EDEN, ANTHONY British Foreign Minister in Churchill's government during World War II.

GALILI, ISRAEL Leader of Palmach and successor to Moshe Sneh as head of the Haganah after August 1946.

GRUNER, DOV One of the Irgun soldiers hanged by the British in 1947.

HASKEL, MICHAEL Jewish businessman, friend and follower of Jabotinsky, South African honorary consul in Jerusalem 1936–39.

JABOTINSKY, VLADIMIR Journalist, novelist, poet, and soldier, originator of Jewish Legion in World War I. Leader of Revisionist Opposition to Zionist Establishment and mentor of the Irgun Zvai Leumi until his death in 1940.

LANDAU, HAIM (Avraham) Chief of staff of Irgun Zvai Leumi during revolt against Britain.

LANKIN, ELIAHU Commander of the Irgun outside of Palestine 1947–48, and of the contingent on the *Altalena* arms ship (June 1948).

MERIDOR, YAACOV Commander of the Irgun 1941–43.

PAGLIN, AMIHAI (Giddy) Chief of operations of the Irgun (1946–48).

RAZIEL, DAVID Commander of the Irgun (1937–41), initiated the campaign of reprisals for Arab attacks, proclaimed a truce with Britain on outbreak of World War II. Killed while on a British mission in Iraq in May 1941.

SHERTOK, MOSHE Head of the political department of the Jewish Agency 1933–48.

SILVER, RABBI ABBA HILLEL U. S. Zionist leader and head of the Zionist Emergency Committee in U.S. during the period of conflict with Britain.

SNEH, DR. MOSHE Head of the Haganah 1943–46. Resigned when Jewish Agency Executive decided to end armed resistance to Britain in August 1946, but remained a member of the Jewish Agency Executive till December 1947.

STAVSKY, ABRAHAM Victim of false accusation of murder of Zionist leader Arlosoroff (1933) later active in rescuing Jews from Nazi Europe, killed on the *Altalena* June 1948.

STERN, AVRAHAM Poet and leader of the Lohamei Herut Israel (LEHI), captured and killed by British police, February 1942.

TAVIN, YAACOV (Eli) Head of Irgun Intelligence to 1945, later head of Organization Department in Europe, there organized operations against Britain, notably the blowing up of the British embassy in Rome, October 1946.

WEIZMANN, DR. CHAIM Famed chemist and President of the World Zionist Organization almost uninterruptedly from 1921 to 1946. Chief Zionist negotiator for the Balfour Declaration by the British Government in 1917 and prime mover for granting Palestine Mandate to Britain.

BIBLIOGRAPHY

This bibliography, although not complete, includes basic material that supplements what I have written and enables those interested to read at firsthand the opposing versions of events and points of view.

IN ENGLISH

ALDINGTON, RICHARD *Lawrence of Arabia* (Collins, London, 1955)

ATTLEE, CLEMENT *As It Happened* (Heinemann, London, 1954)

BEGIN, MENAHEM *The Revolt* (W. H. Allen, London, 1951)

BERNADOTTE, FOLKE *To Jerusalem* (Hodder & Stoughton, London, 1951)

BRAND, YOEL *Advocate for the Dead* (Andre Deutsch, London, 1958)

BULLOCK, ALAN *Hitler: A Study in Tyranny* (Odhams, London, 1952) *The Life and Times of Ernest Bevin* (Heinemann, London, 1960)

CALVOCORESSY, PETER *Survey of International Affairs 1947–1948* (Royal Institute of International Affairs, London, 1952)

CHURCHILL, W. S. *The Second World War,* 6 Vols. (Cassell, London) (1948–53)

CHORLEY, KATHERINE *Armies and the Art of Revolution* (Faber, London, 1943)

COHEN, GEULA *Woman of Violence* (Holt, Rinehart & Winston, New York, 1966)

CROSSMAN, R. H. S. *Palestine Mission* (Hamish Hamilton, London, 1946) *A Nation Reborn* (Hamish Hamilton, London, 1962)

CRUM, BARTLEY *Behind the Silken Curtain* (Simon & Schuster, New York, 1947)

DALTON, HUGH *High Tide and After* (Muller, London, 1962)

EDEN, ANTHONY *The Reckoning* (Cassell, London, 1965)

FORRESTAL, J. V. *The Forrestal Diaries* (Viking, New York, 1951)

FRANK, GEROLD *The Deed* (Simon & Schuster, New York, 1963)

FRANKENSTEIN, ERNST *Justice for My People* (Nicholson & Watson, London, 1943)

HAY, MALCOLM *Europe and the Jews* (previous title: *The Foot of Pride*) (Beacon Press, New York, 1950)

HOSKINS, HALFORD L. *Middle East Oil in U. S. Foreign Policy* (Public Affairs Bulletin No. 89, Washington, 1950)

HOURANI, ALBERT (ed.) *St. Anthony's Papers,* No. 11 (Chatto & Windus, London, 1960)

HULL, CORDELL *Memoirs* (Macmillan, New York, 1948)

JABOTINSKY, VLADIMIR *The War and the Jew* (Dial, New York, 1942) *The Story of the Jewish Legion* (Bernard Ackerman, New York, 1945)

JOSEPH, DOV *The Faithful City* (Simon & Schuster, New York, 1960)

KATZ, DORIS *The Lady Was a Terrorist* (Shiloni, New York, 1953)

KIMCHI, JON and DAVID *Both Sides of the Hill* (Secker & Warburg, London, 1960)

KIRK, GEORGE *Survey of International Affairs: The Middle East 1945–1950* (Royal Institute for International Affairs, London, 1954)

LAWRENCE, T. E. *The Seven Pillars of Wisdom* (Cape, London, 1935)

MACARDLE, DOROTHY *The Irish Rebellion* (Gollancz, London, 1960)

MCDONALD, JAMES G. *My Mission in Israel 1948–51* (Gollancz, London, 1951)

MORRISON, HERBERT *An Autobiography* (Odhams, London, 1960)

SACHAR, HOWARD M. *The Course of Modern Jewish History* (World, New York, 1958)

ST. JOHN, ROBERT *Ben-Gurion* (Doubleday, New York, 1959)

SCHECHTMAN, J. B. *Rebel and Statesman: The Jabotinsky Story,* 2 vols. (Yoseloff, New York, 1956–61)

SHAREF, ZEEV *Three Days* (Allen & Unwin, London, 1960)

SHERWOOD, ROBERT E. *Roosevelt and Hopkins* (Harper, New York, 1950)

SHWADRAN, BENJAMIN *Middle East Oil and the Great Powers* (Praeger, New York, 1955)

STEIN, LEONARD *The Balfour Declaration* (Valentine Mitchell, London, 1961)

SYKES, CHRISTOPHER *Orde Wingate* (Collins, London, 1959)

TRUMAN, HARRY S. *Memoirs,* 2 Vols. (Doubleday, New York, 1956)

WEIZMANN, CHAIM *Trial and Error* (Hamish Hamilton, London, 1949)

WILLIAMS, FRANCIS *Ernest Bevin: Portrait of a Great Englishman* (Hutchinson, London, 1952)

ZAAR, ISAAC *Rescue and Liberation* (Bloch, New York, 1954)

ZIFF, WILLIAM B. *The Rape of Palestine* (Longmans, New York, 1938)

IN HEBREW

BANAI, YAACOV *Hayalim Almonim (Anonymous Soldiers)* (the story of Lehi) (published privately Tel Aviv, 1958)

BAUER, YEHUDA *Diplomatia Umahteret (Diplomacy and Underground)* (Tel Aviv, 1963)

BEN-GURION, DAVID *Bamaarakha (In the Battle Line),* 5 Vols. (speeches) (Tel Aviv, 1957) *Behilahem Israel (When Israel Fought)* (Tel-Aviv, 1951) *Mima'amad le'Am (From Class to People)* (Tel Aviv, 1957)

BEGIN, MENAHEM *Bamahteret (In the Underground),* 4 Vols. (Underground Documents)

BRAND, YOEL and HANSI *Hasatan Vehanefesh (The Soul and the Devil)* (Tel Aviv, 1960)

DEKEL, EPHRAIM *Alilot Shai (Story of Haganah Intelligence)* (Tel Aviv, 1953)

ELDAD, ISRAEL *Ma'aser Rishon (First Tithe)* (Lehi Veterans Group, Tel Aviv, 1963)

JABOTINSKY, ZEEV (Vladimir) *Baderekh Limedina (On the Way to a State)*. Articles. (Jerusalem, 1950) *Basaar (In the Storm)*. Articles. (Jerusalem, 1953). *Ummah Vehevra (Nation and Society)*. Articles and Essays. (Jerusalem, 1950)

LANKIN, ELIAHU *Sippuro shel Mefakked Altalena (The Story of the Commander of the Altalena* (Tel Aviv, 1954)

LAZAR, HAIM *Af-Al-Pi, Sefer Aliya Bet (In Despite of . . . The Book of "Illegal" Immigration)* (Tel Aviv, 1956) *Kibbush Yafo (Conquest of Jaffa)* (Tel Aviv, 1951)

LIVNEH, ELIEZER (with Y. Nedava and Y. Efrati) *Nili: Toldoteha Shel Heazah Medinnit (Nili: The Story of a Daring Political Venture)* (Tel Aviv, 1961)

NEDAVA, YOSEF *Olei Ha'gardom (Those Who Went to the Gallows)* (Tel Aviv, 1952)

OPHIR, YEHOSHUA *Al Hahomot (On the Walls) (The Irgun in Jerusalem in 1948)* (Jabotinsky Institute, Tel Aviv, 1961)

RIVLIN, GERSHON and SINAI, DOV *Hativat Aleksandroni (The Alexandroni Brigade in the War of Independence)* (Tel Aviv, 1964)

DOCUMENTS

Papers on the Foreign Relations of the United States 1943, Vols. 3 & 4 (Washington 1964)

Papers on the Foreign Relations of the United States 1944, Vols. 3 & 4 (Washington 1965)

Palestine Royal Commission, Minutes of Evidence at Public Sessions, md. 37 (London 1937)

NEWSPAPERS AND PERIODICALS

The Times (London) 1940–48

The Jewish Chronicle (London) 1938–48, esp. 1942 onward

The Jewish Standard (London) 1940–48

The Jewish Struggle (London) 1945–46

The Jewish Herald (Johannesburg) 1938–39, 1939–40

Irgunpress 1947–48

Haaretz (Tel Aviv) 1936–48

HEBREW DOCUMENTS

Album Zahal (Israel Defense Army Album) (Tel Aviv, 1958)

Lohamei Herut Israel (Lehi Documents) 2 Vols. (Tel Aviv, 1959)

Meahorei Hapargod (Behind the Curtain) Arab documents on the war with Israel (Tel Aviv, 1954)

Sefer Hapalmach (The Book of the Palmach) 2 Vols. (Tel Aviv, 1956)

Toldot Milhemet Hakomemiut (The History of the War of Independence) (Tel Aviv, 1959)

INDEX